T0301835

Markets, Planning and the Moral Economy

Markets, Planning and the Moral Economy

Business Cycles in the Progressive Era and New Deal

Donald R. Stabile and Andrew F. Kozak

St Mary's College of Maryland, USA

Edward Elgar

Cheltenham, UK • Northampton, MA, USA

Published by
Edward Elgar Publishing Limited
The Lypiatts
15 Lansdown Road
Cheltenham
Glos GL50 2JA
UK

Edward Elgar Publishing, Inc.
William Pratt House
9 Dewey Court
Northampton
Massachusetts 01060
USA

A catalogue record for this book
is available from the British Library

Library of Congress Control Number: 2012939253

ISBN 978 1 78100 676 4

Typeset by Columns Design XML Ltd, Reading
Printed and bound by MPG Books Group, UK

Contents

Acknowledgements

The authors acknowledge their appreciation to St Mary's College of Maryland for the support it has provided in the researching and writing of this book. First, the work involved in this book was greatly aided by paid leaves (sabbaticals) in the spring semester of 2011 for Kozak and the spring semester of 2012 for Stabile. Second, Margot O'Meara, an outstanding St Mary's economics major, worked diligently with us in locating electronic or print versions of the many obscure articles we have used in this book. She also took charge of formatting the final manuscript for publication; in doing so, she identified numerous errors in grammar, punctuation and clarity of expression and thus contributed to the readability of the final version. Third, St Mary's, through its endeavours to become a community, has brought home to us the benefits and costs of what we refer to in this book as the moral economy.

Abbreviations

AAA	Agricultural Adjustment Act
AEA	American Economic Association
FAES	Federated Association of Engineering Societies
FLSA	Fair Labor Standards Act
GDP	gross domestic product
GNP	gross national product
NIRA	National Industrial Recovery Act
NLRA	National Labor Relations Act
NLRB	National Labor Relations Board
NRA	National Recovery Administration
SPA	Socialist Party of America
WIB	War Industries Board

1. Introduction: the moral economy versus the market economy

For over a century in the US opponents of the market economy have attacked it for the excessively immoral behaviour its stress on individualism has allegedly generated. In this book we shall be concerned with the anti-market ideas of the Progressive movement that emerged in the US in the first three decades of the twentieth century and culminated with the New Deal of President Franklin Delano Roosevelt in the 1930s. The Progressive movement and the New Deal were composed of a diverse set of social interest groups, liberal and elitist and democratic or corporatist. The over-arching ideology of the Progressive movement, the glue that held its diverse elements together, we shall argue in this book, was that its members aimed at replacing or at least supplementing the market economy with a moral economy of their own design. In that moral economy, government steward-ship and planning became viewed as a necessary component of the economic system in order to ensure a better life for all.

The Progressive movement arose in response to a number of economic and political forces that came to the fore in the US at the beginning of the twentieth century, such as the growth of large corporations and labour unions, the development of new technology and the increase in the intensity and pervasiveness of business cycles. Our focus will be on business cycles and how they evoked calls for the government to protect its citizens from the market economy that caused them. Because they believed the market economy was immoral, Progressives argued that they followed a moral imperative of protecting society and its poorer members from the unem-ployment and lower income that took place during an economic downturn. Consequently, we shall examine the arguments in favour of government policies for the business cycle that developed during the Progressive Era and New Deal as a way of designing a moral economy that stressed fairness and a stable economy through planning. A moral economy is one whereby economic decisions are made through planning with an attitude of doing what is right and fair in order to achieve social justice. Planning is an essential feature of the moral economy, because its proponents believe that human wisdom as informed by mutual obligations can make collective decisions about what society needs to have produced and do so in a way that avoids recessions.

This work explores the relationship between business cycles and planning as seen through the lenses of economists, pundits, politicians and business leaders during the Progressive Era and New Deal. This exploration centres on what they saw as the nature and causes of business cycles and use of government stewardship including collective decision-making and planning to avoid them. We want to make it clear, however, that our aim is not to establish the legitimacy of the moral economy over the market economy or the reverse. In using the distinction between the moral economy and the market economy we are adopting the rhetoric of moral economy advocates as a way of uncovering what motivated Progressives in the first four decades of the twentieth century, without involving ourselves in the correctness of their arguments that markets are immoral.

THE MARKET ECONOMY

The central assumption of modern economics is that scarcity is a fundamental human problem. To economists scarcity means that we do not have sufficient resources to produce everything human beings would like to have. Because of scarcity, goods and services must be rationed through a process where individuals, organizations and societies make choices as to how to use the resources that are available to them. Market advocates argue that the market economy is a superior way for making choices about what to produce with our limited resources, by letting each individual's or organization's willingness and ability to buy or sell at market prices allocate (ration) goods and services. Economic production, moreover, is enhanced through the division of labour, through which individuals and businesses cooperate to produce a good or service. The market economy relies on competition among individuals and firms to sell at the lowest possible price, but there must also be cooperation with consumers and other producers to make the sale take place. The market economy uses monetary incentives and competition to organize and order the social priorities of what to produce, how to produce it and who gets it. Prices in the market economy signal those priorities and government intervention that affects prices will disrupt these signals and alter the rationing process.

For the market to work effectively there needs to be the appropriate institutional setting. The primary requirement is the institution of private property, including the right of property-owners to use their property as they see fit. In this way they are free to determine how to put their wealth to its best use in terms of what signals the market economy sends them without any hindrance. Advocates of the market economy, however, recognize that government is also a necessary institution for the market economy, albeit a limited one. Government must provide laws to protect property rights, enforce those laws and contracts made under them and eliminate unscrupulous behaviour among the elements of the market economy. Those advocates also recognize that property rights may allow individuals who are successful in meeting what the market economy favours to accumulate and keep wealth. As long as the wealth is honestly gained from meeting the social needs that the market economy has established it is acceptable.

As an underlying philosophy, market advocates hold that human beings respond to economic incentives more reliably than they respond to moral imperatives. This response to incentives is often viewed as following a path of simple self-interest with the individual not caring about other persons. But, as anyone who has ever tried to sell something, a product or their own labour in the marketplace would know, to be successful in selling one must always be thinking of others to determine what it is that they will want to purchase. Self-interest is a complex mix of self-regard for making the most money combined with catering to consumers or employers. The types of incentives that will appeal to this complex mix of motivations are varied, and markets are exceptional in creating this wide array of incentives. But incentives will not work if individuals are immoral. Some may cheat. Therefore, as long as there are legal and ethical codes to prevent cheating the market economy functions acceptably. The role of the government should be limited to maintaining and enforcing a legal system that promotes free trade. As long as trade is voluntary, market exchanges allow everyone to gain.

One important element of the market economy is that it contains very high incentives for innovation. Once market conditions of supply and demand in a particular market settle down into a routine, profits will reach a relatively stable level. To earn higher profits, firms and their leaders must innovate by either finding a way to produce the same goods or services more cheaply or through the development of a new product that consumers will want. Joseph Schumpeter (see Chapter 4) recognized this stress on technological change as a key function of entrepreneurs and labelled it the process of creative destruction. Entrepreneurs are rarely the inventors of new methods but they have the drive to implement them. In return, they earn high profits by creating new industries in the market economy even as they destroy older industries that cannot compete with them. The process of creative destruction puts wealth in new areas where it will do the most good for society. It also means that the wealth that an individual builds up through market activities can be lost very quickly from the process of creative destruction. One of the findings of this book is that advocates for the moral economy based their argument for planning on the need to control the destructive phase of creative destruction, even though technological change had greatly revolutionized society and raised the standard of living for all of its members.

Another important point regarding the virtues of the market economy that its proponents make is the way it can handle the business cycle. The theory they rely on is Say's Law of Markets. Say's Law is captured by the familiar circular flow model covered in virtually every introductory economics textbook. In this model, all of the costs of production – labour, land, capital and entrepreneurial skill – become someone's income: wages, rent, interest and profit. In turn, this income is spent on the items that have been produced and returned to businesses as revenues. The end result is that a full employment economy always generates the income necessary to cover the cost and purchase of everything produced. Overproduction or under-consumption cannot be a persistent problem. If some of the income generated by production is not spent but is saved, financial markets will adjust the price of saving, that is, interest rates, so that someone else will borrow the saved money and spend it. Prices of products may also have to fall to stimulate spending on consumption or investment goods. In the end, a prolonged period of insufficient demand cannot exist in a market economy as long as prices are flexible.

Up to the Great Depression of the 1930s, the consensus view among economists was that there could not be a sustained period of general overproduction of goods and services resulting in a sustained period of high unemployment. There could, of course, be overproduction of certain goods, Hula Hoops, for example, when consumer preferences were changing to skateboards. But through changes in the prices of Hula Hoops and skate-boards, income earned in Hula Hoop production would be spent on skateboards. Unemployment would occur in the Hula Hoop industry but employment would increase in the skateboard industry. The long-run result is no prolonged period of unemployment.

We shall see later that Schumpeter tied the process of creative destruction to business cycles. When entrepreneurs are creating a new industry, they cause a boom in that industry that spreads to other parts of the economy. When the creation of the new industry is complete, production in that industry expands and prices fall. At the same time, firms and industries that compete with the new industry will have to reduce prices and some of them will go bankrupt. A recession may occur during this adjustment to a new structure in the economy. As long as prices are enabled to adjust in the manner predicted by Say's Law, the recession caused by creative destruc-tion will take care of itself. Many of the ills included in business cycles that

Progressives wanted to curb were simply the process of creative destruction working itself out through the market economy.

THE MORAL ECONOMY

For much of human history great thinkers have espoused the case for a moral economy. Plato, for example, clearly disliked the competition of the market economy and the persons who used it to make profits, because he believed that the pursuit of wealth was inimical to creating an effective society based on virtuous behaviour. Aristotle also placed a high priority on moral behaviour, but made a distinction between market activities that were acceptable because their goal was to meet the basic needs of life without which virtue was impossible and those that were not acceptable because their goal was profit and wealth (Stabile 2008, 12–15). For the next two millennia, the teachings of Christianity, which took a dour view of money making, paralleled the economic ideas of Aristotle and Plato, favouring a moral economy over the market economy by setting forth the idea of the just price and the just wage.

Those ideas did not put money making to an end. For most of those two millennia, the market economy developed until it became too powerful to ignore. We give Adam Smith credit for providing the first intellectual defence of the market economy. We must remember, however, that he was a moral philosopher and that his first book, *The Theory of Moral Sentiments*, was a highly regarded treatise on how humans developed moral behaviour. In it, he offered a succinct definition of a moral economy:

> All the members of human society stand in need of each others assistance, and are likewise exposed to mutual injuries. Where the necessary assistance is reciprocally afforded from love, from gratitude, from friendship, and esteem, the society flourishes and is happy. All the different members of it are bound together by the agreeable bands of love and affection, and are, as it were, drawn to one common centre of mutual good offices. (Smith 1759 [1976], pp. 85–6)

The moral economy must be based on morals and the bonds of love and mutual assistance with each person caring about every other person.

This moral economy, however, was not the type of economy Smith found in the cities of Glasgow and Edinburgh. That world used buying and selling in the marketplace to exist and it was the world that preoccupied Smith in *The Wealth of Nations*. He anticipated this world in the second part of the above quotation:

But though the necessary assistance should not be afforded from such generous
and disinterested motives, though among the different members of the society
there should be no mutual love and affection, the society, though less happy and
agreeable, will not necessarily be dissolved. Society may subsist among different men, as among different merchants, from a sense of its utility, without any
mutual love or affection; and though no man in it should owe any obligation, or
be bound in gratitude to any other, it may still be upheld by a mercenary
exchange of good offices according to an agreed valuation. (Smith 1759 [1976],
pp. 85–6)

In the urbanized, industrial economy that was emerging while he was
writing, the bonds of family and friendship were breaking apart through the
development of social distance and Smith's genius was in showing how the
market economy replaced them with exchange transactions and provided an
increased standard of living for all members of society. When society did
not have a moral sense of mutual assistance, the market economy would
suffice by using the incentives of self-interest to provide its members with
what they needed to live. Put differently, the division of labour and
specialization were necessary for economic growth. But at the same
time, specialization increased the social distance between people. Donald
Frey describes this process as follows: 'As social distance increased,
self-interest was needed to replace the weakened bonds of human
sympathy' (Frey 2009, p. 36).

The economy and economics changed substantially in the century after
Smith wrote *The Wealth of Nations*, moving further away from the idea of a
moral economy. In the market economy, through the process of creative
destruction, technological innovations in transportation, communication
and production transformed the economy from one with a few small
factories of Smith's day to an industrial society where capitalists combined
large quantities of labour and capital in a mass production economy with
many large firms. In addition, this economy did not grow smoothly but
showed the boom and bust of the business cycle. Economists began writing
about these elements of what was then a new economy. Their ideas
expanded on Smith's theory of markets, including the development of Say's
Law.

Still, the moral economy did not disappear. Instead, it was transformed
into the socialism and communism championed by individuals such as
Robert Owen, Pierre Saint-Simon and Karl Marx, with their call for
communal or national economic planning. They wanted to replicate a moral
economy that took over the economic gains of the market economy and
used planning to offset the human deprivation they saw in the market
economy. Although advocates of small villages of cooperation such as
Owen experimented with planning, those arguing for national planning

were less transparent on how they would organize a system of planning. Marx, for example, insisted that the pattern of the market economy at the time of a transformation to socialism would determine how planning would take place. In this context we see the Progressive Era as the designing phase for the reforms that were needed for US society to regain the moral economy that thinkers from Plato to Marx had envisioned. Could the modern economy, these latter-day visionaries asked, be run under moral rules and in a way that avoided business cycles?

MORAL ECONOMY OR MORAL HAZARD

The moral economy, however, has not been without its own excesses. For over two millennia, the moral economy held sway and immoral behaviour in the form of intolerance of intellectual achievement and exploitation of peasants and slaves took place under its social order. During the twentieth century the followers of Marx caused the death of millions of persons in their efforts to build the moral economy of communism in Russia and China. In considering whether the moral economy is feasible, we can look to its origins among the Greek philosophers. To Plato and Aristotle, the term economics referred to household management, an economy of small-scale production on estates that was organized by family relations, where a benevolent male parent made all of the plans for the family. At heart all schemes of the moral economy ask why the entire economy cannot be run like a family, without market relations of buying and selling.

Consider the case of a family planning a holiday dinner. If the dinner takes place at a family member's home, he will usually take care of the dinner or at least the main courses. Typically a benevolent parent would host the meal and plan it. Other members of the family may bring servings of food, dessert or wine. Because of close family ties, they would all know what each other liked and would bring food that met each other's tastes. The decisions of how the dinner would be organized take place under the rules of the moral economy, with the tasks of cleaning up being assigned somehow. The members of the family would be motivated by mutual bonds of love and affection. There might be a family member who did not contribute to the meal but who still enjoyed it. Other members of the family would know the person well enough to either take measures to prevent a repeat occurrence at future meals or to accept the transgression good naturedly. The dinner plans might call for more food than was necessary, but family members could share the leftovers. If the family members did not like the meal they could make a case for changes in next year's meal to those who planned the meal.

The family in our hypothetical example exhibits the features of a system of planning. There is an overriding group goal of a happy family dinner. Someone gathers information about what family members want to eat. That information is then assembled into a menu that sets priorities in terms of whose wants will be met first. The decisions in making the plan can be made cooperatively by all of the family members or by delegation to a subset of them. These cooperative decisions will determine what is to be produced, who will produce it and who will get what share of the final output, the dinner. The process of allocating or rationing the food is relatively easy to accomplish in a family without using prices or monetary incentives, although we have left out the problem of how the raw material for the meal was produced. In the household economy of Plato and Aristotle it was produced on self-sufficient estates through the work of slaves.

The question that proponents of the moral economy need to address is how the moral economy of the family can be scaled up into plans for an entire economy. Businesses in a market economy are always using innovation to scale up to a national level. They can scale up by expanding an existing facility or opening one or more duplicate facilities. As long as there are no barriers to entry, other potential businesses can add to the totality of economic production. This spontaneous expansion of business will depend on economic incentives of profits; a savvy owner will also work from a business plan that estimates those profits. Plans that go wrong will be eliminated by bankruptcy. The market treats failure less kindly than a family would, that is, the moral economy is much nicer than the market economy.

Advocates for the moral economy desire to restore the kindness of family relations to a national economy. To do so, however, they believe that the best approach would be to let businesses scale up their operations to a national or even a global scale through the operation of the market economy. Then society, somehow, can take over those businesses and transform them into the moral economy. That was the approach Marx eventually set forth and we shall see in this book that a variety of Progressive thinkers took the same approach, pushing for the nationalization of existing industry as the path to the moral economy.

This point makes it appear that the moral economy and the market economy must operate as separate spheres. Throughout this book we shall describe advocates for a moral economy who were satisfied to use planning to coordinate market activities into a cooperative system that combined morals and markets into a mixed economy. They cited the lack of overall planning in market activities as adequate evidence that markets needed to be regulated or supplemented by government programmes of the moral economy. Two important assumptions in this anti-market attitude were that the government's behaviour is more moral than business behaviour and that the persons being helped by the government recognize the mutual obligation to behave morally. Advocates of a moral economy believe that humans are basically good and the social institutions of the moral economy will bring about moral behaviour automatically, without investigating the validity of their underlying assumptions.

The issues we raise regarding the risks of immoral behaviour in the moral economy have a name: moral hazard. A moral hazard takes place when a person has an incentive to behave immorally, as is the case when the person is protected from the negative consequences of bad decisions; the hazard means that she will not take as many precautions to avoid the risk of her behaviour because her damages will be limited by the protection. Such a person, it is argued, has no incentive to behave responsibly. Once the government begins protecting society from the risks of the business cycle, its members may no longer take steps on their own to protect themselves. Advocates of the market economy assume that humans have a variety of character flaws that tempts them to anti-social behaviour. Consequently, they believe that government planning is not feasible because there is a moral hazard that irresponsible behaviour will make government programmes costly and ineffective. They also find a moral hazard attached to the political leaders in government, who may expand government programmes to fight a recession as a way to keep themselves in office by appealing to a broad range of voters. Market activities can include immoral behaviour from business. But bringing in the government to replace markets with morals and planning may simply substitute one form of moral hazard for another. Blending morals and markets may bring about the best features of both but runs the risk of irresponsible politicians and a populace not imbued with a sense of mutual obligation turning a moral imperative into a moral hazard.

The point we are making is that the intersection between morals and markets is a fine line not easily drawn. The moral economy requires that all of its members share the moral imperative that mutual assistance is the primary goal of society or else it will too easily fall prey to moral hazard where persons who receive assistance do not take the steps needed to make that assistance unnecessary. The market economy avoids this difficulty by making each individual responsible for his own assistance and for the risks of not living up to that responsibility; but without morals the individual may become unscrupulous in how he meets that responsibility. A mixed economy that combines morals and markets, by trying to play two roles, may instead play neither role convincingly.

OVERVIEW OF THE BOOK

In this book we shall examine the intellectual history of business cycles and planning during the Progressive Era and the New Deal from a variety of perspectives captured in our stereotypes of the moral economy versus the market economy. The moral economy is represented by the Progressive reformers, willing to plan the economy in order to avoid business cycles, and our focus is on them. We shall not, however, forget advocates for the market economy who opposed the moral economy with its government planning and we shall also let them have their say. We shall explore these opposing views on the relationship between business cycles and planning by considering a variety of views on the nature of business cycles and the programmes for dealing with them. Those programmes would require intervention by government, which raises an issue about the ability of government to plan the economy.

Our focus is on the discussion of business cycles and planning by selected economists, pundits, politicians and business leaders. In choosing the subjects of our study our goal is to incorporate the leading ideas on both sides of the fence behind the movement to reform the market economy in the first four decades of the twentieth century. Chapter 2 introduces two important individuals behind the debate over the effectiveness and the morality of a market economy, Edward Bellamy and William Graham Sumner. Bellamy, we argue, provided a model of the moral economy that formed an intrinsic, if tacit, part of the reform side of the moral economy; Sumner countered Bellamy with a socially informed exposition of the market economy. Chapter 3 explores the nature of business cycles and planning as a solution to them from the moral economy perspective of Thorstein Veblen, Theodore Roosevelt, Wesley Clair Mitchell and John Maurice Clark. Chapter 4 examines the main ideas behind the causes of business cycles from a market economy perspective, as found in the ideas of Irving Fisher, Henry Ford, William T. Foster and Waddill Catchings, and Joseph A. Schumpeter. Chapter 5 discusses the idea of planning, starting with the scientific management of Frederick W. Taylor and exploring the ideas of socialist intellectuals and the Progressive intellectual, Walter Lippmann, culminating with government planning in World War I with the War Industries Board (WIB). Chapter 6 continues the study of planning in the 1920s through consideration of Herbert Hoover, Rexford Tugwell, Stuart Chase and Walter Lippmann. Chapter 7 summarizes this debate by way of a general overview of the Great Depression and the way in which Progressives focused on the underconsumption theory of Foster and Catchings as an explanation for the depression; we also review efforts to use the

WIB as a model for how to use planning to end the depression. In Chapter 8 we present the political and economic background of Franklin D. Roosevelt and describe his attitude towards government planning. Chapters 9–11 look at the debate over the New Deal's fledgling experiment in planning under the National Industrial Recovery Act (NIRA) and the National Recovery Administration (NRA). We shall see that many participants in the debate over the moral economy versus the market economy judged this programme of planning to have been inadequate even before it was declared unconstitutional by the US Supreme Court. When it ended, the Roosevelt administration was left with fiscal policy as a way to control the business cycle and Chapter 12 considers the contribution of John Maynard Keynes to fiscal policy, including his advocacy of planning, as well as how his ideas were initially received in the US. Chapter 13 presents an assessment of the New Deal by key figures from previous chapters. We conclude with an Epilogue that draws lessons for today from the legacy of the New Deal and the failure of planning.

In each chapter we shall be reviewing interpretations by supporters, opponents and analysts of the Progressive Era and New Deal policies and programmes aimed at economic security through control over the business cycle by planning. We offer a representative sample of the variety of points of view that were expressed at the time, and we must stress that there was a great deal of variety. Our selection of subjects ranges from well-known politicians and business leaders to obscure economists. Where possible we have tried to give biographical details of each person. Although the persons whose writings we review had a diversity of views on the reforms of the Progressive Era and New Deal, some of them unique, we have divided them into our two polar fields of the moral economy and the market economy. Not surprisingly, the proponents of the moral economy favoured the planning efforts of the New Deal in the NIRA, even though many of them thought it did not go far enough towards their ideal. Advocates for a market economy retained their belief in the effectiveness of the market economy and highlighted the flaws in the NRA. The issue, then as now, was learning to draw the line between the moral economy and the market economy while avoiding the middle ground where moral imperatives become moral hazards.

2. The moral economy in the nineteenth century: Bellamy versus Sumner

The idea of the moral economy existed in many forms throughout human history. As a result, its lineage is difficult to trace from any particular source. In the US during the last three decades of the nineteenth century, for example, there were a variety of political movements that placed government action and some form of socialism on the political agenda. To some extent, this penchant for socialist thinking and activist government came from many academics in the US studying in Europe. In Europe they learned socialist ideas that were more common on that continent due to the influence of thinkers such as Robert Owen, Pierre Saint-Simon and Karl Marx. Many academics studied in Germany where they saw first-hand the activist government of Otto von Bismarck and especially the social welfare programmes that Germany developed to take care of the poor.

Given this readiness to attribute a European influence on US intellectuals, it is often overlooked that in the US there was a home-grown version of the moral economy set forth by Edward Bellamy. In this chapter we describe Bellamy's vision of a cooperative commonwealth that he saw coming about in the US. That vision was influential among US intellectuals, for it gave them a model of the moral economy that, while rarely acknowledged, formed a background for thinking about the moral economy during the early decades of the twentieth century. We shall use Bellamy's vision as our model of what we are calling the moral economy. His writings were very popular.

Also popular, at the time he wrote, was the idea of the market economy. In this chapter we follow our discussion of Bellamy's moral economy with a version of the market economy set forth by William Graham Sumner, a conservative academic. Sumner's model of the market economy offered a countering voice to Bellamy and the Progressives.

EDWARD BELLAMY AND THE MORAL ECONOMY

Edward Bellamy (1850–98) was a newspaper editor and novelist from Massachusetts. His most popular book, *Looking Backward*, published in 1888, tells the story of Julian West, who falls asleep in the nineteenth century and does not wake up until the year 2000. He awakens to a new US, organized as a cooperative commonwealth. The book struck a chord in the US and became a bestseller; Bellamyite 'Nationalization Clubs' sprang up throughout the nation, with 161 charted by 1891 (Stabile 1988, pp. 213–15). Encouraged by this success, in 1898 Bellamy produced another book, *Equality*, as a sequel to *Looking Backward*, to elaborate on his ideas and respond to criticisms of them.

Both books gave a model of the moral economy in the US that had a great influence on Progressive thinkers and reformers, even after the Bellamyite movement died out. In his introduction to *Looking Backward* written in the 1920s, Progressive journalist Heywood Broun observed that a large number of his 'radical friends' admitted to him that the book was 'the first thing that got me started thinking about Socialism' (Broun 1926, p. i). A decade later, Thurman Arnold, a stalwart of the New Deal, supported the idea of Bellamy's importance to the Progressive spirit in his book, *The Folklore of Capitalism*, when he stated, 'Edward Bellamy … was the forerunner of the N.R.A [National Recovery Administration]' (Arnold 1937 [1968], p. 221).

In the books, Bellamy used West as a way to compare what existed in his day to what might be found in the moral economy. For example, West was an idle gentleman, living on wealth accumulated by his grandfather. Time had increased West's wealth through the magical process of investment income and compound interest. Bellamy called this system 'a species of tax in perpetuity upon the product of those engaged in industry which a person possessing or inheriting money was able to levy' (Bellamy 1888 [1926], p. 9). The rich became rich at a cost to the poor, which implied that their wealth was immoral. West remarked that in the days of the market economy it was commonly said 'that nobody could honestly acquire a million dollars.' As a result, Bellamy felt that the wealthy 'had no moral right to [their wealth] as based upon dessert' (Bellamy 1898 [2005], pp. 1681–95).

Bellamy's opposition was not to the market economy directly but to the way it had evolved into a 'plutocracy' through the accumulation and concentration of wealth. On his account, 'Free competition in business had ceased to exist. Personal initiative in private enterprise, which formerly had been open to all, was restricted to the capitalists, and to the larger capitalists at that' (Bellamy 1898 [2005], p. 4586). To support this account, he cited data from the US Census of 1890 to show that the wealthiest 9 per cent of the population owned 75 per cent of the wealth (Bellamy 1898 [2005], pp. 4724–30). He has West forcefully state, 'These figures were enough to turn the very stones into revolutionists' (Bellamy 1898 [2005], p. 4745).

To establish a peaceful transition from the market economy to the moral economy, Bellamy started from a trend that was apparent in the US in his day, the growth of large businesses. As the control of the economy came to be held by a few wealthy capitalists, labour strife increased. Under a system of small business, individual workers knew their employers and worked well with them. As businesses began to grow in scope and scale, workers formed unions in response, which led to strikes and violence. Moreover, big business trampled over smaller companies, and they diminished in number. Everyone disliked the power big business was gaining, but recognized that large corporations were very efficient producers of goods at low prices (Bellamy 1888 [1926], p. 55). When the consolidation of business reached the point where there were only a few corporations left, the nation took them over as 'a single syndicate representing the people, to be conducted in the common interest for the common profit' (Bellamy 1888 [1926], p. 56). Bellamy later elaborated on the general achievement of the cooperative commonwealth as follows: 'The industrial and commercial system by which the labour of a great population is organized and directed constitutes a complex machine. If the machine is constructed unscientifically, it will result in loss and disaster' (Bellamy 1898 [2005], pp. 1998–2000). The market economy had developed haphazardly and was thus prone to problems. By design, the planning of the moral economy would be more effective.

In *Equality* Bellamy gave a more detailed process of the transition to the cooperative commonwealth. The first step was the nationalization of semi-public service industries, such as water works, electricity and railroads; this initial step transformed many workers into public employees and showed that the government could manage industry effectively. Then the government took over retail outlets, but still purchased products from private business. Each time the economy went into a recession, however, the government bought up idle factories at low prices. Once that was accomplished and everyone saw how well the new economic system performed, many small private businesses and farms clamoured for the government to take them over. Finally, the few enclaves of private business that remained were confiscated (Bellamy 1898 [2005], pp. 5202–50). In this way a market economy was transformed into a planning system run by the government with a goal of enhancing general welfare instead of maximizing profit.

In that system society was organized on a military basis with each person required to serve a 24-year work life. Bellamy wrote, 'When the nation became the sole employer, all the citizens, by virtue of their citizenship, became employees, to be distributed according to the needs of industry' (Bellamy 1888 [1926], p. 62). Workers did not find this system to be compulsory, because they were motivated by the same spirit of service and patriotism that soldiers had. Anyone who tried to avoid work would not have a way to provide for his existence. Workers were all paid the same wage under the principle that individual differences in productivity were due to natural differences in strength and intelligence; what mattered was that workers all did their best. Workers who performed well would rise through the ranks of the army to higher levels of responsibility. Technical professionals, such as engineers, were included as part of the industrial army.

The industrial army was organized into guilds for each trade, headed by a general. The guilds were then organized in related trades. There were ten of these larger divisions, headed by a higher ranking general. These ten generals formed a national council, which was headed by a president, who had risen through the ranks and served as overall general of the army. All generals were elected, not by the workers they led, but by the workers from the branch of industry the general led who had finished their work lives. The president was elected from one of the ten members of the national council. To help the president, an inspectorate investigated complaints about defective goods, ineffective leadership or evasions of work duties; the inspectorate used a system of pervasive investigation to find such transgressions on its own. The president served a five-year term, typically from age 40 to 45. At the end of that term a national congress would be called to review the president's report of the performance of the industrial army. The congress also reviewed reports from the ten generals on the national council, and if it disapproved a report, that general was ineligible to serve as president. Under the new system there were no parties or politicians nor demagoguery and corruption. Because social conditions had changed, human motivation also changed. By removing profit from business, the new system removed temptation from politics (Bellamy 1888 [1926], pp. 60–61). In addition, political leaders would be hemmed in by recall elections and a democratic system where citizens voted on every law passed by those leaders (Bellamy 1898 [2005], pp. 4036–42).

Even though workers were part of an army, they could choose their occupation based on their personal aptitudes. Workers served three years of menial labour. Then they could indicate their top three choices for a trade or profession and be certain to be trained for one of them. If some occupations became overcrowded and others had shortages of workers, the national council would determine that the one with shortages might be too hard and would alter its working conditions. With equal pay, money could not serve as an incentive to attract workers to an occupation, but working conditions could be used to attract them. Workers would also be motivated with badges of merit that they could wear discreetly. For those workers who did not perform at their best, Bellamy offered the following solution:

> As for actual neglect of work, positively bad work, or other overt remissness on the part of men incapable of generous motives, the discipline of the industrial army is far too strict to allow anything whatever of the sort. A man able to do duty, and persistently refusing, is sentenced to solitary imprisonment on bread and water till he consents. (Bellamy 1888 [1926], p. 128)

The moral hazard of slacking was not acceptable. Under the planning system 'a complex mutual dependence becomes the universal rule' (Bellamy 1888 [1926], p. 132) and everyone must be a part of it. In his later book, Bellamy elaborated on the new attitude towards work: 'Labor for others in the name of love and kindness, and labor with others for a common end in which all are mutually interested, and labor for its own joy, are alike honorable' (Bellamy 1898 [2005], p. 1522). Women worked under the same system as men, only in a different army with female officers (Bellamy 1888 [1926], pp. 256–8). Freed from dependence on a male for their survival, women become more liberated.

The use of coercion to avoid moral hazard might indicate that Bellamy was neglecting the issue of economic incentives. In *Equality* he offered two points on the issue. First, under the market economy the economic incentives workers faced were extremely harsh; they had to work long hours for low pay and the alternative was starvation. Solitary confinement with bread and water might seem mild in comparison. Second, under the moral economy work became a moral obligation. Bellamy wrote, 'Now that all work is for the common fund, the one who evades or scamps his work robs every one of his fellows. A man had better hang himself nowadays than get the reputation of a shirk (Bellamy 1898 [2005], pp. 5743–5).

Workers would receive their pay in the form of credits placed on a card, Bellamy actually called it a 'credit card.' Workers in need of items would go to a distribution centre where they could examine the array of samples of needed items, order a selection and have it delivered from a central warehouse to their residence, with the cost deducted from their credit card. Meals were eaten in communal dining halls with payment also by credit card; waiters would be workers in their three-year tour of menial work. The government would not be in charge of deciding what to produce, but would base production on what workers consumed in distribution centres and at communal dining halls. If a small group of workers wanted something that was not being produced, they could petition the government to have it added to the production schedule. Prices of goods would be based on the cost of production, with no profit included. Bellamy argued that by eliminating many of the unnecessary costs of the market economy – banks, multiple distribution systems, middlemen, crime based on privation, the need for a military – the government could produce basic items at a very low cost (Bellamy 1888 [1926], pp. 87–8, 198–215).

Another way the cooperative commonwealth could save money was through the elimination of fads and fashions in consumption. Bellamy argued that the wealthy set the trends in fashion in the market economy but that the lower classes soon emulated them. To maintain their distinction the wealthy would create another fashion but as soon as the lower classes emulated it, they would again find something new. On the vicious cycle would go, causing the market economy to use too many resources in catering to what Bellamy thought of as the whims of the wealthy. In the cooperative commonwealth everyone bought standard items, especially in clothing, but individuals who wanted to express their own tastes could design an article of apparel and have it produced, thanks to the greater productivity of the moral economy. In the moral economy jewellery became passé (Bellamy 1898 [2005], pp. 900–950). Proponents of the moral economy often blamed the wealthy for the wastefulness of luxury spending.

A worker could save credits from one year to the next and borrow a few credits in advance, for large purchases, but there was no need for saving or the accumulation of wealth. As Bellamy described it, 'No man any more has any care for the morrow, either for himself or his children, for the nation guarantees the nurture, education, and comfortable maintenance of every citizen from the cradle to the grave' (Bellamy 1888 [1926], p. 90). Thriftiness was no longer a virtue, and few persons would accumulate personal possessions as they would need to spend credits on larger homes or storage space to house them.

One special reason why there was not a need for saving was the solution to the business cycle. Bellamy referred here to what he called business crises that took place every five to ten years and eliminated weak companies, crippled strong ones and brought hard times to workers. These crises would be followed by short periods of prosperity, followed in turn by another crisis. As the economies of the world developed and became interconnected, these crises became worldwide. The growth in size of business also meant crises became more frequent. Economists of the time concluded that these crises could not be avoided and were a necessary evil (Bellamy 1888 [1926], pp. 224–44).

One of the main causes of the business cycles, Bellamy argued, was the lack of an overall direction of industrial production, which meant that its development was not coordinated; corporations often were out of step with each other and would produce more than was demanded by consumers.

Indeed, that was often the case because the profits businesses took meant that workers and farmers would not be paid enough to purchase all that was produced; even wealthy business owners who spent on luxuries could not make up the shortfall in consumption. According to Say's Law a fall in prices should increase consumption and eliminate the problem. Bellamy, however, argued that before they would resort to cutting prices and losing profits, business would first cut wages, which to him meant the price cuts came too late. As a consequence, price cuts could not restore consumption, profits would fall and the result would be unemployment (Bellamy 1898 [2005], pp. 2338–60). This was a constant problem in the market economy, but when it became widespread it caused a crisis of overproduction. Workers would be laid off, and with reduced incomes, could no longer purchase products, which added to the problem of overproduction and continued the downward spiral until the crisis was full blown.

The credit system of capitalism reinforced the problem because credit was a promise to pay money but could expand beyond the supply of money needed for trade. As a result, businessmen could use credit to increase their factories until overproduction existed. The resulting decline in prices meant that the promise of payment could not be kept, and credit defaults would spread through the economy causing more business failures and layoffs, adding to the crisis. Yet, credit was necessary to organize the large firms of the economy to take advantage of their higher productivity. Higher productivity, however, led to the problem of not enough consumption and too much production. Bellamy sarcastically noted that the market economy would be better off if it would take its excess wealth and burn it. Instead, he forecast that it was headed for permanent stagnation (Bellamy 1898 [2005], pp. 2712–40).

The cooperative commonwealth, Bellamy went on, eliminated the problem of the business cycle through planning. Overproduction was not possible. If one industry produced too much, no workers would be laid off. Surplus workers in that industry would be transferred to another industry where they could add to its output. Since they did not lose any pay they could still use their credit cards for purchases. In addition, the cooperative commonwealth would be able to stockpile the excess production of the industry until it could eventually be sold. Finally, the commonwealth did not use credit in the way capitalism did. Credit existed, but only in the form of real goods, not as promises to pay money that could be used to create overcapacity in industry. Bellamy described the system as follows:

> Out of the annual product the amount necessary for the support of the people is taken, and the requisite labor to produce the next year's consumption provided for. The residue of the material and labor represents what can be safely expended

in improvements. If the crops are bad, the surplus for that year is less than usual, that is all. Except for slight occasional effects of such natural causes, there are no fluctuations of business; the material prosperity of the nation flows on uninterruptedly from generation to generation, like an ever broadening and deepening river. (Bellamy 1888 [1926], p. 238)

Through national planning the cooperative commonwealth was able to avoid all the wastes of the business cycle by keeping capital and labour constantly employed.

Planning would also bring control over the process of creative destruction. Bellamy recognized that innovation had played a large part in making the market economy productive. He observed, however, that many elements of the market economy were hostile to innovation due to the destructive phase of the process of creative destruction. Business owners did not like it when innovations made their factories obsolete and without value. Because most innovations had increased productivity by replacing workers with machines, labour opposed them for fear of job loss. All of the innovations since the industrial revolution, he argued, had not improved the lot of workers nor ended poverty. Moreover, innovations added to the problems caused by overproduction and underconsumption by increasing them both. The cooperative commonwealth ended the hostility towards innovation by planning their introduction in a way that protected workers from the destructive phase of creative destruction (Bellamy 1898 [2005], pp. 3260–578). Although he made a case for the cooperative commonwealth having a friendlier environment for innovation, Bellamy did not explain how the inventive genius behind innovation would develop.

Regardless, from Bellamy's perspective the national organization of industry under a single control gave it the power of 'a disciplined army under one general.' With this discipline, the nation grew rich and could spend its vast surplus not on individual ostentation, but on 'public works and pleasures in which all share' (Bellamy 1888 [1926], p. 243). By eliminating the wastes of the business cycle and using the power of combined effort, the commonwealth greatly increased its productive capacity and could do much good for the people in common.

We return to Aristotle's idea that individuals would work to produce what they used for meeting basic needs but did not need to get involved in the profit-seeking methods of trade. They could live in the system of mutual obligations that Adam Smith did not think likely to exist in the modern world, where economic cooperation took place 'reciprocally afforded from love, from gratitude, from friendship, and esteem' and 'the society flourishes and is happy' (Smith 1759 [1976], pp. 85–6).

As a model of society, however, Bellamy's cooperative commonwealth has the fault of all utopias. They are all authoritarian in the sense that everyone in them follows the orders of an author such as Bellamy. In particular, in Bellamy's cooperative commonwealth individual consumers learned that they could get along without the fashions, fads and frills that are such a strong feature of the market economy. This enlightened consumerism made the planning of production for use much easier. If the goal was to provide every member of the society with basic food, clothing and shelter, then the task of planning an economy became simple. Planning for an economy where consumers were allowed to express their individual tastes and preferences through the purchase of a wide array of consumer goods was much more difficult. Moreover, Bellamy's national council of planners would have the wisdom to handle this difficult problem, because he said they would. A worker who did not go along with the plans would receive 'solitary imprisonment on bread and water till he consents' (Bellamy 1888 [1926], p. 128). In return for consenting he would be given economic security.

Finally, we must point out a fundamental assumption that Bellamy made: the government can produce a moral economy based on mutual obligation. Underlying that assumption was the idea that politicians became moral agents who would not be driven by personal self-interest the way greedy businessmen were. Moreover, the officers of the industrial army – engineers, managers and accountants to name a few – would also develop the technical skills and moral outlook that the cooperative commonwealth required of them.

Bellamy's view regarding the topics of this book – the nature of business cycles and the need for economic planning – are clear. Bellamy was a strong proponent of the moral economy. His community of mutual assistance reduced the role of individualism in economic decision-making and required government stewardship in order to eliminate the profit incentive and enhance the general welfare. Economic planning by able leaders of government enterprises would eliminate the wastefulness of overproduction of a market economy and thus eliminate the occurrence of business cycles.

WILLIAM GRAHAM SUMNER AND THE MARKET ECONOMY

Although Bellamy's vision of a moral economy gained some traction in the US it experienced criticism. Here we review the writings of William Graham Sumner (1840–1910) as an indicator of what market adherents made of Bellamy's moral economy. Sumner was a long-time professor of sociology at Yale University. He considered sociology to be a broad science of society and he spent much of his life studying economics as part of that science. He was a prolific writer and public speaker and his ideas were popular and influential. We shall see in the later chapters that two of his students at Yale, Thorstein Veblen and Irving Fisher, became prominent economists. More recently, Sumner has regained prominence as the source of the title of Amity Shlaes's book on the New Deal, *The Forgotten Man* (2007).

Sumner felt so strongly about the difficulties presented by Bellamy's moral economy he wrote but never completed or published a satire on a cooperative commonwealth. The satire consisted of a series of articles from a socialist newspaper, the *New Era*, with a motto, 'Let the Rich Pay! Let the Poor Enjoy!' The cooperative commonwealth he presented was economically inefficient and socially interventionist. Many of the 'articles' reported on the activities of a Board of Ethical Control, including a case where a 'pestilent preacher has been condemned to the chain gang' and a report that the members of the Board of Ethical Control would stay in office for ten years instead of having annual elections as previously intended. One article reported, 'The Cooperative Railroad Commission, having found a mechanic to repair the locomotive, announce that they will recommence regular weekly trips to Yonkers on next Monday. A train will start at 9 a.m. or as soon thereafter as convenient' (Sumner 1969, pp. 442–6). Bellamy's moral economy took away freedom with no corresponding increase in efficiency was Sumner's opinion.

Freedom was important to Sumner, especially freedom to pursue economic activity. He defined liberty as 'the security given to each man that if he employs his energies to sustain the struggles on behalf of himself and those he cares for, he shall dispose of the product exclusively as he chooses' (Sumner 1914a, p. 32). The individual's ability to use his efforts in the best way possible and to be able to enjoy all the benefits of those efforts was Sumner's standard for the attainment of social justice. To him, equality did not equate to social justice because it destroyed this liberty. For Sumner, one way an individual might use the benefits of his efforts was to save and thereby accumulate capital. Since capital gave its possessor advantages over those without it, it led to inequality. Socialists set their goal as to give everyone a 'right to whatever he needs' (Sumner 1914a, p. 34). The only way to attain that goal of equality was to eliminate capital and create an economic system where 'all are equally miserable' (Sumner 1914a, p. 32). Sumner was sceptical about efforts to change the market economy, which, he observed, was 'the outcome of the efforts of men for thousands of years to work together' (Sumner 1904 [1914], p. 57).

That scepticism ran through all of Sumner's writings and especially his writings on the forgotten man. To Sumner, the forgotten man was the person who, in the market economy, pays for government policies and social experiments on behalf of special interests. He wrote,

> The type and formula of most schemes of philanthropy and humanitarianism is this: A and B put their heads together to decide what C shall do for D. The radical vice of all these schemes, from a sociological point of view, is that C is not allowed a voice in the matter, and his position, character, and interests, as well as the ultimate effects on society through C's interests are entirely overlooked. I call C the Forgotten Man. (Sumner 1883b [1982], p. 107)

From Sumner's perspective, whenever well-minded persons decide to help a group they feel is needy, that is, when they try to bring about a moral economy and social justice, they overlook the fact that society must be thought to be made up of many parts that must all be held together. Changing one part of society to help a chosen group will set off consequences, many of them unintended and potentially negative, in other parts of society. Social justice cannot be judged by the positive benefits a policy has for the chosen group, but must be measured by a holistic accounting of the impact of the policy on all members of society.

Within Sumner's economic thinking there was a Darwinian notion of market competition as a struggle for survival that separated the fit from the unfit. Its key human component was the individual, whose sole obligation was to enter the competitive economic struggle in order to ensure his survival and the survival of his family. In that struggle the unfit fell by the wayside and efforts to help them must come at the expense of the fit, that is, the forgotten man. He meant more than that, however, for it was the forgotten man who carried the economy forward by being fit while efforts to help the unfit held the economy back. The government could not help the unfit except by taking money from the fit. This reduced the capital of the fit and, since capital to Sumner was the key ingredient in the advance of civilization, 'Every bit of capital, therefore, which is given to a shiftless and inefficient member of society, who makes no return for it, is diverted from a reproductive use' (Sumner 1883b [1982], p. 108).

It was thus folly to denounce capital and the persons who owned it. The concentration of wealth that Bellamy and others deplored was essential to the growth of the industrial economy with its large firms. That concentration did two things. It accumulated the capital needed to create the large firms needed for the mass production of goods and it put that capital into the hands of managers of those firms who had proved they were fit to run things (Sumner 1902 [1914], pp. 81–2). Socialists believed that concentrations of wealth implied greater poverty and that capital was easy to accumulate no matter what form the economy took, which meant that the redistribution of income had no negative consequences (Sumner 1887b [1914], p. 66). Sumner disagreed. To him, the accumulation of capital depended on virtues such as hard work, thrift and prudence and the only way to get more capital was through the expansion of those virtues (Sumner 1914b, pp. 200–2). Since wealth was a result of those virtues, he concluded, 'It is not wicked to be rich' (Sumner 1914a, p. 27).

The point Sumner was making is that every economic activity in the market economy, including government policies to redress perceived social ills, creates winners and losers. When the market economy creates winners and losers, however, that is done under the freedom of the market economy where by definition the winners are the fit and the losers are the unfit. Government policies to reverse this Darwinian and thus to Sumner 'natural' outcome by helping losers at the expense of winners were not 'natural' and caused harm to society. To bring home the effect of a tax on the forgotten man, for example, Sumner considered a man with an income of 1000 dollars a year, out of which he saved 100 dollars. Suppose the government levied a ten-dollar a year tax on him. Would he, Sumner asked, pay for the tax out of the 900 dollars he was using to live on, and thus reduce his current standard of living, or would he reduce his savings to pay the tax and sacrifice his future standard of living? In the first case industries that produced what the forgotten man was no longer buying would suffer. In the second case economic growth would be inhibited (Sumner 1885 [1969], p. 32).

The problem Sumner was raising is what economists call the difficulty of making interpersonal utility comparisons. When the government takes money from one person, causing a decline in his welfare, to give to another, creating a gain in his welfare, how do we know that the gain is greater than the decline? Social philanthropists and government reformers may assume that the gain is greater than the decline, but Sumner believed the reverse, arguing that the individual knew best what to do with his money. Thus he considered it 'mischief' to use taxes for 'parks, libraries, and other grand things.' The government official who did so was determining that the forgotten man would 'have less clothes and more library or park' (Sumner 1885 [1969], pp. 32–3).

Included in Sumner's view of the market economy was a theory of economic growth and development through the accumulation of capital and the development of new technology. In anticipation of Joseph Schumpeter (see Chapter 4), he recognized that this growth and development was a process of creative destruction whereby advances were 'won by pain and distress.' Every new product or method of production 'displaces the acquired skill of the men who formerly performed the service.' The gain accrued to society 'but it imposes on some men the necessity of finding new means of livelihood, and if these men are advanced in life, the necessity may be harsh in the extreme.' The transition to a new occupation took time and might involve lower paid jobs. This process also destroyed capital invested in the old ways (Sumner 1879 [1969], pp. 221–2). The late nineteenth century was an era of prosperity as a result of this process of creative destruction, and the result was a reduction in the costs of many items that were being mass produced, which meant a better life for all members of society (Sumner 1885 [1969], p. 56). Sumner predicted, correctly, that the next quarter century would be even more prosperous, as long as politicians and social reformers did not attempt to alter the process of creative destruction.

Sumner worried, however, that they would make the attempt, because the hardships caused by creative destruction resulted in situations where reformers like Bellamy thought that economic competition was much too harsh in the way it treated the 'weak.' Sumner sarcastically debunked this view by writing, 'If we do not like the survival of the fittest we have only one possible alternative, and that is the survival of the unfittest' (Sumner 1879 [1969], pp. 224–5). A programme for saving the unfit by redistributing wealth from the rich to the poor was incompatible with economic growth and development. To do so, he argued, would be to 'act like an army invading a hostile country, which should shoot its own advance guard' (Sumner 1883a, p. 94).

His argument applied even during economic recessions. In the recession of 1896 he chided politicians for claiming that 'discontent and distress prevail to an extent never before known in the history of the country,' calling the claim 'distinctly untrue.' Moreover, the cause of the recession was government policies related to the coinage of silver and the impact they had on credit markets and business (Sumner 1896a [1969], p. 149). When government interfered with private business transactions it added to the risk and uncertainty of business and caused economic distress.

In addition to wrong-headed government policies, recessions resulted when capital was invested in businesses that did not prosper, with the result that the capital was lost. Those businesses had made contractual obligations to other businesses, and when they failed and did not meet their obligations, those other businesses also failed and their failures spread throughout the economy leading to other failures. Much of the problem, Sumner pointed out, came from businesses following fads and overinvesting in a new or rapidly growing industry, we might now call it a bubble, until the industry ended in collapse. Businessmen made a mistake in where and how much they invested their capital and they paid for their mistake through failure, even though the failure spread through the entire economy (Sumner 1896a [1969], pp. 150–52).

The problem Sumner saw was that the market economy had become increasingly interconnected and highly organized, with problems in one industry spreading quickly to other industries and then to other countries. Moreover, since the economy was dynamic and always creating new products, new technology and new business systems, business needed to cope effectively with economic change. Business would make many mistakes in an economy with creative destruction, but those mistakes would be corrected by failure. Businessmen who failed were unfit and needed to be allowed to fail.

Should workers who were employed in those industries pay for the mistakes of their employers? They did pay, and Sumner had a subtle explanation for why they did. Before the rise of industry and factory work, labour took place in the form of independent artisans. These artisans, because they worked with their own capital and took individual orders for their products, had direct contact with the market. It did not take much knowledge for artisans to know when they saw fewer customers. Fewer customers gave them a signal that it was time to find a new occupation. In a factory system where the workers earned wages they had less direct contact with market conditions. If a market decline hit their industry, the employer might have to reduce wages or eliminate jobs, but the worker, without knowledge of the market, might see the wage reduction as the employer's 'arbitrary and cruel act' (Sumner 1879 [1969], p. 228).

To help workers deal with this situation Sumner looked favourably on unions. He argued that they could take over many responsibilities that were being taken care of by government regulations, such as safety issues, hours of work, child labour and so on (Sumner 1883b [1982], pp. 82–3). More importantly, unions could perform the function of helping workers learn about market conditions and how they impacted wages. In this case, as long as union strikes avoided the type of violence that was criminal, they were not bad, but were a way for workers to 'test the market.' 'Supply and demand,' Sumner wrote, 'does not mean that social forces will operate of themselves.' Instead, economic agents had to fight for their market-derived earnings or risk losing them and labour was no exception. He continued, 'The other social interests are in the constant habit of testing the market, in order to get all they can out of it. A strike, rationally begun and rationally conducted, only does the same thing for the wage-earning interest' (Sumner 1887a [1969], p. 252). To him, however, a strike was reasonable only if employers were not able to replace the strikers with workers at a lower wage than the strikers demanded. If they were, the strikers were asking for too

much (Sumner 1896b [1914], p. 99). Unions, in other words, were necessary for workers to get the wages that market conditions warranted and
served the same function of responding to market fluctuations that the
independent artisans had done individually for themselves.

Union efforts to gain market wages were as much help as workers should
expect to get in their struggles for survival. That did not mean that others did
not try to give them help. Politicians could easily use the distress of workers
as a way to create social programmes. Sumner described them as follows:
'It is a very popular thing to tell men that they have a grievance. That most of
them find it hard to earn as much as they would like to spend goes without
saying. Now comes the wily orator and tells them this is somebody's fault'
(Sumner 1896a [1969], p. 153). Politicians were always presenting policies
to the public that would make the country prosperous. The policies included
government spending and there was always some segment of the public that
would support them because it was in its interest. Sumner wrote:

> The silver miners, finding that their product is losing value in the market, get the
> government to go into the market as a great buyer in the hope of sustaining the
> price. The national government is called on to buy or hire unsalable ships; to dig
> canals which will not pay; to educate illiterates in the states which have not done
> their duty at the expense of the states which have done their duty as to education;
> to buy up telegraphs which no longer pay; and to provide the capital for
> enterprises of which private individuals are to win the profits. (Sumner 1883c
> [1969], pp. 488–9)

Economic gains came from the accumulation of capital and the process of
creative destruction. Men who accumulated capital through a work and
saving ethic were the keystone of fitness. Persons without that ethic were
unfit. They, however, demanded the same outcome for themselves as they
saw taking place among the rich and successful. 'In their view,' Sumner
wrote, 'they have a right, not only to *pursue* happiness, but to *get* it; and if
they fail to get it, they think they have a claim to the aid of other men'
(Sumner 1883b [1982], p. 14, emphasis in original). The mutual assistance
of the moral economy could come from charity or from government
programs. Sumner had doubts that charity was beneficial to the poor but had
no doubts about the efficacy of government programmes. He wrote, 'The
question whether voluntary charity is mischievous or not is one thing; the
question whether legislation which forces one man to aid another is right
and wise, as well as economically beneficial, is quite another question'
(Sumner 1883b [1982], p. 18). Under such social legislation the government became 'the protector and guardian of certain classes' while those
who implemented the legislation were the reformers who proposed it
(Sumner 1883b [1982], pp. 20–2).

In pushing for this intervention, proponents of activist government presented the state 'as a superior power, able and ready to get us out of trouble.' Sumner asked,

> Is the state a source of moral energy which can contribute what is needed? Can it bring to us from some outside source that, by the facts of the case, we lack? If it can, then indeed it is the most beneficent patron we possess. (Sumner 1914b, p. 202)

To Sumner, however, the government was an arena where human passions ruled over economic considerations. He was non-partisan in his criticisms of politicians' penchant to use the government to intervene in the economy, writing: 'In this country the party which is "in" always interferes, and the party which is "out" favours non-interference' (Sumner 1883b [1982], p. 85). He also recognized the dangers of a government controlled by wealthy business interests by criticizing 'plutocratic doctrines' (Sumner 1883b [1982], p. 91) and pointing out that the 'lobby is the army of the plutocracy' (Sumner 1883b [1982], p. 93). Wealth gave power to its possessors that might be abused and it was necessary to erect safeguards against that abuse.

He did not, however, criticize voluntary efforts to help the poor through charity, ruling out of discussion any questions of whether charity did any good or not. To him, it was acceptable for a person such as himself to exercise 'my own sympathies under my own reason and conscience,' but it was not acceptable 'what another man forces me to do of a sympathetic character, because his reason and conscience approve of it' (Sumner 1883b [1982], p. 136). Humans owed each other help and sympathy out of personal feelings, but not out of governmental edict. All that government owed individuals was the guarantee of rights, with the proviso that 'rights do not pertain to *results*, but only to *chances*' (Sumner 1883b [1982], p. 141, emphasis in original).

In this way, Sumner hoped to show his contemporaries that in their quest for Bellamy's moral economy they were headed down a road back to the serfdom of feudalism. As for the morals involved in the market economy, Sumner argued that since capital was necessary for economic growth and development, 'the increase of capital is therefore the expansion of *chances* that intellectual, moral, and spiritual good may be won. The moral question is: How will the chances be used' (Sumner 1885 [1969], p. 98, emphasis in original). Affluence was a necessary condition for moral behavior, and the market economy was the path to affluence. How the affluent used the moral opportunities their wealth gave them was up to them.

Sumner offered a clear and strong case for the advantages of the market economy. The market economy he admired had its faults, but many of them were self-corrected. Business owners misused their capital by investing it unwisely, but the market treated them harshly with failure. Widespread failure might cause a recession, but eventually the accumulation of capital and the process of creative destruction would bring about economic growth. Large firms gained market power, but new firms arose to compete with them, as long as government did not give them a legal form of protection.

Sumner's views regarding the topics of this book – the nature of business cycles and the need for economic planning – are clear. Sumner was a strong proponent of the market economy. Government stewardship and planning reduced individual freedom and could only lessen the general welfare. With a constant innovation of new products and new technologies government planners like business planners would find it hard to cope effectively with economic change. Furthermore, in an economy with creative destruction and change as constants and necessary for economic growth, planning could only be less than perfect, thus requiring the notion of failure and business cycles as part of the overall market process. What Sumner left out was an estimate of how long it would take for the market process to work. It might take decades for competitors to challenge large firms with market power, and recessions might last long enough that people would grow tired of waiting for the market to work. Under those conditions it is indeed not surprising that government leaders would be driven to act and the populace would be willing to have them act.

CONCLUSION

Sumner and Bellamy represent prototypes of two different attitudes that we shall find as part of the intellectual history of the Progressive Era and New Deal. Bellamy will represent the Progressive reformers, willing to remake society in order to eliminate business cycles and help the poor. He offered a clear model of a moral economy. Any person who supports a moral economy must be prepared to go as far as Bellamy did to bring it about through government ownership of the means of production, including his assumption that politics would become more moral, as would all of human behaviour. They must also accept his use of coercion where human behaviour was not up to the standards the moral economy required.

Supporters of the market economy should be willing to agree with the harsh results that Sumner found as part of the market where competition separates the fit from the unfit and the unfit must rely on the voluntary charity of the fit for any chance of survival. Although we are less concerned with this viewpoint in this book, we shall present ideas of supporters of the market economy. Not everyone who favoured the market economy, however, went as far as Sumner did in championing its virtues. They tried to find the middle ground where one can try to draw a fine line of markets and morals, hoping to get the best of both worlds but risking the possibility of getting the worst of morals and markets.

3. The business cycle: moral economy perspectives

As the nineteenth century turned into the twentieth century, the market economy in the US made a transition from production by small firms serving local customers to the greater use of large-scale firms and mass production for a national market. To create these large firms, either from internal growth or by merger and acquisition, business leaders began to use credit and the sale of stock as a source of funds. As a result, a system of financial capital was put into place, a system that has never abated. Under this system banking, credit and the stock market became more important elements of the market economy. The problem of economic crises continued, however, as the economy saw recessions such as the Panic of 1907 that seemingly started on Wall Street.

In this chapter we shall review the development of business cycle theory in the early twentieth century. Our focus is on the moral economy perspective of three individuals trained in economics and one politician. All four took the view that business cycles were a part of the market economy and to eliminate them the market economy had to be changed through government programmes that would serve to counteract them. We start with a broad social thinker who saw the potential for the market economy to evolve into a system of national planning that Edward Bellamy desired, and he was one of William Graham Sumner's former students.

THORSTEIN VEBLEN: BUSINESS CYCLES AND PLANNING

Thorstein Veblen (1857–1929) has long retained a reputation as a maverick economist. He began his academic career at Carleton College, where he studied economics with the noted economist John Bates Clark. In graduate school at Yale he took economics from Sumner, who encouraged him to become an economist. But Veblen's first interest was in philosophy, and he completed a doctorate by writing a dissertation on Immanuel Kant. Unable to find a teaching job in philosophy, he spent a long period on his family's farm in Minnesota, idly reading. Among the books he read was Bellamy's

Looking Backward and it changed his life. He returned to graduate school at Cornell to study economics and spent an unsettled career teaching at a number of universities (Dorfman 1972, pp. 46–53, 79).

The economics Veblen taught, however, bore little resemblance to the economics he had studied with Clark and Sumner. Like Sumner, Veblen based his economics on Darwinism, but with a twist. Veblen's Darwinism focused on the evolutionary growth of the economy through a process of cumulative causation and applied to group survival and not to individual fitness. Instead, Veblen saw competition and the market economy as being unstable and evolving into a more stable system. The main force for bringing about economic evolution was technology, because technological innovation constantly shook up the world.

What apparently made his economics so different was that Veblen had been influenced by Bellamy. As noted in Chapter 2, Bellamy had argued that the wealthy spent a great deal of their time and money on fads and fashions, creating a great deal of waste in the market economy. In addition, through their use of credit and through their cutting back on production when they could not sell all they produced, they added to the direct wastes of the market economy and caused the additional wastes of the business cycle. Veblen's works in economics were informed by these two points Bellamy made.

We can see the first point clearly in Veblen's most influential book, *The Theory of the Leisure Class* (Veblen 1899 [1973]). In it he satirized the consumption behaviour of the affluent as designed to show off their wealth by displays of what he called conspicuous consumption. While we might construe this as class warfare, Veblen observed that the rest of society emulated the conspicuous consumption patterns of the wealthy in order to be thought worthy. As a result, the market economy was extremely wasteful. We shall see in subsequent chapters that Veblen's views on this process of displaying wealth would influence a variety of social thinkers.

The second point is more detailed and relates to Veblen's theory of business cycles, which he presented in two articles, 'Industrial and pecuniary employments' and 'On the nature of capital' (Veblen 1901 [1932], pp. 279–323, 1908 [1932], pp. 352–86) and in his book, *The Theory of Business Enterprise* (Veblen 1904 [1935]). He started with a premise that Sumner and Bellamy would have recognized, the growth of large corporations was changing the economy. Underlying that growth was the technology of mass production, which Veblen referred to as 'the machine process.' The machine processes, he maintained, was creating larger units of production, with business being transformed from the small family firm or partnership to the large corporation. These large firms had become interconnected to the point that what one firm did had an impact on other firms

(Veblen 1904 [1935], pp. 47, 165–6). The problem was that the coordination of those large firms depended on monetary relationships in product markets and in financial markets. In Veblen's analysis, businessmen had previously been the proprietors of small firms seeking to earn a profit from the sale of goods and services that society needed. Their productive efficiency, as Sumner argued, made them fit to be the leaders of the economy.

In the new industrial economy, as members of a corporate system, they became financial experts in an effort to enhance the value of their firms (Veblen 1901 [1932], pp. 279–323). Because the corporation was valued on the basis of its stock price, businessmen had the objective of enhancing the stock market value of their firms. In the business system of the market economy ownership of physical capital gave businessmen a right to capture the benefits of technology for their firms. They used their control over technology to gain market power and charge higher prices to consumers, thereby earning higher profits. These profits in turn gave the capital of the corporation its stock market value. To Veblen, the value of capital was based on its 'income yielding capacity' as determined by the stock market (Veblen 1908 [1932], pp. 355–63). Physical capital embodying technology had productive value in providing goods and services for society. It had stock market value based on estimates of future profits. Since the stock market was psychological, the value it placed on capital was subjective. The subjective nature of the value of capital, however, did not keep businessmen from treating it as a real value and finding ways to enhance that value. One way to add value to capital was with credit, Veblen observed, by which businessmen used leverage to augment the capital that they had originally invested in a firm.

Leverage exists when a business uses debt to expand, increase profits and enhance the value of its stock. The idea is that its revenues will increase by enough to pay back the debt and interest on it, and leave a surplus to increase the earnings on which the stock's price depends. The risk of leverage comes about when profits do not increase by enough to cover the interest payment. Then the firm will have to pay the interest from profits, reducing earnings and the price of the stock. If the debt cannot be repaid, lenders may take over the business, the biggest risk of all. Leverage can add to the return investors get from their stock, but it also adds to the risk of owning the stock.

As Veblen saw it, through leverage, capitalists could use debt to expand their firms or buy out other firms. This use of credit could not create goods and services, however. Veblen argued that expansions of credit could only cause price increases and he was interested in how business leaders and investors responded to those price increases. His view was that they interpreted inflationary price increases as a real gain. Moreover, when investors interpreted those inflationary gains as increasing future income flows, they bought more stocks. That in turn increased the market value of the capital in any business, allowing it to increase its leverage even more. According to Veblen, the use of leverage set off a process of cumulative causation that had risky implications for society. Business leaders used credit to increase the stock market value of their firms. This increased value of their firms enabled them to take on even more credit, and the additional leverage continued the expansion of stock prices. A stock market boom took place, based on the illusion that the expansion of credit and business were sustainable. That illusion resulted in a period of 'irrational exuberance,' to use a recent term. Only when the earnings on that high market capitalization could not live up to investors' expectations would the capitalized earning power embedded in stock prices decline (Veblen 1904 [1935], pp. 99–131). Then there would be a collapse in the stock market and in the economy. Over-leveraged firms went bankrupt or were bought by firms that were solvent and the process would begin again. Business cycles were caused by financial instability from credit and leverage.

From this perspective, the market economy of large firms whose stock was publicly traded was inherently unstable due to leverage and the irrational exuberance it created. Once a credit bubble among large firms ended, it spread throughout the economy and the world due to the interconnectedness of all business entities. Credit and leverage made the system of financial capital inherently unstable.

What was to be done? In his publications Veblen wrote with an air of the detachment of a scientist, so for him the question was what was likely to happen. As a Darwinian, he anticipated that the economy would evolve, but in what direction? During each business cycle, he answered, some businesses became bankrupt and only stronger businesses survived. These survivors, moreover, grew larger and took over other firms through mergers and acquisitions. Would this trend eventually lead to a Bellamy world of nationalization? Veblen felt he had established that businessmen were no longer fit to run the economy because their habits of thought in terms of stock market valuations disrupted the interconnected market economy and made it unstable. Who then might become fit enough to run this system? That was the question Veblen asked.

Throughout his career Veblen endeavoured to identify social groups who would develop an industrial outlook that would set aside business habits of thought and take a social approach to production, that is, to replace the market economy with a moral one. One of his earliest articles investigated Bellamy's followers as possibly taking over the economy, but he gave up on them (Stabile 1988, pp. 213–15). He then turned to labour. In looking at labourers, Veblen found it to be a hopeful sign that they worked with the methods of modern production. Due to the advanced technology of mass production, what Veblen called the machine process, workers had to engage in rational thinking to function. Under the influence of their working with technology workers might become more rational and question the fitness of their bosses. Working through their unions, they sought to place limits on the rights of property underpinning business (Veblen 1904 [1935], pp. 155–7). When he looked at unions, Veblen was impressed by their outlook in having social values. Workers and their unions were attacking the market economy through strikes and by voting socialist at the time (1900–04), Veblen wrote, which is why he focused on them. To him, they were apparently developing a sceptical outlook regarding the validity of arguments in favour of the market economy.

Under the influence of this scepticism workers would become susceptible to socialist ideas. Their work with the machinery of mass production enabled them to think systematically as well as sceptically. Consequently, they would be able to see that the economy was an interconnected system much as the factories in which they worked were an interconnected system. Here Veblen turned the tables on Sumner. During the competitive era business owners competed and provided for society's needs. Indeed, they competed too well, because through the process of creative destruction they introduced new technologies to enhance their productive efficiency. Technology, however, produced large firms and required the use of finance and credit leverage to purchase even larger pieces of machinery. Business leaders then became distracted by the stock market and lost their focus on producing to meet society's needs. Their fitness as speculators in their own stock made them unfit to manage production. But the technology they introduced helped workers gain the outlook needed to manage production. Those workers would see the value of socialist thinking and help bring about Bellamy's moral economy.

Veblen was too critical a thinker to accept that the trends he had outlined meant the inevitability of the moral economy. Business leaders had options for forestalling the erosion of their power and influence. The most salient one was the government and military spending. Veblen recognized the power of patriotism to influence workers, as brought out by military activities such as the Spanish-American War. The use of patriotism could blunt socialist fervour among workers. In addition, Veblen identified an important factor that might lead the US down the road to militarism. The productive efficiency of modern technology was so great that it produced a surplus beyond the capability of the US society to consume. Government had to be called in to purchase this surplus, but Veblen believed that military expenditure was the most justifiable way for it to spend. Government spending on the military could offset the business cycle. Veblen observed that the government spending to fight the Spanish-American War had ended a recession and 'brought prosperity to the business community' (Veblen 1904 [1935], p. 198).

Militarism, however, imposed a harsh rule on society and made business leaders subservient to the government (Veblen 1904 [1935], p. 166). Consequently, Veblen's social forecast argued that Sumner's vision of the market economy was not sustainable. Instead, the market economy would evolve towards the overall control of a military system or the overall planning of Bellamy's moral economy. Veblen followed Bellamy in seeing a trend in the US economy towards a system of national planning run by a set of scientifically minded administrators (Veblen 1904 [1935], p. 9), but he also saw another potential scenario whereby Bellamy's moral economy with its industrial army might be sidetracked by a militarism that turned society into an armed camp. He did not think the market economy under the rule of competition could persist. Importantly, given Veblen's view that over time the market economy would be characterized by a lack of competition or might eventually be ruled by militarism, we conclude that Veblen viewed it as less than moral.

THEODORE ROOSEVELT STOPS A PANIC

Theodore Roosevelt (1858–1919) had a highly public career as a cowboy, soldier, author, police commissioner and politician before becoming president of the US. During his years as president (1901–09) many of the reforms of the Progressives were enacted, such as the Pure Food and Drug Act. Roosevelt's view of the role of the federal government was that the president had a duty to broaden his influence and to use that influence to ensure the welfare of all members of the US society (Roosevelt 1916, p. 371). He used this expanded view of the federal government to counteract the Panic of 1907.

Even before the turn of the twentieth century, the US economy had started a process of industrialization that brought about a period of impressive growth. To foster that growth, banks became larger in size to be able to accommodate the direct borrowing needs of large corporations and to handle the underwriting of stocks and bonds that the corporations sold to raise money. A new era of finance was ushered in, one based on leverage. Banks are especially reliant on leverage, because they borrow the money of depositors by paying them interest on their deposits and lend the money to businesses or individuals at a higher interest rate. Where depositors can withdraw their money at a moment's notice, banks are especially vulnerable to the risks of leverage, for their borrowing is short term while many of their loans are long term.

This use of leverage is especially risky in a financial system that is increasingly interconnected. In addition to borrowing from depositors, banks might borrow from other banks in the normal course of business. If the systemic use of leverage suffered a weak spot in any bank, it could readily spread to other banks. This systemic risk was especially dangerous at the beginning of the twentieth century, because the US did not have a central bank. This created a problem for banks in the Panic of 1907.

The Panic of 1907 centred on New York and its severity depended on how banks and bankers responded to it. The leading figure in the response was J.P. Morgan. After the Knickerbocker Trust Company failed by not being able to pay its depositors, Morgan drew a line with the Trust Company of America and ensured that it was able to remain solvent. Morgan and his colleagues worked with the Secretary of the Treasury George Cortelyou to have the federal treasury deposit $25 million in gold in New York banks to add to their liquidity. As a result of the work of Morgan and the federal government, the Panic subsided by November 1907.

Roosevelt left behind his own account of how he used the federal government to take action in trying to head off the Panic of 1907. He recognized that 'severe business disturbances and financial stringency' had started in New York City and then spread over the country, causing damage to the economy and threatening to bring the economic system to a halt. Because of government intervention, the Panic was stopped before it became 'a disaster fraught with untold misery and woe to all our people.' Roosevelt and Cortelyou felt their duty was 'to prevent appalling disaster by checking the spread of the panic before it grew so that nothing could check it' (Roosevelt 1916, pp. 452–3).

Roosevelt believed that it was necessary to restore confidence to end the Panic and that was what the financier J.P. Morgan was trying to do. One problem was that several banks were on shaky ground and some of their holdings of corporate stock had become worthless. To eliminate those worthless stocks, the leaders of US Steel had agreed to swap their stock for the worthless stock, but that would give them a greater ownership of the Tennessee Coal and Iron Company, which might be construed as giving the Steel Company enhanced market power. Roosevelt did not agree with this construction and approved the transaction. He wrote, 'The action was emphatically for the general good. It offered the only chance for arresting the panic, and it did arrest the panic' (Roosevelt 1916, pp. 455–7).

Roosevelt by his actions established a principle that when business failures had the capacity to bring down the economic system, the federal government should take a role in preventing those failures. Roosevelt did not promote direct government funding of those failed businesses but would permit other businesses to intervene to keep them from failing. As an interventionist in economic affairs Roosevelt would likely have incurred the wrath of Sumner. Sumner would have seen Roosevelt's interventions as violating the laissez-faire principles of the market economy. To Roosevelt, the days of the laissez-faire economics were over, having been ended by the growth of large businesses. He never doubted that government had the wisdom to intervene in the economy, albeit indirectly, when an economic crisis took place. The form of this intervention was government help for the voluntary actions of the business community to bailout firms that were at risk of failure and thereby avoid the systemic risk such failures might cause. Large corporations might be guided, regulated or controlled, but to Roosevelt there was no need for the government to own them as Bellamy had argued. In this way Roosevelt tried to draw that fine line between markets and morals.

WESLEY MITCHELL STUDIES THE BUSINESS CYCLE

Wesley Claire Mitchell (1874–1948) attended the University of Chicago where he studied with Veblen. Once he had finished his graduate work he began research about the problem of the fluctuations in the economy that appeared at irregular intervals. His first book on the subject, *Business Cycles*, was published in 1913 and made him the reigning expert on the topic. He would later help start and then direct the National Bureau of Economic Research to collect and analyse data on the US economy to a degree never before undertaken.

Business Cycles is a thorough examination of the economic fluctuations in the US and European economies. In it Mitchell reviewed all previous theories of the business cycle. He then observed that the problem was that those theories were all 'plausible but which are valid?' The best way to determine their validity was 'by study of the facts they purport to interpret' (Mitchell 1913 [1970], p. 19). Rather than set up a test of each theory, Mitchell would use them to inform his study as to which data about the economy he would collect.

Before investigating his data, Mitchell set forth a sketch of the main features of the market economy by dividing it into the business side, which dealt with the flows of money, prices and profits, and the industry side, which handled the technical operation of producing goods and services. The business side of money and profits dominated the industry side of production and it was in the handling of money that Mitchell would find the cause of business cycles. In the business side the goal was to make a profit based on the monetary value of the capital used in the business. At the same time, businesses were becoming integrated into a unified system where no business could act independently of another. These interconnections were held together through financial relationships from contracts to buy and sell raw materials to the use of stock ownership that made it easier for companies to own or control each other. This system of large corporations owned by stockholders was unified 'by business men in quest of profits.' Given that the market economy was run by profit-seeking businessmen, 'an investigation into the ebb and flow of contemporary economic activity must concern itself primarily with the phenomena of business traffic – that is, money-making' (Mitchell 1913 [1970], p. 26).

Under this approach prosperity depended on whatever factors had an impact on business profits. Profits in turn depended on the relationships among a number of prices, that is, the price the business sold its product for versus the prices the business paid for everything it bought to make the product. These prices and the profits they led to held together all the interrelated parts of the market economy. In addition, because these larger businesses employed credit to function, they were supervised by the commercial banks that loaned them money or by the investment banks that underwrote their stocks and bonds. These banks could keep track of how well the business functioned under a system of financial control (Mitchell 1913 [1970], p. 35).

Government entered the economic system with a different guidebook. Its function was to promote public welfare. It, too, had to operate under a system of money in terms of how much it spent to promote public welfare. Still, government had to base its sense of the public welfare in terms of what government leaders thought were the important needs of society, while businesses had to decide what customers wanted to buy. If that was the only difference, however, 'society would probably be organized on the basis of state socialism' rather than by the market economy. But there was another difference, the 'government is far less efficient in pursuing its aim of social welfare than business enterprise in pursuing its aim of making money' (Mitchell 1913 [1970], p. 36). Consequently, the idea of having government control the economy had not been popular. Government did not have the weeding out process that failure brings in the way the market economy did (Mitchell 1913 [1970], p. 38).

Because there was no government control over business, many criticized the business system for being 'planless.' Mitchell disagreed. Within each business unit planning took place. Business leaders used money to hire all the experts needed to execute that planning, with the result that within each firm production was coordinated to a greater degree than ever before. As firms grew larger and controlled more industrial facilities, the process of planning by experts expanded. But the process did not expand quite far enough. The problem was in coordinating the production activities of all businesses. Coordination of the overall economy remained dependent on the activities of individual businesses seeking to make profits, but 'profit is an uncertain, flickering light.' Coordination by prices and profits thus 'confuses the guidance of economic activity by interjecting a large element of chance into every business venture' (Mitchell 1913 [1970], p. 39). These risks grew larger because large firms required more time to gear up for production, but that was the trend in the market economy.

With the economic background of the market economy described, Mitchell then provided his readers with a long survey of business cycles from 1873 to 1911. His overall goal was to analyse how the different sets of data influenced the profitability of business, for that was the key variable in how well the economy functioned. When business was not profitable, the economy did not prosper. Consequently, Mitchell considered all of the forces that had an impact on the profits of businesses and how those businesses responded to declining profits and the threat of bankruptcy. When they responded favourably to their profit outlook, the economy gained upward momentum, while an unfavourable response led to downward momentum in the economy. In addition, the lack of coordination among firms over price changes led to lags in those changes during recessions or recoveries, which created short-term profit opportunities for some firms and losses for others.

In terms of what to do about business cycles, Mitchell noted three proposals to ameliorate the business cycle in the US: reform of the banking system; the use of expenditures by the government and by the railroads to counteract the decline in spending that brought on a recession; and efforts to stabilize the dollar. Banking reform was necessary, and on the agenda in the US through the creation of the Federal Reserve Act while Mitchell was writing. The other proposals had not been tried in great enough degree to determine their efficacy (Mitchell 1913 [1970], p. 588). He did not propose a system of national economic planning, even though he had indicated that a lack of overall planning could be construed as a potential cause of business cycles.

Mitchell's lack of a proposal for national economic planning can readily be attributed to his recognition that socialism was not popular in the US, due in part to a mistrust of the efficiency of government compared to business. Let us recall that he had concerns over government being efficient and being able to eliminate failed policies (Mitchell 1913 [1970], pp. 36, 38). Still, he was not opposed to government intervention in the economy. We can see this in his analysis of government programmes to combat the recession of 1920–21.

At its annual meeting for 1922 the American Economic Association held a session on the recession of 1920–21 and Mitchell was one of the main presenters. He pointed out that as long as the US economy was based on a system of money and credit, it was doubtful that business cycles could be eliminated. But there was a prospect of mitigating some of the problems that recessions caused. Policies to control the causes of business cycles would be difficult but there was hope for improvement 'by prudent management of processes which are subject to control' (Mitchell 1922, p. 21). For example, in the US a centralization of banking had been initiated by the Federal Reserve Act of 1913. In the 1920–21 recession the Federal Reserve 'was put to the test and found adequate' (Mitchell 1922, p. 21). The lesson Mitchell drew from the experiences of the US economy with central banking was that it enabled the Federal Reserve to keep a financial crisis from becoming a panic. A government-sponsored central bank could help control the business cycle.

The next phase in controlling the business cycle was in keeping the economy from having too great an expansion and Mitchell believed that politicians and business leaders were thinking about 'prevention as well as cure.' As Secretary of Commerce, Herbert Hoover had held a Conference on Unemployment, which worked on ways 'for framing a preventive program' (Mitchell 1922, p. 22). In the preventive programmes there had been a stress on taking steps to head off a recession during the later stages of a boom, as the economy approached full employment of workers and factories.

The main point about the recession of 1920–21 made by persons wanting to follow the programme of prevention was that the Federal Reserve had not raised interest rates quickly enough in 1919 to slow down the boom of that period. To some extent, the action of the Federal Reserve had been hampered by a need to keep interest rates low to help the federal government sell its last issue of bonds to finance World War I. Mitchell observed, 'we are justified in hoping that in the future such exigencies will seldom arise to prevent the Federal Reserve Board from adopting the policy which seems wise in the economic interest of the public' (Mitchell 1922, p. 22). The leaders at the Federal Reserve recognized that it was important to increase interest rates before the economic boom got out of hand as a way of reducing the magnitude of the recession that would follow (Mitchell 1922, pp. 23–4). Critics of the Federal Reserve today argue that its failure to remember this simple rule helped to create the housing boom, the end of which brought about the great recession of 2007–09.

In addition to monetary policy, there were other policies that showed promise. The first policy Mitchell reviewed was the timing of 'the long-range planning of public works, with intent to get a larger part of such undertakings executed in periods of depression' (Mitchell 1922, p. 26). Several states in the US had adopted this plan and a bill for similar action by the federal government had been proposed in Congress. The idea of the plan was twofold: it would keep government projects from adding to the boom by postponing construction projects and it would use them to create jobs during a recession. Mitchell maintained that a large amount of government projects could be timed 'on the basis of the business cycle without detriment to social welfare' (Mitchell 1922, pp. 26–7).

Mitchell's proposal represented a counter-cyclical government spending programme whereby the government would run a budget surplus during periods of prosperity and then spend the accumulated surplus on public works projects to create jobs during a recession. It was also part of Mitchell's work on the business cycle and unemployment undertaken for the Presidential Conference on Unemployment called by Herbert Hoover as Secretary of Commerce. Mitchell, however, was overly optimistic on public works legislation by the federal government. Bills to implement this public works policy were introduced in Congress several times in the 1920s, but none was enacted (Rothbard 2000, pp. 2881–911).

He also indicated that it might be feasible to encourage businesses to take the same counter-cyclical approach by retaining earnings during recoveries and expanding their factories with capital spending programmes during a recession. But that approach would require that some agency be capable of convincing them that this counter-cyclical investment programme was in their interest, as they mostly expanded their investment plans during the heady days of the boom period. Another counter-cyclical policy Mitchell found interesting was the new plans of unemployment insurance being proposed in a number of states. Because these plans charged businesses insurance premiums that were based on their labour turnover rates, they gave 'the employer an inducement to stabilize his working force' by not hiring too many workers during the boom and laying off fewer of them during the recession (Mitchell 1922, p. 28). In addition, the unemployment benefits would help workers who were unemployed maintain a portion of their purchasing power.

Mitchell ended with a series of challenges to economists. From his perspective, the wastes of the business cycle related to problems inherent in having a market economy based on money and profits. This use of money went 'straight to the heart of the difficulty which we must face in our efforts to control the business cycle.' Mitchell described the problem as one where labour was idle when it wanted work and plant and equipment were unused while owners wanted to produce. 'For with all its efficiency,' he went on, 'the Money Economy has a fundamental defect ... when for any reason it is not profitable to make goods we are forced to sacrifice our will as human beings to our will as money makers' (Mitchell 1922, p. 31). By merely recognizing this fundamental issue, Mitchell foresaw a future where economists would study the market economy to understand how its rules kept efforts to control the business cycle from being implemented. Once economists identified those rules as a set of human institutions, they could be changed. That was the task Mitchell set before his fellow economists and he had confidence in their ability to fulfil it (Mitchell 1922, p. 32).

Mitchell was optimistic that the growth of economic knowledge could foster a greater capability for controlling the business cycle. His support of the Federal Reserve as an effective agency for controlling the economy as well as his interest in counter-cyclical fiscal policy by the government were harbingers of things to come in economics and the economy. His recognition of the need for some agency to prompt businesses to adopt a counter-cyclical investment policy hints at a need for some type of planning system for the economy. Mitchell's mentor Veblen had stated this need more strongly than Mitchell, perhaps because Veblen had been influenced by Bellamy. Although not explicitly stated, it seems safe to assume that Mitchell thought planning would be helpful to offset some of the sharp edges of a market economy.

JOHN MAURICE CLARK: OVERHEAD COSTS AND THE BUSINESS CYCLE

One economist who took up Mitchell's challenge to gather more information about economic institutions was John Maurice Clark (1884–1963), who had a long career at Columbia University. His most prominent book, *Studies in the Economics of Overhead Costs* (Clark 1923a), was an analysis of how businesses and the market economy handled overhead costs, the fixed costs of production.

From his study of overhead costs, Clark pointed to two causes of business cycles. The first cause related to the problem that expenditures for the capital equipment that constituted overhead were concentrated into short time periods. Whenever a business had an increase in demand at a time when it was operating at full capacity, it would build new facilities to increase its productive capacity. But new facilities were a considerable expense, which meant that small changes in consumer demand could lead to larger changes in investment demand. Clark referred to this as the accelerator (Clark 1923a, pp. 389–90).

The result of this accelerator process was that booms and recessions had reinforcing effects that amplified their total force. During a boom a rise in consumer demand increased the demand for capital equipment, and the producers of capital equipment would expand and hire more workers, whose pay would add to consumer demand and lead to more demand for capital equipment and so on. As consumer demand levelled off, however, the demand for capital equipment would decline, leading to contractions in the production of capital equipment, the unemployment of workers in the capital equipment industries, lower consumer demand and the beginning of a recessionary spiral. Businessmen would like to buy capital during the trough of the recession when prices were low, as Mitchell had argued they should, but they could never be sure when the bottom had been reached (Clark 1923a, p. 397). With this perspective Clark could conclude that the market economy was not a good way to control the business cycle, and he proposed national planning as a way to control it instead. But there was a second way overhead costs contributed to those cycles.

In an unusual use of overhead costs Clark applied it to labour. He stated the case as follows: 'There is a minimum of maintenance of the laborer's health and working capacity which must be borne by someone, whether the laborer works or not' or else 'the community suffers a loss through the deterioration of its working power' (Clark 1923a, p. 16). Workers were responsible for their own sustainability. When their wages were not adequate to maintain them or when they became unemployed, if the community did not make additional provisions for them, members of the labour force might deteriorate.

Businesses shifted many of the costs of maintaining labour onto society through layoffs and wage reductions, leaving it to society to help sustain the workforce. To avoid this cost shifting a community approach to industrial production was needed. As an illustration of a community approach, Clark wrote, 'If all industry was integrated and owned by workers … . It would be clear to worker-owners that the real cost of labour could not be materially reduced by unemployment' (Clark 1923a, p. 402). Workers knew that laying them off did not reduce their costs of living, but shifted them. Clark did not see a market solution to this problem. He wrote, 'The overhead cost of labor is a collective burden upon industry in general, but the market does not allocate to each employer the share for which his own enterprise is responsible' (Clark 1923a, p. 372).

In a separate article in 1923 Clark analysed how his theory of overhead costs shed light on what happened during a recession. To do so, he pointed out that to workers and the community as a whole wages were an overhead cost while for businesses those same wages represented a variable cost that depended on the number of workers they hired (Clark 1923b, pp. 50–51). Clark saw that issue in terms of how business viewed those costs versus how society should view them. He argued, 'We may say that most of the ultimate costs of labor to the laborer and to the community are constant costs and that they are translated into variable costs to the employer by our customary system of wages' (Clark 1923b, p. 54). What was needed was a coordinated programme to convert wages into a fixed cost for business and Clark suggested that unions should use their bargaining power to win a wage system that gave workers 'a substantial minimum retainer plus a moderate charge proportioned to work actually done' (Clark 1923b, p. 58). If a part of the wage rate was converted into an overhead cost for business, then the variable costs of labour would be lower and it would be worth keeping those workers actively producing even if prices were low. If all firms in the economy followed this approach, they would all keep producing and the recession might be avoided as the result would be a 'general stabilization' of wages, prices and total demand (Clark 1923b, p. 59). Idle factories and workers during a recession were a waste that could be avoided with the proper system of social cost accounting.

But how would such a system of social cost accounting be implemented? Clark believed that wage bargains were the result of the unequal strength of workers compared to employers, which made it a national problem requiring government intervention through planning with a goal of mandating a 'social minimum' in terms of a standard of living (Clark 1926, p. 176). To offset the business cycles' overhead costs created, Clark deemed it necessary to have a system of social planning using national councils. To him, that system did not require the type of planning that Bellamy wanted, but it did go much further than Mitchell and even Veblen in pushing for a form of planning as a remedy for the business cycle.

CONCLUSION

What are the causes of business cycles? For Veblen, following Bellamy, excessive credit was the culprit. Both saw excessive credit generating overproduction. This overproduction, caused by a lack of coordination among firms, created a situation whereby prices would fall and businesses would be unable to pay off their debts resulting in layoffs and closings. These layoffs and closings exacerbated the overproduction problem because workers could not buy the products to reduce the overproduction. Once business earnings no longer matched investors' expectations a stock market bust and a business cycle downturn was inevitable.

On the other hand, Mitchell and Clark saw the cause of business cycles in the production side of the economy. Mitchell argued that in an economy based on market incentives any event that threatened the profitability of business had the potential to cause a downturn. Once a downturn took place in one industry, the interconnected economy ensured that it would become widespread, however. It was the market economy as a whole that generated business cycles. Mitchell was cautious about identifying any commonality in events that led to negative impacts on profits and downturns in economic activity. In his words, 'it is probable that the economists of each generation will see reason to recast the theory of business cycles which they learned in their youth' (Mitchell 1913 [1970], p. 583).

Clark's analysis of business cycles saw them coming from misallocation of capital during prosperous times. Businesses experiencing an increase in demand for their products would increase their investment in new capital equipment in order to satisfy the increased demand. This process tended to concentrate business spending in short time periods and was labelled by Clark as the accelerator principle. Once consumer demand levelled off the demand for capital equipment would also fall, generating unemployment in the capital goods industry and eventually in the consumer products industry. The result was the inevitable downturn of the business cycle. His idea that labour was an overhead cost for society but a variable cost for business added to the problem of the business cycle, because business would lay off workers as soon as a downturn began, adding to the decline in demand for consumer products.

All three of our economists in this chapter posed the crucial question: is the market economy a fair way to organize economic life? For Veblen, the market economy was destined to create a system of a few large firms dominating economic outcomes and without competition how could workers and consumers be guaranteed a fair wage and price? Clark saw a basic unfairness in market economies since markets could not address the need for business to incur the 'overhead' cost of labour. In the market economy businesses simply pushed this cost on to the community at large. Veblen and Clark looked for national economic planning to take care of the problems caused by business cycles, although neither of them set forth a theory of how planning took place.

Mitchell saw markets as acceptable ways to organize economic life, but believed that limitations on markets such as some planning might be helpful to offset some of the rough edges of a market economy. The problem was in deciding who would do the planning. Mitchell was sceptical that government had the capability to plan an economy effectively. Still, Roosevelt's actions in 1907 and government-sponsored agencies such as the Federal Reserve were becoming adept in adjusting the economy. Moreover, it was possible for the government to use counter-cyclical spending programmes on public works projects to offset the decline of business during a downturn and perhaps ameliorate its impact. Business cycles were intrinsic to the market economy with its emphasis on profits, but it would take much more study by economists of how to change economic institutions before anything resembling the moral economy could be brought about.

4. The business cycle: market economy perspectives

Advocates for a moral economy felt they were on strong ground by arguing that recurrent business cycles were a part of the market economy and that replacing the market economy with the moral economy was necessary to avoid the damage those cycles caused in terms of the unemployment of workers and the underemployment of capital. Proponents of the market economy, however, would not have accepted this verdict. They did not ever argue that the market economy worked perfectly. We saw in Chapter 2 that William Graham Sumner recognized that the businesses that made up the market economy often made mistakes and misallocated capital. When those mistakes were large and spilled over into other industries, as was very likely in an interconnected market economy, a recession would result. The recession, however, would correct the mistakes that businesses made, albeit ruthlessly. The corrections of the business cycle were part of the economic process of weeding out bad businesses, that is, those that erred too greatly.

In this chapter we shall continue to review the development of business cycle theory in the early twentieth century. Our focus is on individuals who looked at business cycles from the perspective of proponents of the market economy. They identified business cycles as part of the market economy but believed that they were an acceptable cost when compared to the advantages the market economy had for bringing about prosperity. Our starting point is with another of Sumner's students, Irving Fisher.

IRVING FISHER DEFENDS THE MARKET ECONOMY

Irving Fisher (1867–1947) would be included on any list of prominent early economists from the US. He attended Yale University with a major in mathematics and went on to earn a mathematics PhD. As Veblen before him, Fisher took an economics course from Sumner and liked Sumner and the course very much. When he was searching about for a PhD dissertation topic, he sought Sumner's advice. Sumner, no mathematician himself, encouraged Fisher to do work in mathematical economics (Allen 1993,

p. 53). Fisher eventually converted himself into a theoretical economist who also did pioneering work in economic statistics.

From Adam Smith on until the end of the nineteenth century, economists had tried to explain why capital earned an income in a way that avoided the appearance of chicanery or exploitation that opponents of the market economy like Marx insisted it carried. Fisher offered a new explanation in 1906, when he published his initial major work, *The Nature of Capital and Income*, which he dedicated to Sumner. He labelled it as his effort to give the concepts of capital and income a rational basis (Fisher 1906 [1930], p. vii).

In the market economy, he argued, a major form of wealth was capital. In previous eras the value of capital, like that of any form of wealth, equalled its exchange price, the amount for which it could be sold at any given time (Fisher 1906 [1930], pp. 3–13). The owner of a small business could find out how much his capital was worth only by selling it. Financial markets had changed the valuation of capital by their use of securities as a way of owning wealth. In the corporate system being developed in the US the transfer of ownership in the form of shares of stock had become easy and commonplace. This constant transfer of ownership offered a continual value of the capital of a business. It enabled Fisher to argue that the value of capital used in a publicly owned business would be equal to its stock market value and the profits that businesses collected and paid out to stockholders represented a return on the value their capital added to society in the form of goods and services.

What was the basis for stock market valuations of capital? To answer this question, Fisher stressed the relationship between capital and income. The sequence for that relationship started when businesses used physical capital to produce goods and services. When they sold those goods and services at their market price, businesses earned income. The discounted value of that income as a flow in the future set the value of capital. The future may turn out differently but the current value of capital was based on a current estimate of an expected future flow of income (Fisher 1906 [1930], pp. 185–8). In a certain world with a sure flow of future income and a fixed and permanent rate of interest, the value of capital was the present value of the future income from the specified capital discounted at the established interest rate (Fisher 1906 [1930], pp. 202, 211).

In this certain world changes in the value of capital resulted from changes in the interest rate or in the flow of future income. An uncertain world, such as businesses faced, included risk. Fisher described the problem of valuing financial assets under conditions of risk as follows: 'If we take the history of the prices of stocks and bonds, we shall find it chiefly to consist of a record of changing estimates of futurity, due to what is called chance' (Fisher 1906

[1930], p. 265). All owners of stock operated under conditions of risk, as no future income was certain. To use this view of risk in valuing stock, Fisher pointed out that the two variables used in valuing it, the future interest rate and future incomes, were unknowable. The problem of changes in the interest rate was handled by using the current rate, but unforeseen changes in the rate of interest caused changes in the value of stock. Because interest rates did not fluctuate greatly, however, the main source of risk in stock valuation concerned future income. To value a security, in theory, an investor in stock could use statistical tools to estimate the probability that future income would fall outside a given range (Fisher 1906 [1930], pp. 406–10). Since the probabilities used in making this type of calculation were subjective, Fisher acknowledged that most investors used a rule-of-thumb approach. Still, he believed that 'the mere guessing about future income conditions [should] be replaced by making use of the modern statistical applications of probability' (Fisher 1906 [1930], pp. 281–2, 410).

The point Fisher was making has a modern name: efficient markets theory. Under this theory, financial markets, like all markets, are not capricious but random. We cannot predict where they will move from day to day, but in the long run they price stocks and the value of capital correctly. Persons like Veblen, who thought financial markets added to the instability of the market system, were wrong. The stock of a business might shoot up very rapidly, as investors judged that its future income would pay a return that was high enough to compensate them for the risk of buying the stock, based on new information. Such opportunities were short-lived, Fisher continued, 'because of the existence of competition, by which the special advantage of individuals through special knowledge, foresight, etc., is offset by the vigilance of their rivals' (Fisher 1906 [1930], p. 321). Whatever the starting point of a stock price, over time its value would follow a trend, except that the influence of risk would cause it to move up or down as investors gained 'new information' or their 'confidence in the future receives a shock' (Fisher 1906 [1930], pp. 321–2).

Fisher's work stands as a counterpoint to Bellamy and Veblen. To them, the market economy was chaotic, disorderly and prone to ruinous business cycles brought on when finance got out of hand. For Fisher, however, there was a rational order underlying all the changes going on in the economy, including the stock market. To see that rational underlying order was the function of scientific economics as informed by mathematics and statistics. To use modern terms, the opponents of the market economy were being 'fooled by randomness' into thinking that what they saw was systemic risk getting out of hand when what it really represented was the functioning of efficient markets.

If financial markets were efficient, they were eliminated as a cause of economic recessions. Given his concern for economic reality, how did Fisher explain those recessions? Fisher did offer several explanations for business cycles during his long career. Here we focus on the one he presented early in his career in his book, *The Purchasing Power of Money* (Fisher 1911). His starting point was with the quantity theory of money, which showed how changes in the money supply would cause inflation (Fisher 1911, pp. 25–7).

Previous economic thinkers had not considered inflation as being related to recessions. Fisher took the view that changes in the money supply caused changes in prices, but there was a time lag before the full impact on prices took place. As a result, interest rates did not adjust to inflation as rapidly as they should, thus lowering the real cost of borrowing for businesses. In addition, during a period of inflation, a businessman should find the prices he charged going up at the same rate as his costs of production, which would keep his real level of profits the same. Fisher, however, noted that 'the business man's profits will rise more than this because the rate of interest he has to pay will not adjust itself immediately' (Fisher 1911, p. 59). The cost of borrowing money fell relative to other prices because interest rates lagged behind price changes. Businessmen in that situation would borrow and expand their businesses. The borrowing and expansion of businesses would further increase the money supply and add to inflation. With interest rates still lagging behind, further borrowing would take place and banks, feeling that rising interest rates would add to their profits, continued to lend (Fisher 1911, pp. 58–60), even though they lost money due to the lag in interest rate increases behind inflation. All of this expansion of business led to an increase in total economic output but there remained limits to how fast output could expand.

These limits helped put an end to the prosperity brought about by the increase in the supply of money. Fisher wrote, 'The expansion coming from this cycle of causes cannot proceed forever' (Fisher 1911, p. 64). Eventually the rate of interest would increase and when it fully adjusted for price increases, economic conditions would change. Banks would find their reserves insufficient to support a large amount of loans and raise interest rates to their proper level to account for the inflation. At this higher interest rate businessmen no longer made profits and stopped borrowing and expanding their business. Some businesses not able to borrow funds to keep operating would wind up in bankruptcy. When they did, savers would worry about the solvency of the banks that had their money and start a run. To protect themselves, banks would cut back on loans and increase interest rates even further. Businesses that were desperate would pay the higher rate of interest, but be pushed closer to bankruptcy as well. The end result was a collapse in business confidence, but for Fisher the decline in business confidence stemmed directly from the 'belated adjustment of the interest rate' (Fisher 1911, p. 66).

Once the collapse came, prices would begin to fall. Now the problem was that interest rates again lagged behind price decreases, with the result that they stayed too high compared to the expected profitability of business. The previous process reversed itself until the interest rate declined in line with the fall in prices. Once the economy hit a bottom in the recession, the process of inflation and expansion would begin again (Fisher 1911, pp. 68–71).

From this approach, Fisher determined that the economy went through these cycles about every ten years. In these ten-year cycles the economy fluctuated back and forth trying to find equilibrium. It would find such an equilibrium point through the self-correcting process of the market, but there were always forces that prevented the corrections from taking place. The most common of those forces, Fisher noted, were increases in the quantity of money. The solution he offered was that if banks should be 'conservative in making loans during the periods of rising prices,' the process of expansion would not be so great 'and the succeeding fall is apt to be less' (Fisher 1911, p. 71). Fisher, however, never identified an economic force that would cause bankers to be conservative in making loans during inflationary periods. He merely hoped that bankers would lose their money illusion and become more proficient at their jobs.

Fisher represents an updated version of Sumner that defended the market economy while admitting that it contained flaws that made it risky. The biggest flaw was that economic decisions looked towards the future by being based on future income, but the future was unknowable. Mistakes and the risks attached to them would be made, but the market economy was efficient in correcting those mistakes. The problem was in how long it took for economic actors to recognize their mistakes and to take remedial action. To the extent that economics developed as a scientific discipline and became more influential among businessmen, they might recognize their mistakes more quickly and reduce the risk their decisions about the future caused for them and for the economy. In the context of this work, Fisher's view of the market economy as self-correcting and efficient represents an acceptable, fair and moral outcome. In particular, profits were a 'fair' result as a return on capital investment because capital added to society's goods and services and generated a higher standard of living.

HENRY FORD EXPERIENCES A RECESSION

Henry Ford (1863–1947) still stands clearly as a paradigm of what made manufacturing in the US one of the most remarkable stories of the twentieth century. Born on a family farm in Michigan, Ford was always tinkering with machines. Eventually he tinkered enough to build an automobile. Additional tinkering led him to the assembly line and the mass production of his 'Model T,' the car that turned the world into drivers and made Ford a classic example of creative destruction. To Ford, his low-cost cars were the key factor in 'the commercial success of the Ford Motor Company' (Ford 1922, 'Introduction').

   Not every business succeeded and to Ford the key ingredient in business failures was a reliance on finance. He recalled that when he started in the automobile business finance had just started making inroads into business and 'many corporations were being floated and financed.' His view was that a business should start out small and grow through the reinvestment of profits. That approach set him against the grain of 'modern' business methods, which he described as follows:

> The plan at that time most in favor was to start off with the largest possible capitalization and then sell all the stock and all the bonds that could be sold. Whatever money happened to be left over after all the stock and bond-selling expenses and promoters' charges and all that, went grudgingly into the foundation of the business. A good business was not one that did good work and earned a fair profit. A good business was one that would give the opportunity for the floating of a large amount of stocks and bonds at high prices. It was the stocks and bonds, not the work, that mattered. I could not see how a new business or an old business could be expected to be able to charge into its product a great big bond interest and then sell the product at a fair price. I have never been able to see that. (Ford 1922, Chapter 2)

Ford's strictures on finance led to his explanation of the business cycle. He recognized that the economy and the businesses that constituted it often grew 'by fits and starts.' Some persons called a recession a period of overproduction, but Ford disagreed. What was called overproduction was 'great stocks of goods at too high prices.' To him, this was not overproduction, but 'bad manufacturing or bad financing.' Bad manufacturing and bad financing meant that business had lost sight of production for consumers and focused on making money through finance. The system of finance was the cause of recessions and it was that system that needed to be changed if recessions were to be mitigated. He wrote: 'It is perfectly possible, with the reorganization of business and finance that is bound to come about, to take the ill effect of seasons, if not the seasons, out of industry, and also the periodic depressions' (Ford 1922, Chapter 9).

In his own business Ford had avoided booms and busts by increasing production and sales each year no matter what the economic conditions were. During the recession of 1920–21, for example, Ford sold over a million cars, five times the number sold during the last 'normal period' before World War I, 1913–14. In doing so, Ford claimed to be 'not much concerned with the statistics and the theories of the economists on the recurring cycles of prosperity and depression.' They called the periods when prices are high 'prosperous.' But prosperity existed only when prices were in line with incomes. The Ford approach was: 'If the prices of goods are above the incomes of the people, then get the prices down to the incomes' (Ford 1922, Chapter 9). If the manufacturer put the consumer first, he would cut prices when the consumer did not buy what he wanted to sell. But manufacturers who had to pay interest on bonds or dividends on stock did not feel that they were able to cut prices.

Ford believed that for most businesses reductions in wages were the easiest way to cut costs and thus prices. Instead, they should recognize that a recession was a challenge to business to come up with ways to make labour more productive to cut costs. Whenever a recession hit the economy, someone had to take a reduction in income. Ford believed that business should take the loss, but to him it was not really a loss when businesses used past profits to survive and were then able to gain higher profits in the future when the recession was over. What stopped businesses from cutting prices was finance (Ford 1922, Chapter 11).

As an example of how to handle hard times, Ford detailed his own experiences during the 1920–21 recession. In December 1920 there were more automobile plants closed than open and many of the closed ones were in the control of bankers. As sales slowed during 1921, Ford began to cut prices to below his costs. He noted:

> We received a deal of criticism. It was said that we were disturbing conditions. That is exactly what we were trying to do. We wanted to do our part in bringing prices from an artificial to a natural level. I am firmly of the opinion that if at this time or earlier manufacturers and distributors had all made drastic cuts in their prices and had put through thorough house-cleanings we should not have so long a business depression. Hanging on in the hope of getting higher prices simply delayed adjustment. (Ford 1922, Chapter 12)

Prices eventually fell but if business had cut prices when Ford did, they would have taken their losses early in the recession but then would have been in a position to stimulate demand through further price cuts. The businesses that held out on price reductions had to pay interest on their inventories, which cost them additional losses. As a result, unemployment increased, further reducing consumer demand (Ford 1922, Chapter 12).

At Ford, sales at first increased due to the price cuts, but soon they began to decline due to poor overall economic conditions. He continued to produce cars, but in December 1921 shut down operations for six weeks. During that time he began a reorganization of the company to cut back costs. Although there were layoffs, by January 1922 sales had picked up and Ford called back a skeleton crew to begin production. At the same time, he had eliminated waste and when full production was achieved worker productivity had increased and office staff had been reduced. As a result, he concluded, 'We cut the overhead charge from $146 a car to $93 a car.' To him that meant 'by the elimination of waste, it is possible to make an "impossible" price' (Ford 1922, Chapter 12). Thus, he had made the point that a business could develop its own resources and not have to use credit (Ford 1922, Chapter 12).

The danger of finance was that bankers became involved in a business. Bankers, he went on, 'think solely in terms of money. They think of a factory as making money, not goods. They want to watch the money, not the efficiency of production.' To a banker, reducing prices meant a loss of profits; bankers did not take to the long-term view that a sacrifice in profits in the short term could lead to greater profits in the future. Bankers were no more capable than the average business leader, but through the use of credit bankers were in control of business. Indeed, there had been an expansion of banker control over business and that had been aided by the Federal Reserve System giving banks a large amount of credit (Ford 1922, Chapter 12).

Ford in his writing presented himself as a modern business leader with old-fashioned ideas. He had created his company through hard work and thrift and then succeeded by giving consumers what they wanted – dependable cars at lower prices. In this regard, he exemplified both Say's Law and the process of creative destruction. The modern view of business involved expansion through credit and leverage. Companies that practised the modern view, however, were especially vulnerable when a recession came. Many of them failed under tight economic conditions and could not repay their loans. Their failures led to the failure of other firms, which made the recession worse. When companies failed, moreover, they had to lay off their workers, causing misery throughout the economy. Here Ford might have agreed with Edward Bellamy and Thorstein Veblen that credit in the market economy added to its instability. But he would not have gone as far as Bellamy in seeking national planning as a solution. Rather, he would have reformed the credit system – he did not say how – to end the problems it caused. Whether that meant Ford branded credit and those who used it as immoral was arguable. The use of credit by many businesses, however, made him question the efficacy of their management.

FOSTER AND CATCHINGS AND THE DILEMMA OF THRIFT

Although the 1920s saw a great deal of prosperity, they were also marked by several recessions. Halfway through the decade, William Trufant Foster (1879–1950) and Waddill Catchings (1879–1960) published a series of books (Foster and Catchings 1924, 1925, 1928) that presented the paradoxical idea that recessions were due to the way savings reduced spending by consumers. Foster was an academic who eventually became president of Reed College, while Catchings had a long career as an investment banker. They stated their point quite clearly in the preface of their book, *Profits*: 'Why must industry as a whole slow down because of "overproduction" when millions are suffering from "underconsumption?"' Their answer was that at some point in 'a period of increased productivity' the time came 'when the people who want the goods which have already been produced lack the money wherewith to purchase them.' That was an obvious answer, but the real question then became: '*What causes this deficiency of purchasing power?*' (Foster and Catchings 1925, p. v, emphasis in original). Their answer was that savings meant a reduction in consumption and was the primary cause of the underconsumption that produced recessions.

To argue their case, Foster and Catching set forth a theoretical apparatus they called the 'circuit flow of money and the annual equation' (Foster and Catchings 1925, p. 246). The 'circuit flow of money' is similar to what Keynesian economists now call the multiplier (see Chapter 12). Every time a consumer spent, he generated income for a business, which then used that income to hire workers, who then spent their income on goods, generating more income for business and so on (Foster and Catchings 1925, p. 252). The 'annual equation' represented the idea that in the economy as a whole aggregate demand must equal aggregate supply or as Foster and Catchings put it, 'products find their way to consumers as rapidly as they are produced' (Foster and Catchings 1925, p. 248). To demonstrate how the two ideas combined in a stable economy, Foster and Catchings offered a diagram of 'the circuit flow of money' (Foster and Catchings 1925, p. 255), an elaborate version of the circular flow diagram that is now standard in introductory textbooks in economics. Their real concern, however, was with breaks in the circuit flow, today referred to as leakages, that led to instability in the economy. The key leakage that altered the flow was savings.

They first considered business saving, that is, retained earnings, in a long chapter that analysed a variety of scenarios of business saving. In all of them they concluded that if a business 'earns profits from sales to consumers, and uses the profits in such a way that they are not returned to consumers, dollar for dollar, within the period in question, consumers have no means of buying the output without a fall in prices.' In addition, if a business increased its production without increasing 'its payments to consumers within the period in question, consumers cannot possibly buy the output at the current price-level' (Foster and Catchings 1925, p. 282).

In looking at savings by consumers in another chapter, Foster and Catchings first indicated that even if consumers spent all of their income on consumption, they would not remedy the problem caused by business saving. Foster and Catchings recognized that individuals save by putting their money into some form of financial asset, from savings in a bank to stocks in corporations. These forms of savings were placed back into the economy in the form of borrowing for investment by business. Investments in business, however, aimed at increasing their productive capacity and thus added to the problem by putting even more consumer goods into the market at a time when underconsumption was prevalent (Foster and Catchings 1925, p. 291). The 'circuit flow' required that when a business took in money for goods it must spend that money not to increase the productive capacity of its factories but to hire workers who would use it to buy more goods. The expansion of production by building new factories created jobs and income for consumers to spend, which added to prosperity and kept the economy growing for longer than it would have by counteracting some degree of underconsumption, but eventually some of that income would be removed from the 'circuit flow' as savings, and the prosperity would end.

When they plugged the savings of consumers and the savings of business into the 'annual equation' that total production must equal total consumption, they reached the following conclusion:

> The first requirement is that all profits, if there are any profits, shall be returned to consumers. The second requirement is that consumers shall spend all the money they receive. Under these conditions, however, savings are impossible either for corporations or for individuals. Yet both corporations and individuals must save. This, then, is the dilemma of thrift. (Foster and Catchings 1925, p. 296)

They would later put the dilemma in terms of a catchphrase, 'A Penny saved is sometimes a Penny lost' (Foster and Catchings 1925, p. 400).

Foster and Catchings investigated many of the ways that had been suggested as a solution to their 'dilemma of thrift.' To the argument of Say's

Law that a lack of consumer spending would cause the price of goods to fall, encouraging more spending, they responded that falling prices put business-men in a fear of falling profits, which discouraged them from producing and led to cutbacks in output and layoffs, reducing consumer spending even more. Another approach would be government ownership under a Bellamy-like programme of production 'for use and not for profit,' but they insisted that government ownership would likely result in lower production because there would not be 'the spur of competition and the profit motive' (Foster and Catchings 1925, pp. 305–6).

Government fiscal policies of taxing and spending would also be ineffec-tive. They noted that many felt taxation, another potential leakage, to be responsible for underconsumption, but tax policy was not the problem (Foster and Catchings 1925, p. 335). Taxation took money from people who might have spent it, and then the government spent the money buying goods and services. In a similar way, government spending financed by borrow-ing, that is, deficit spending, could not change the problem of under-consumption. The government borrowed money from one group of consumers, reducing their spending, and spent in ways that gave income to other consumers to spend. Government spending was never used to produce items for sale. In terms of consumer goods markets, however, government loans or taxes could 'neither offset a deficiency in consumer demand nor create one' (Foster and Catchings 1925, p. 338).

Foster and Catchings went on to consider the idea that government should adjust its spending to offset the business cycle by saving in good times and spending when consumer demand fell. Such a policy was sound when it added to consumer spending when that was what was needed and it might delay a recession. The government could not sustain its spending for long enough to solve the problem of underconsumption and the recession it ultimately brought. At best, it could stabilize the economy for a time by making spending more steady over the course of a few years, but such spending 'does not in the long run offset the deficiencies in demand' (Foster and Catchings 1925, p. 340). Government spending on public works pro-jects at the right time limited the economy to 'moderate declines' where 'there might have been a collapse.' But because taxes took money away from individuals and 'the people collectively spend their money more wastefully than they do individually,' the government and its leaders 'should devise better methods of dealing with the problem of deficient consumer demand than constant increases in public expenditures' (Foster and Catch-ings 1925, pp. 347–8).

Another explanation for the problem of underconsumption was the unequal distribution of income. Even with their extravagant spending, the wealthy could not buy all that was produced. By redistributing their money to the poor, the lack of demand for goods would be addressed. Recall from Chapter 2 that Bellamy had used this argument as part of his explanation for business cycles.

The problem with this argument, Foster and Catchings noted, was that it did not alter the total income, which was already insufficient to purchase all that was produced. A wider distribution of wealth, however, might make a difference. If stock ownership were more widespread, dividends fell into more hands and more of those dividends would be spent on consumption instead of being saved. This might offset some of the underconsumption but 'even if every member of society were a capitalist, this would not offset deficiencies of consumer income which have already been caused by the use of individual and corporate savings to increase production' (Foster and Catchings 1925, pp. 355–7).

One approach that business was developing at the time was the use of consumer credit to allow consumers to purchase goods by borrowing. Consumer credit, however, could not be 'extended indefinitely.' Foster and Catchings insisted, 'What people need is the means of paying for goods, rather than the means of acquiring goods for which they cannot pay' (Foster and Catchings 1925, p. 411). In a later book they looked at consumer credit in more detail. They found that by letting some people buy more than their current income permitted, the problem of underconsumption was offset and the use of consumer credit kept the economy 'from a marked business recession' at the time, that is, 1928 (Foster and Catchings 1928, p. 62). But the gains in sales from consumer credit were not permanent.

Foster and Catchings found that credit increased the risk to business by making it concerned with the issue of what to do when a recession came and consumers could not make their payments. To make the case further that consumer credit could not solve underconsumption, they pointed out that when consumers had to pay off their loans, they would reduce their spending. If businesses tried to offset this reduction by extensions of additional credit to consumers, they might still increase their sales for a time, but then that meant a greater decline in sales at some point in the future as even more consumers cut back their spending to pay off loans. Foster and Catchings stated the problem this way: 'A given dose of instalment sales, like a given dose of any other stimulant, may be very stimulating; but to get the same effect again and again, the dose must be larger and larger' (Foster and Catchings 1928, p. 68). No consumer could increase his use of credit buying indefinitely.

There are many problems with the underconsumption argument expressed by Foster and Catchings, especially its disregard of Say's Law (see Chapter 1). Our concern in this book, however, is not with analytical correctness but with influence and here Foster and Catchings rate high honours. In later chapters we shall see that their arguments had an influence on the economic policies of Herbert Hoover and the New Deal to maintain consumption. Eventually, John Maynard Keynes addressed the issue of underconsumption with greater analytical sophistication than Foster and Catchings did (see Chapter 12). Nevertheless, Foster and Catchings pushed business cycle theory away from financial markets and into the broader economy. In doing so they helped foster an approach to macroeconomics that used imbalances in economic aggregates as an explanation for business cycles.

JOSEPH SCHUMPETER, THE ENTREPRENEUR AND THE BUSINESS CYCLE

Joseph Schumpeter (1883–1950) presents a difficulty in terms of where to place him in this book, because it is not easy to determine when he became influential in US economic thinking. He was born in Austria-Hungary in what is now the Czech Republic. He was educated at the University of Vienna and served as minister of finance for Austria. After being a faculty member at several European universities, in 1932 he moved to the US to be professor of economics at Harvard University where he remained for the rest of his life. His influence in the US came earlier, however. His views on economics and business cycles were presented early in his career in a book published in German in 1911 and his ideas became known to US economists at this time (Wicker 1911, pp. 318–20; McCrea 1913, pp. 520–29).

Schumpeter's enduring reputation rests on his theory of the entrepreneur and the entrepreneur's role in the process of creative destruction. We saw in Chapter 2 that Bellamy and Sumner had outlined the process of creative destruction. Schumpeter elaborated on the process more fully than they ever did. One statement in English of Schumpeter's theory of creative destruction and its relationship to business cycles can be found in a 1927 review of a book on business cycles by the noted economist, A.C. Pigou. Schumpeter used the review as an opportunity to start 'from his own views' (Schumpeter 1927, p. 290). To Schumpeter, the economic process that constituted the theory of economic equilibrium used by most economists did not contain any factors that would lead to a business cycle. Equilibrium conditions might change upward from population increases or the accumulation of capital and decreases in these two vital factors might bring about economic decline. In those cases the economic system would accommodate to the changes by finding a new equilibrium, either higher or lower than before. But that would be a one-time change and not a series of recurring cycles (Schumpeter 1927, p. 290).

Instead, Schumpeter thought business cycles were part of the economic system as an effect of the process of creative destruction (Schumpeter 1927, p. 295). Schumpeter argued that economists will 'have explained the cycle when we have explained those booms which are so clearly before our eyes ever since (at least) the Napoleonic wars.' He added, 'Those booms consist in the carrying out of innovations in the industrial and commercial organism.' By innovations Schumpeter meant changes in methods of production and transportation, changes in industrial organization, the production of a new good or service, the opening of new markets or the development of new sources of raw materials (Schumpeter 1927, p. 295). Innovations arose as part of the economic process, according to Schumpeter, and they set off booms of prosperity that ultimately lead to recessions.

Moreover, Schumpeter argued, innovations would not produce booms, if they took place continuously in time. In that case, the disturbance caused by innovation would be small and not able to set off a period of prosperity. Instead, innovation in industrial and commercial methods took place in leaps, 'because as soon as any step in a new direction has been successfully made, it at once and thereby becomes easy to follow' (Schumpeter 1927, p. 297). Business activities tended to be routine matters until some person came up with a new way of doing things. Once that new way became known, it would be easy to imitate and as more businesses took up the new approach they would be building new factories, buying raw materials and hiring new workers, all of which would set off a boom. Schumpeter described the situation succinctly, 'The first success draws other people in its wake and finally crowds of them, which is what the boom consists in' (Schumpeter 1927, p. 298). Competition by innovators would force the members of the crowd to adopt the new methods as the best way to save themselves. The process started when businessmen created a new business and undersold the old ones and the older businesses had to adopt or face bankruptcy.

The change of business methods with its resulting period of prosperity was only part of the story. The other part was the role played by banks and credit (Schumpeter 1927, pp. 300–301). By expanding credit, banks increased the purchasing power of business, which led to a period of inflation. But this type of inflation, Schumpeter argued, differed from the inflation set off by the government printing money. With bank credit, the additional purchasing power would be used to outbid other businesses for existing commodities and labour, which would make prices rise. In the case of government produced inflation, the process of increasing the money supply might last for an indefinite period. With bank credit advanced to business, however, the inflationary pressure ended in a process of 'self-deflation.'

Schumpeter described the process as follows. Entrepreneurs got credit from banks to spend on factors of production, causing their prices to rise and increasing the income of workers and owners of capital goods. This caused the prices of resources to rise 'until enough means of production have been, by the rise of prices, wrung from those firms which had them (Schumpeter 1927, p. 302). The innovators would be willing to pay those higher prices for resources because they could use them to greater advantage than the older firms. If they were able to so use them successfully, however, they would be able to pay back what they borrowed plus interest, and the purchasing power created by bank credit would be eliminated, which is what Schumpeter meant by 'self-deflation' (Schumpeter 1927, p. 303).

Since there was no other source for the demand for credit creation but the entrepreneur, the entrepreneur was responsible for both the boom and the recession that followed it. The periods of depression that followed every boom were set off because the changes brought about by innovation, especially those involving the building of new factories, were up and working. This new productive capacity led to a downward movement of prices as a first phase of 'self-deflation.' At the same time, banks began to 'expect difficulties arising with their debtors but also anticipate difficulties with depositors and sources of rediscount' (Schumpeter 1927, p. 306). The ensuing withdrawal of credit added to the 'self-deflation' and the economy entered a recession.

Given that banks were in business to lend money to worthy creditors, Schumpeter did not see a 'possibility of stopping any normal boom by a proper management of credit' (Schumpeter 1927, p. 307). Nor should banks want to cut off a boom by curtailing credit. To Schumpeter, a boom was part of the economic process by which the economy developed new products and production methods. New methods of production and new products enriched the lives of all members of an economy, increased their standards of living and created the wherewithal for future innovation. Rather than being something to be avoided, the business cycle was a sign of the benefits of economic development. Still, Schumpeter felt it necessary to say that while the business cycle should not be considered entirely negative, 'serving no social interests,' it did 'its work at very great costs' (Schumpeter 1927, p. 308).

It was possible that some of those costs could be reduced by government policy. Government intervention, however, would slow down the pace of innovation but some economists and politicians might consider reduced innovation a reasonable price to pay for avoiding the excessive harm a recession caused. One such policy would be to raise interest rates during a boom, and Schumpeter pointed to the US experience in the 1920s as a sign that a monetary policy of increased interest rates could cause a boom to slow down. But this policy was 'really an instrument only for fighting disturbances which are small and do not last too long' and only small changes in interest rates by a central bank were politically feasible. Banks could add to a slowdown in a boom by raising interest rates by more than the central bank did (Schumpeter 1927, p. 308). The point Schumpeter was making was that there were limits to the effectiveness of monetary policy, especially in how stringent it had to be to stifle a boom that was set off by innovation.

In 1928 Schumpeter published another article in English that elaborated on the entrepreneur and justified the profits the entrepreneur made. The process of creative destruction led to a new world for the economy. Schumpeter wrote, 'What we, unscientifically, call economic progress means essentially putting productive resources to uses hitherto untried in practice, and withdrawing them from the uses they have served so far' (Schumpeter 1928, p. 378). Behind the process was 'successful innovation,' which Schumpeter considered to be 'a feat not of intellect, but of will. It is a special case of the social phenomenon of leadership' (Schumpeter 1928, p. 379) Economic leadership carried none of the glamour of other types of social, political or intellectual leadership, which made it less easy to honour or defend. It was also very rare and not to be confused with an aptitude for routine work that was typical of much of business management. For this reason, Schumpeter differentiated between the entrepreneurial function and the managerial function. That way he then distinguished between the profits entrepreneurs earned and what managers were paid. As a result, he could argue that 'it is this entrepreneurs' profit which is the primary source of industrial fortunes, the history of every one of which consists of, or leads back to, successful acts of innovation' (Schumpeter 1928, p. 380).

In coming to this conclusion, Schumpeter set forth an explanation of profits that was different from other thinkers of his era. Unlike them, he made profits the value added to society by the changes in technology brought about by entrepreneurs, with the value added being found in cheaper and better products of mass consumption. Creative destruction, however, did destroy older industries and make the workers and capital in those industries obsolete. The result might be lower wages and unemployment for those workers, something which they and their supporters were likely to protest as a social problem. Many of the ills that Progressives were fighting against came from the process of creative destruction whereby entrepreneurs produced technological change.

CONCLUSION

Like the advocates of the moral economy, the thinkers in this chapter also asked: what are the causes of business cycles? Though the specific details they offered varied, our experts on business cycles can be categorized as those who saw business cycles as a problem of the real side of the economy and those who saw them as a problem of the monetary side of the economy. Interestingly, for the most part, those who saw the causes of business cycles as problems of the monetary side of the economy, such as Bellamy and Veblen, were also those who viewed market economies as unfair and immoral. Fisher, however, was the exception. Fisher, in looking at the same monetary side of the economy as Bellamy and Veblen, saw the problem as interest rates lagging behind price changes. In this way, Fisher saw the problem as a mistake that bankers made, but it was a mistake that had the potential to be remedied by the efficiency of the market economy, much as Henry Ford argued.

On the other hand, Foster and Catchings and Schumpeter saw the cause of business cycles in the production side of the economy. For Foster and Catchings, savings was the culprit. They did not see a remedy to this dilemma and viewed it as something that had to be accepted along with the benefits the market economy brought to the world. We shall see in later chapters that political leaders in the US accepted their underconsumption argument as the best explanation for the Great Depression.

For Schumpeter, business cycles were simply a part of the economic system as an effect of the process of creative destruction. Innovations took place in leaps and did not occur continuously over time, which set off booms of prosperity ultimately leading to downturns in the business cycle. Downturns took place when innovations displaced older businesses and their methods with a flood of new and cheaper products. For Schumpeter, the market economy may create losers and generate failures but this was a necessary part of creative destruction that allowed society to increase its standard of living. Supporting this favourable view of market economies, Fisher recognized the flaws of markets as well as the risks created by markets but, nonetheless, saw markets as self-correcting and efficient. Along this line of thinking, Foster and Catchings simply favoured market economies because the benefits far outweighed the costs. In sum, with all of its rough edges and unequal outcomes this group of experts saw the benefits generated from market economies as far outweighing any other framework for organizing economic life.

The basic idea that advocates for the market economy set forth was that government intervention in the economy was rarely needed, because markets were basically efficient in correcting mistakes and taking care of recessions if they were given enough time. Fisher was especially vocal in presenting this view of the market economy. By the 1920s, he believed that the market economy was so efficient – the Federal Reserve was doing a good job of keeping interest rates in line with inflation – that perhaps the prosperity of the 1920s would become permanent. As a result of this view, when the stock market declined in September 1929 Fisher made a call that has been used many times ever since to denigrate him and any other economist who believes in the efficiency of markets: 'Stock prices have reached what looks like a permanently high plateau' ('Fisher sees stocks permanently high', 1929, p. 2). To him, the decline in stock prices would be short-lived.

We now know that Fisher was wrong in his call on the market. Fisher's incorrect call and the way the economy did not respond quickly to end the recession that began in August 1929 gave the upper hand to advocates of the moral economy by diminishing claims that markets were efficient. In other words, Fisher's off the mark prediction about the stock market undermined his view that markets were efficient and gave ammunition to the intellectual attacks on the market economy in the 1930s. Those attacks provided momentum for Progressive thinkers to develop 'planning' models for the moral economy. The ideas behind these planning models that developed in the first three decades of the twentieth century are explored in the next two chapters.

5. The Progressive push for planning: 1900 to 1920

The Progressive Era from 1900 to 1920 saw a revised role of the federal government in the US with regard to economic affairs, as it became more active and interventionist. The Progressives were not quite followers of Edward Bellamy in terms of government ownership of the means of production. Instead, they tried to find a way to blend markets with morals through planning. The advocates for planning were intellectuals, who thought long and wrote deeply about social issues. The Progressive Era had more than its share of these pundits, who sought to become influential in higher political circles.

One area where Progressive political leaders needed ideas was with the problem of business cycles. We saw in Chapter 3 that business cycle theorists with a moral economy perspective hinted at planning as a solution to economic downturns, but they were not sure who would do the planning. We describe in this chapter how Progressive pundits hit upon an answer to the problem of who would plan the economy through the growth of scientific expertise as an instrument of planning. Early in the twentieth century Frederick W. Taylor developed his principles of scientific management to show that there was a science of management that could be experimented with, studied and learned and then applied to business management and public administration as a planning tool. Eventually, pundits would argue in favour of the extension of planning to the total economy of the US.

FREDERICK W. TAYLOR AND SCIENTIFIC MANAGEMENT

Frederick W. Taylor (1856–1915) was born into an upper-class family from Philadelphia. He followed the family tradition of attending an elite boarding school but then broke with that tradition by not attending Harvard University. Instead, he took a job in a steel mill and learned engineering in the shop as an apprentice, a path often taken in his day because academic programmes in engineering were not readily available. Eventually, he would complete a degree in engineering through home-study courses at the Stevens Institute of Technology. Meanwhile, working in a machine shop taught him that workers did not always perform at their highest level. Instead, they often slacked off and because their work was not easily monitored they got away with it. Efforts to give them an incentive to work harder by paying them 'piece-work,' that is, paying a set amount for each item they produced, often failed. Either the workers would band together and agree on a proper amount for each to produce or, if they worked harder to earn more pay, employers would eventually reduce the piece-rate to get more work for less pay.

Taylor hoped to end all that through a scientific study of work. In his book, *The Principles of Scientific Management*, he offered numerous examples of how he studied in minute detail work such as shovelling or loading iron ingots into freight cars (Taylor 1911 [1919], pp. 138–9). His aim was to design the right way to work with the right workers and the right tools. Once he had established that design, the amount of work that the right worker could accomplish in a day would be determined. Given a standard amount of work in terms of items produced, it would be easy to establish a standard rate of pay that would be fair to both the worker and the employer. In this way, engineers could ensure efficiency and profitability to the business, solve the labour issue and secure a place for themselves in corporate management.

In that secure place Taylor and his followers would revolutionize corporate thinking and become better managers than those that existed at the time. For once these efficiency experts had found the best way for workers to produce, they had to plan the operations of the entire organization. The tools to be used had to be determined down to the smallest detail. The management representative on the shop floor, the foreman, had become obsolete. He was too autocratic and had to be replaced by a functional foreman who used scientific knowledge in place of the rules of thumb of an old-style foreman. Since many managers had risen from the ranks of foremen, they too had an old-fashioned view of work and workers. Taylor had in mind that business adopt the functional expert approach of scientific management. Within each department of the corporation one person would be put in charge of deciding the issues on which he was the functional expert. The use of this functional expert would achieve the broader perspective of scientific analysis and Taylor thought it important for all persons in business, from workers to top managers, to gain respect for scientific expertise in all areas of human affairs (Stabile 1984, pp. 42–5).

Taylor's efforts to earn this respect for himself and his methods did not follow a smooth path. Unions opposed, often successfully, his methods in the businesses where he personally tried to apply them, and union leaders initiated a public campaign against the efficiency experts. An attempt by the highly scientific DuPont Co. to apply scientific management in its explosives manufacturing was short-lived (Stabile 1987, pp. 365–86). Then Taylor and his followers got a break. One of those followers, Harrington Emerson, had worked for the Santa Fe Railroad. In 1910 he testified before the Interstate Commerce Commission in hearings to determine if the railroads needed a rate increase. Emerson claimed that a rate increase was not needed because the railroads could save a million dollars a day by using scientific management. Shortly thereafter, Emerson repeated his evidence at a meeting of the National Civic Federation, an organization of Progressive reformers (Stabile 1984, pp. 54–5).

Emerson's dramatic statements set off an outburst of interest in scientific management and it was featured in cover stories in several leading Progressive magazines. Taylor was called to testify in Congress. His followers began to offer other examples of how scientific management could be used to improve society. Taylor insisted that once the public became knowledgeable of the true situation in business it would insist that 'justice be done' to all of society by demanding 'the largest efficiency from both employers and employees.' Public opinion, he added, would 'force the new order of things upon both employer and employee' (Taylor 1911 [1919], pp. 138–9).

In its early days, however, the allure of scientific management in general was more promise than application. At its heart Taylorism focused on the idea that monetary incentives would motivate workers to cooperate with the efficiency experts. Instead, workers and managers resisted this approach. But it did serve as a model of how scientific expertise could be used to solve a vexing social problem.

SOCIALISM AND THE TECHNOLOGICAL IMPERATIVE

At the corporate level Taylor's scientific management aimed at attaining efficiency by planning production through scientific expertise. If business managers could plan production smoothly and if workers were paid a scientifically determined wage, many of the fluctuations in business profitability and workers' income could be eliminated. The problem with this approach was that it needed to be generalized. As Bellamy had argued, business operated in a web of interrelated production. What happened in one firm had an impact on all other firms. The promise of scientific management in one firm might be offset by events that took place in other firms. The social issues brought about by large corporations would have to be solved by scientific planning in every firm as well as overall planning of all firms. That was the implication Bellamy would have drawn from

Taylor's methods, even though Taylor never went that far. Other thinkers in the US at the time, specifically socialists, did draw that implication.

The US has never had a labour party. It has, however, had a socialist party and we will see that its socialist party was not strictly a labour party. Still, during the Progressive Era there was a vibrant movement for socialism in the US. Eugene V. Debs was usually the candidate of the Socialist Party of America (SPA) and he garnered from 1 to 6 per cent of the votes in presidential elections during the period. There were factions within the SPA, however, who thought socialism would evolve through reforms of capitalism and those who insisted that socialism would come about from a revolution. The reform element of the socialists took a line similar to Bellamy that when the number of trusts was few the government would nationalize them and run them as one big syndicate under an industrial army of workers. From this approach, socialism would come about from winning an election on the appeal of the idea that nationalizing industry would have for voters. To do so, socialists set forth a reform socialism that promised the nationalization of large firms as Bellamy argued (Stabile 1984, pp. 119–48).

This message had an appeal to intellectuals and many of them joined the SPA. They formed a variety of intellectual magazines in which they set forth their ideas about what socialism was and how it would take place. In those magazines they developed a message that they hoped all voters would find persuasive. To be sure, workers would remain their core constituency. Debs had started his career working for railroads. He joined the American Railway Union and led its members in a strike that paralysed the nation until soldiers were called in to force workers back to work. Debs never forgot his roots and would not promote ideas inimical to workers. Still, organized labour that belonged to the American Federation of Labor, under the leadership of Samuel Gompers, was strictly anti-socialist. Debs realized that to win votes he had to appeal to broader groups such as farmers and the middle class. To do this, he and the SPA set forth a reform socialism that would bring about some of the benefits of socialism through the nationalization of large firms and thus gradually bring about the total nationalization of industry that Bellamy argued for (Stabile 1984, pp. 140–48).

Included in this reform socialism were arguments that were aimed at the new middle class of professionals. When Frederick W. Taylor entered the public arena with his scientific management, the socialists took him as a fellow spirit and echoed his calls for making industry more efficient. From this perspective, scientific management improved the efficiency of workers, which would aid the formation of the government-owned industry the socialists sought. Socialists thought that Taylor's approach would be even more effective if workers owned the means of production collectively.

Bellamy had included engineers as part of the industrial army and later socialists agreed. Scientific management was a necessary part of implementing the socialist commonwealth (Stabile 1984, pp. 149–60).

We can see this interest in scientific management in the writings of a prominent socialist pundit, William English Walling. Walling had been influenced by the pragmatism of John Dewey; in his version of the transition to socialism, socialists had to set aside their principle of socialism as a working-class movement and be pragmatic by allying with the professional experts to bring about state socialism. He agreed that scientific management under capitalism aimed at getting more efficiency from workers but did so 'by improving health, skill and intelligence' (Walling 1914, pp. 56–8). He also recognized that state socialism would be 'based on one privilege alone – that of a special and expansive training' (Walling 1914, p. 93). Once state socialism was in place, with scientific experts administering it, those experts would not fear workers as capitalists had but would work to improve their efficiency by enhancing their technical skills. Eventually, all workers would gain skills comparable to those of professional experts and they would be able to overthrow state socialism and convert it to worker socialism.

While there are many problems with this argument, the relevant one here is that the new middle class of professional experts was turning to Progressive reform instead of socialism. Socialists recognized this pattern and believed it would work in their favour. The attitude of Progressive reformers showed a change from the older middle class. The older middle class was against government, while the new Progressive middle class favoured government intervention. This new attitude would help start the US down the path to socialism. At least that is what socialist pundits thought.

From the socialist perspective, socialism involved national planning to avoid the business cycles they thought were inherent to capitalism and a sign of its moral frailty. Socialism, however, would not come about suddenly. Instead, it would be brought about gradually through stages. First, the new middle class of Progressive reformers would work with the old middle class of small business owners against the large trusts and create state capitalism, that is, government regulation of large corporations. Second, a segment of the professional reformers, technical experts such as Taylor and his associates, would administer the state capitalism until, with the help of workers, they eliminated the small business owners and instituted state socialism, government ownership of large corporations and all other businesses. Third, workers would gradually gain the skills needed to run industry and would combine with technical professionals to bring about worker's socialism as depicted by Bellamy.

We shall not concern ourselves with an examination and critique of the socialists' ideas, especially since we have only scratched the surface in setting them out for review. Here we are concerned with their analysis of Progressive reformers. Were Progressive reformers in favour of stronger government and would they take over the government and use it to regulate business as the socialists anticipated?

WALTER LIPPMANN: THE PROGRESSIVE PUNDIT

While the Progressive movement was carried to the public through the efforts of politicians such as Theodore Roosevelt and Woodrow Wilson, its intellectual foundations lay in the writings of pundits who were attracted to the movement. Their overarching goal was the achievement of social and economic efficiency through the application of scientific methods to human activity. As a first step in their goal of social efficiency, the Progressive pundits wanted to eliminate corruption in government at all levels. Hence, their early reforms included the elimination of machine politics through good government, including the use of experts in civil service and the hiring of professional city managers. They soon concluded, however, that the source of many of the social ills they found, including political corruption, was the system of big business that they saw as taking over the economy. Economic efficiency meant to them that the government had to control big business as a means to solving social problems, leading to social efficiency.

Underlying their goal of social efficiency was the philosophy of pragmatism, not in the crude sense of being practical and expedient, but in John Dewey's approach of being experimental in terms of trying new ideas and sticking with the ones that succeeded and discarding those that failed. With this approach, the Progressives could advance reform as a process of social engineering, where impartial experts could look holistically at a social problem in terms of the underlying economic conditions that caused it. Once they understood those conditions, they could formulate a solution to the problem. If the solution worked, the problem was solved. If not, the process would be repeated until a workable solution was found. These impartial experts would learn by doing and bring an enlightened administration to society, especially when it came to regulating the economy.

A leading figure among the Progressive pundits was Walter Lippmann (1889–1974), a Harvard University graduate whose long career in journalism and political writing earned him Pulitzer Prizes in 1958 and 1962. In his youth he wrote on the social issues surrounding Progressive reform, and his book, *Drift and Mastery*, published in 1914, served as a guidebook for Progressives. As the title indicates, Lippmann argued that society could drift along from problem to problem. All around him, Lippmann saw drift, as social upheaval eroded faith in the traditional authorities of society, which had no answers to social problems. To achieve mastery, society had to channel social upheaval towards the building of a better society. Mastery, Lippmann wrote, was 'the substitution of conscious intentions for unconscious striving' (Lippmann 1914 [1961], p. 269). Because the scientific method was conscious it led to mastery: 'The scientific spirit is the discipline of democracy, the escape from drift' (Lippmann 1914 [1961], p. 276). Science was important, he added, because 'The discipline of science is the only one which gives any assurance that from the same set of facts men will come approximately to the same conclusion' (Lippmann 1914 [1961], p. 286).

Thus, society should follow the lead of the Progressives in their application of science to social problems (Lippmann 1914 [1961], pp. 15–17). Experts could reach a scientific consensus about how to solve social problems. In particular, science would be needed to attain national economic efficiency. Lippmann wrote, 'We are entering on another new period now; not alone big business, but all business and farming too, are being criticized for inefficiency, for poor product, and for exploitation of employees' (Lippmann 1914 [1961], p. 27). He further indicated that men like 'Taylor have taken the lead in this new criticism' (Lippmann 1914 [1961], p. 29).

Where previous reformers such as the populists went wrong, Lippmann argued, was in trying to break up large corporations to restore a system of small business and competition. To Lippmann, the optimal size for a firm was a matter for scientific experts in the administration of business to determine and efforts to use anti-trust laws to create an optimally sized competitive industry were not scientific (Lippmann 1914 [1961], pp. 39–43). Large factories and the corporations that integrated them into a productive unit with a large amount of market power, if not a monopoly, might be more efficient than small factories needed to sustain a large number of competitors. These larger units of production were more efficient because they took large-scale collective action under the direction of expert administrators. These new technical administrators took a different view than the old capitalists who had built up the large firms. Their ability to succeed depended on developing their technical skills and using them to achieve productive efficiency, as opposed to the older entrepreneurs who sought profits from unproductive activities such as arbitrarily raising prices that had an adverse impact on other industries. Lippmann noted that large corporations relied on leaders 'who have come in contact with the scientific method. That is an enormous gain over the older manufacturers and merchants' (Lippmann 1914 [1961], pp. 43–4). In addition, these leaders worked for salaries and were less motivated by money and more motivated by work for its own sake.

This use of salaried managers was part of a trend where leading thinkers distrusted old-style businesses run by self-interest. Lippmann reported, 'Men don't trust the profiteer in a crisis' (Lippmann 1914 [1961], p. 29) with the result that the profit motive was being called into question by Progressives. The profit motive might have served well in building up industry, but it worked poorly in reaching the promise of industry, which was why government regulation of business was becoming generally acceptable. The new industrial world of economic integration required new types of managers, who understood science and psychology, and universities were beginning to train them as professionals.

Large corporations were also changing private property, turning it into stock ownership. This caused a separation of ownership from management of the business. Today economists refer to this as the principal-agent problem. As a result, Lippmann argued, 'Private property will melt away; its functions will be taken over by the salaried men that direct, by government commissions, by developing labour unions' (Lippmann 1914 [1961], p. 60). There would be little difference between a corporation owned by stockholders and one owned by the government; stockholders would be indifferent as to whether they owned stock or government bonds and would not stand up for property rights. To those who argued that government was inefficient, Lippmann answered that if it chose administrators with the same care as business and gave them higher pay and greater responsibility, they would become efficient managers of nationalized industries (Lippmann 1914 [1961], p. 62).

The growth of large corporations had created a number of problems. Lippmann did not have a simple solution to those problems, but believed that they could be worked upon most effectively through the development of national planning (Lippmann 1914 [1961], pp. 104–5). National economic planning was crucial to mastery, because it looked at the whole economic system and had clear intentions of where it should go. By using scientific administrators as the staff of national planning, the government could avoid the drift where it employed a variety of solutions from anti-trust to regulation with no clear purpose in mind.

How to pay for it all? For Lippmann there existed a social surplus that consisted of the wasteful activities of business and the parasitism of the wealthy. This wealth could be taken from its holders without causing any harm to industry, because it would not impact the salaried managers who now ran it. Sumner's views that wealth accumulation served society no longer held, and Lippmann made a direct challenge to Sumner's forgotten man, assuming we can think of Andrew Carnegie as forgotten: 'Could the government make better use of Mr. Carnegie's fortune than Mr. Carnegie does?' If so, and Lippmann surely thought it was so, then 'the government is entirely justified in substituting itself for Mr. Carnegie as a dispenser of libraries' (Lippmann 1914 [1961], pp. 108–9). Transferring wealth and income from the idle wealthy such as stockholders and creditors to productive workers and salaried managers would enhance the efficiency of business, much as Bellamy had argued. That was a much better approach than using the anti-trust laws to break up the trusts to restore competition. National planning of production would bring about cooperation among business, instead of wasteful competition.

There was a problem with the cooperation among businesses brought about by scientific administration and Lippmann pointed it out: 'The real problem of collectivism is the difficulty of combining popular control with administrative power' (Lippmann 1914 [1961], p. 45). Here was the main problem facing the Progressives. How can a free society reconcile concentrated administrative control over industry with the US tradition of popular democracy? Lippmann answered by looking to unions. As industry became collected in larger units, the strength of unions would increase and they would push for participation in the decisions being made by administrative experts, as part of the union leaders' recognition that they could cooperate with management to achieve greater efficiency. By working together, unions and professional experts could provide effective management for large collective firms. Because unions were in the tradition of US democracy, their participation in management would ensure that large firms were consistent with that democracy (Lippmann 1914 [1961], pp. 61–5).

Moreover, Lippmann assured his readers, there was nothing to fear from administrative experts using their knowledge to secure power for themselves (Lippmann 1914 [1961], p. 141). Here Lippmann believed that the Progressives were replacing the authority of tradition and dogma with the scientific approach of pragmatism. While it was possible that administrative experts might create a new authority based on science, science had the virtue of being self-critical as long as its practitioners continually challenged existing ideas. Science thus had the ability to attack its own absolutist tendencies. 'When science becomes its own critic,' Lippmann concluded, 'it is able, then, to attack the source of error itself' (Lippmann 1914 [1961], p. 157).

We cannot say for sure how many of the Progressives followed Lippmann's approach. Herbert Croly, whose book *The Promise of American Life* enabled him to speak with as much authority to the Progressives as did Lippmann, also argued that persons trained in science maintained very high ideals in their work (Croly 1914, p. 434). Croly was a founding editor of *The New Republic* and was likely the author of its editorials that favoured national economic planning during World War I (see below). More to the point, both Lippmann and Croly along with Dewey imbued the Progressives with a sense that their reforms were scientific as long as they were considered to be social experiments, a testing of new ideas to determine their social validity. That was a powerful message for the Progressives to hear and to take to heart as they looked for reforms to regulate the economy. Whether a scientific economy was a moral economy they never doubted.

WORLD WAR I AND NATIONAL PLANNING

When World War I began, Progressives believed that it would give them an opportunity to continue their movement for reform in the US. The war stirred up patriotism and made the public more loyal to the government; this community spirit surely could be transferred to public approval of other government programmes. Moreover, to fight the war the government had to use national planning. In the integrated, technological economy that the US had become that planning would require the use of scientific administrators. The planned economy that Progressives such as Lippmann had been writing about would help win the war. When the peace came, it would not be easily discarded.

Even before the US entered the war, a group of engineers and business leaders began campaigning for a programme to ensure that the country would be prepared to enter the war. This group in 1916 formed the Council for National Defense. The Council tried to take an inventory of national resources but businesses failed to cooperate with this effort and other programs the Council set in place. H.L. Gantt, a member of the Council and a follower of Taylor, criticized business in a way that Progressives would have approved. He wrote, 'If the industries are not properly managed for the benefit of the whole community, no amount of military preparedness will avail in a real war' (Gantt 1916, pp. 804–8). To Gantt and many Progressives, the war would show the way towards an economy that produced for the community as a whole.

Meanwhile, preparedness for the war foundered from a lack of cooperation from individual business leaders, and Progressives searched for ways to instil support for community efficiency among the public. In a long article in *The New Republic* Lippmann observed, 'The war has given large numbers of Americans a new instinct for order, purpose, discipline' (Lippmann 1916, p. 62). The problem was in finding a way to channel this new instinct into support for the federal government. A new set of social ideals that would make the public feel more strongly attached to the national government was needed. To nurture those social ideals, Lippmann recommended that the federal government take over the railway system. In an approach similar to Bellamy's (see Chapter 2) he argued that the system in its current state was poorly run and that reorganization of the railroads into a national system would provide the country with a new national spirit. In addition, he wrote, 'The government would then have the instrument and power for controlling and stimulating business' (Lippmann 1916, p. 66). To the obvious objection that government operation of the railroads would be inefficient, Lippmann responded that through practice the government would become more efficient. The Progressive ideal of scientific administration by experts was easily attainable by the government. In doing so, the federal government would create a new form of democracy where 'inefficiency and waste and lack of public spirit are crimes against the state' (Lippmann 1916, p. 66).

When the war came, the government through the WIB did take over the railroads and a good deal more including shipping and the distribution of food and fuel. Labour unions were brought into the fold with the promise of collective bargaining in the war industries. At the same time, government efforts to sell bonds to fund the war stirred up a patriotic fervour that often went overboard in the way it squelched dissent, exhibiting the militarism that Veblen had warned against (see Chapter 3). Still, Progressives joined the war effort in action as well as in the spirit they thought it brought to economic affairs. They framed their efforts with a new term, 'Industrial Democracy,' and argued that true democracy must be economic as well as political, which required that the country 'establish democracy in the commercial government which is the real government of the state' (Richberg 1917, p. 49).

The New Republic, then a pillar of Progressive thinking, noted the way government was taking charge of industry and took it as a sign that Progressive pundits had been right in labelling business as inefficient. Taking over business to plan for the war was necessary, and there would have to be a debate over whether this government takeover should be made permanent. Progressives had no right to insist that the nationalization of business that the war made necessary should be retained as permanent without a debate, but they were 'entitled to demand that the automatic restoration of the *status quo ante* should not be promised or expected' (*The New Republic* 1918, p. 331). The proper place for the debate would be the presidential election of 1920. They felt certain that the experience of the war would clearly show the inefficiency of current business practices and the efficacy of national planning.

Their hopes for victory included their anticipation that they could win support from labour. Progressives realized that they were a middle-class movement and that to win elections they needed to gain support from other social classes. The war effort had helped labour and its unions and taught them that they could be part of Industrial Democracy. Unions and their workers did not yet have the scientific expertise needed to be active participants in the planning that Industrial Democracy needed. They would have to be represented by the managers who would run the industrial units of that Industrial Democracy until workers could appreciate how the efficiency and prosperity of their unit depended on their efforts (Stabile 1984, p. 91). Unions and workers had fought with managers due to 'the arbitrary and unscientific dogmatism of the efficiency engineers' ('Editorial notes,' 1916, pp. 75–6). What the scientific managers overlooked was that supply and demand forces would offset any efforts to set wages scientifically, something labour understood. That was why planning was necessary. The result would be the integration of national unity in production that these pundits saw as the fruition of their collaboration with the government in the war effort. Whether they recognized it or not, the Progressive pundits anticipated that after the war they would begin the development of Bellamy's cooperative commonwealth under a new name of Industrial Democracy.

Socialists began thinking along similar lines. The members of the SPA voted overwhelmingly to oppose US participation in World War I and its leader, Eugene Debs, would be sent to prison for his speeches decrying worker participation in a capitalist war. Pundits in the party either abandoned it, as did Walling, or at least abandoned its party line. They reasoned that they could use the war to achieve their goal of socialism. Harry Laidler, a founder of the Intercollegiate Socialist Society and long-time head of the League for Industrial Democracy, recommended that socialists become involved with the government's efforts to win the war to make wartime planning pave the way for the cooperative commonwealth (Laidler 1917, pp. 4–7). Achievement of government collectivism in the US as a forerunner to state socialism became the common theme of these socialists.

The idea that the government control of the economy during World War I could become a permanent approach to national economic planning that was consistent with Bellamy's moral economy captivated the minds of Progressive pundits. We shall see in the next chapter that advocates for planning presented the WIB as a model for what they believed planning could accomplish. In later chapters we show that the WIB remained in the minds of the promoters of planning and the moral economy. To understand how the WIB functioned, we turn to the man who was in charge of it.

BERNARD BARUCH AND ECONOMIC PLANNING: WORLD WAR I

Bernard Baruch (1870–1965) at first glance would seem an odd person to be an oracle of national economic planning. He was born in Camden, South Carolina, but his father, a physician, moved the family to New York City in 1881. After graduating from the City College of New York, Baruch had a legendary career as a speculator in financial securities, not the sort of person politicians, especially Democratic Party politicians, would take to heart. Yet he eventually became known as an adviser to presidents. Baruch's career in politics came about both from his ability and political connections. Having been born in the South when the Democratic Party monopolized that region, he remained loyal to the party throughout his life. By the time he was 30, he had piled up a fortune through multiple deals engineered on Wall Street. In his memoirs, however, he indicated that he became influenced by his father's idealism, which 'held ethical values and usefulness to the community in higher esteem' rather than money making. He grew restless spending all his time in financial affairs and went against the common view of business, laissez-faire, which 'did not encourage either a high opinion of government service or a sense of social responsibility' (Baruch 1960, p. 2).

Armed with a new spirit of service and a large bankroll, Baruch began getting involved in politics first at the local level and eventually at the national level. As a major contributor to the Democratic Party, he met Woodrow Wilson during the campaign for the Democratic nomination in 1912 and liked him, especially his views on business with its distinction between large corporations that were necessary for efficiency and those that were not. When Wilson won the election, Baruch occasionally helped him out and was a major contributor to his re-election campaign (Baruch 1960, pp. 8–13).

As the war began in Europe, Baruch began thinking of what it would take in terms of war mobilization if the US entered the war. He had a vision of a 'centralized government organization, manned by experts' being in charge of the war (Baruch 1960, p. 23). In September 1915 he made the first of many visits to the White House in his life, this one to sell Wilson his war planning idea. Wilson liked the idea but since it was not in concert with his plans for promoting peace, he did not give it support at the time. Eventually, in July 1917 Congress set up a Council of National Defense with an Advisory Committee of businessmen and other civic leaders, including Baruch. This system was put in place several months before the US entered the war and its organizational structure of committees and subcommittees for each vital industry was a forerunner for the WIB that was established in

1918 and eventually planned the economy during the war. We are not concerned here with the actual workings of the WIB and its mission, 'To control and regulate industry in all its direct and indirect relations to the war and to the nation' (Baruch 1921 [1941], p. 4). Rather, we are interested in the economic philosophy inherent to the need for wartime planning.

The underlying philosophy of the WIB, according to Baruch who was in charge of it, was an abandonment of the market economy. He wrote:

> The law of supply and demand is as vital to the economics of war as it is to the economics of peace. But there is this crucial difference. In peacetime the free working of the market place can be trusted to keep the economy in balance. The law of supply and demand has *time* in which to operate. But in war that equilibrium must be achieved by conscious direction – for war, with its ravenous demands, destroys the normal balance and denies us time. (Baruch 1960, pp. 53–4, emphasis in original)

The WIB gave direction to both supply and demand through control of both by its ability to set priorities in production and transportation. It could decide, for example, that steel could not be used to build a theatre when warships were a priority. When efforts to curtail the production of automobiles under a voluntary programme faltered, Baruch threatened to have the railroads, which the federal government controlled, stop their service to automobile factories, and the automakers went along with the plan (Baruch 1960, pp. 55–61). In his report on the WIB after the war he indicated that the priority system represented 'a new method of control over the products of industry' (Baruch 1921 [1941], p. 21). That system worked well because the WIB was staffed by capable men who 'in private life had been managers rather than owners of large industrial undertakings' (Baruch 1921 [1941], p. 28). Baruch also used his negotiating skills to keep business from raising prices (Baruch 1960, pp. 63–8).

Under the direction of the WIB, the US government was able to mount an effective mobilization campaign to fight the war. More important to the theme of this book, this program of wartime planning portended what economic planning could accomplish, at least during an emergency. Moreover, its overall program of control over industrial production came close to Bellamy's moral economy. The federal government did not nationalize industry. It did take over the railroads, however, and used its control over the transportation system to gain business compliance with its plans. Progressive pundits hoped the WIB would usher in an era of national economic planning.

Baruch apparently shared their vision. In his memoirs he wrote:

> The lessons to be learned from WIB were not confined to questions of war. The WIB experience had a great influence upon the thinking of business and government. WIB had demonstrated the effectiveness of industrial cooperation and the advantage of government planning and direction. (Baruch 1960, p. 74)

The government was not inefficient in economic planning was the overall lesson and it could be used to serve the country at any moment of danger and not just in wartime. The WIB provided a countering view to the market economy, which previously dominated economic and political thought in the US.

CONCLUSION

Both the Progressives and the socialists we have surveyed in this chapter developed the idea that planning under the direction of scientific experts was the proper model for the moral economy. They differed over how far this direction could go and over the extent to which workers could partici-pate in the planning methods they were devising for their moral economy. Armed with this model, they thought that the planning by the WIB during World War I would bring about a new social order with increased govern-ment control over the economy coordinating overall industrial activity. Within separate industries scientific managers, engineers with a humanistic approach to labour, would bring about a democratic approach to production through a combination of experts and workers into a cohesive force. The parts of the programme interlocked to achieve the integration of national unity in production that these pundits saw as the fruition of their col-laboration with the government in the war effort.

They were greatly disappointed. The WIB was formed in the US in June 1917 to coordinate the government's purchase of war materials. Much of wartime production, however, took place through cost-plus contracts to individual businesses, and Baruch, the antithesis of all the advocates of planning stood for, became the head of the WIB. Baruch succeeded very well in this position by using his many contacts in the business world to ensure that the business community cooperated with the war effort. Even though Baruch recognized the benefits of national planning, the WIB never fully regulated business during the war and shut down within a week of the armistice (Stabile 1984, p. 95). The final disappointment came later when the presidential election saw the victory of Warren G. Harding and his slogan of a return to normalcy.

6. The Progressive push for planning: 1920 to 1930

Warren G. Harding ran for president of the US in 1920 on the promise of a return to normalcy. If by normalcy he meant a return to economic prosperity, he delivered. The 1920s were a period of economic growth and prosperity never seen before in the US. The Federal Reserve index of industrial production went from 81 in January 1920 to 114 in July 1929 – a 40.6 per cent increase; real income grew at an average of 4.6 per cent a year from 1920 to 1929 (Parker 2007, p. 2), and 1929 was the best year the US economy had experienced up to that time. Economic recessions were common during the 1920s. The first began in January 1920 and a recovery did not begin until July 1921; other recessions took place from May 1923 to July 1924, October 1926 to November 1927 and the final downturn began in August 1929. These recessions took up 52 months of the ten-year period.

In addition to being a decade of economic growth, the 1920s were also a decade of economic transformation, brought about by the development of new technologies in production and in product development. The automobile came of age in the 1920s, and the radio and films launched new industries. A contemporary estimate by Joseph Schumpeter found that 90 per cent of the change in economic activity in the 1920s came from the automobile, chemical and electrical industries (Schumpeter 1964, p. 305). As a result, economic conditions in the US were very good. Until the 1929 crash, leaders in the federal government could justifiably claim that their policies in support of the market economy had worked very well and that Calvin Coolidge had got it right when he said the business of America was business. The 1920s started out by being billed as a return to normalcy, but in terms of economic growth and technological change they were anything but normal. Herbert Hoover ran for president in 1928 on a platform of prosperity and the continuation of the government policies that had brought it; he won a substantial victory. Confidence in the market economy remained high throughout the decade.

Not everyone had that confidence. The triumph of the market economy in the US in the 1920s did not silence its critics. They continued to find places where the market economy was weak and prosperity was not shared by every person in the US. Moreover, in the 1920s world events gave them alternative models to propose in place of the market economy. Lincoln Steffens (1866–1936), a staunch Progressive and muckraking journalist, famously said in1921, 'I have been over into the future, and it works.' He was referring to the Soviet Union where Vladimir Lenin, Leon Trotsky and Joseph Stalin were transforming Russia into a socialist economy. Not long after, Benito Mussolini took power in Italy and put in place a variant of socialism that he called fascism, and Steffens applauded Mussolini as much as he did the Soviet Union (Goldberg 2007, p. 103).

Both these events may have had a marked impression on intellectuals in the US, not so much because they indicated new ideas for how to organize an economy, but because they represented ideas with which Progressives were already familiar. Mussolini, for example, indicated that one of the four major influences on his thinking was William James (Stewart 1928, p. 845), who popularized the philosophy of pragmatism that Progressives used to justify their social experimentation. The notion that the market economy did not produce satisfactory economic results remained a component of advocates for the moral economy in the 1920s.

HERBERT HOOVER PROMOTES VOLUNTARY PLANNING

Herbert Hoover (1874–1964) had a career that reinforces the idea that the US is a land of opportunity. Born into a modest family background in the small town of West Branch, Iowa, he was orphaned at age nine. He moved to Oregon and worked in his uncle's store. When Stanford University opened its doors in 1891, he enrolled and graduated with a degree in geology. For him, the best use of a geology degree was in mining and he worked for many years as a mining engineer, becoming affluent in the process. Perhaps because of his Quaker background, he then had a career in public and humanitarian service, starting with his organizing a food relief programme for Belgium in 1914 during the early days of World War I. When the US entered the war, Hoover became head of the US Food Administration. From 1921–9 he was Secretary of Commerce. In 1928 he was elected president, serving one term, 1929–33. Bernard Baruch, who headed up the WIB that organized production in World War I and thus worked with Hoover, called him 'one of the ablest men in Washington' (Baruch 1960, p. 88).

The part of Hoover's life we are concerned with in this chapter started in 1920. In July of that year an editorial in *Industrial Management* announced 'A great event in engineering history' ('Editorial,' 1920, p. 74). Progressive engineers had been studying the amount of waste in industry and formed an umbrella organization, the Federated Association of Engineering Societies

(FAES) to see what could be done about it. Hoover agreed to be the leader of the FAES. Its goal was to provide information that would enable the US to have a more effective industrial system.

The ideology behind the FAES had been building for years. A decade earlier, efficiency experts promoting the ideas of Frederick W. Taylor had entered the public arena to promote planning as a way to achieve greater efficiency in production and had believed that the planning that won World War I had shown how effective it could be in organizing production. To engineers and to Hoover, engineering and planning had become an essential part of economic production. Engineers were always coming up with new ways to apply science to production that created industries and jobs, but did so in a way that upset the equilibrium of the entire economy as part of the process of creative destruction. In the market economy, however, the changes brought about by creative destruction rippled through the economy by altering wages, prices and profits. Business leaders resisted those changes and so did workers and their unions.

Hoover and the FAES would counter that resistance by providing management and labour with information about how beneficial the changes would be to society as a whole (Stabile 1986, p. 821). Hoover outlined his hopes as follows: 'If we could secure cooperation throughout all our economic groups we should have provided a new economic system, based neither on the capitalism of Adam Smith nor the socialism of Karl Marx' (Hoover 1921, p. 225). The main effort by the FAES was a book-length study of waste in industry, which indicated that 'management had the greatest opportunity and hence the greatest responsibility for eliminating waste in industry' and needed to cooperate with labour to meet its responsibility (Committee on Elimination of Waste in Industry of FAES 1922, pp. 8–9).

When President Harding appointed Hoover as Secretary of Commerce in 1921, the FAES programme decreased in intensity. Hoover, however, saw his new post as an opportunity to gain greater prominence for the work of efficiency in industry through cooperation. His goal was to develop an economic system that prevented business cycles. As Secretary of Commerce, Hoover convened a President's Conference on Unemployment to explore how the government, business and labour could cooperate to solve the problems of unemployment. The conference produced two studies pertinent to the theme of this book. One was on business cycles and unemployment, authored by the business cycle expert Wesley Mitchell, and the other was on the use of public works as an antidote to recessions, produced by Otto T. Mallery (Rothbard 2000, pp. 2847–902).

Hoover's chief approach for voluntary cooperation was to encourage trade associations, organizations of businesses that made up a particular industry. Hoover was a strong proponent of trade associations and believed that the information they shared would help alleviate the severity of business cycles. His intent was to make it feasible for every industry in the US to use its trade associations and the information they provided to promote better decision-making by industry planning groups. The result he anticipated would be industrial efficiency and intelligent competition. In two separate cases the US Supreme Court upheld most of the practices trade associations used, vindicating Hoover's approach (Stabile 2000, p. 422).

To Hoover, the abuses that businessmen imposed on the market economy were very small in comparison to the overall economy, an example of the maxim that a small portion of any group causes most of the problems. Because of the attention they gave this small amount of abuse, opponents of business called for national planning as a remedy. Hoover believed that voluntary associations would be able to set and enforce standards of behaviour for members to the industry. In a 7 November 1924, speech he observed, 'The very publication of codes of ethics by many associations ... the condemnation of specific unfair practices, the insistence upon a higher plane of relationships between employer and employee – all of them are at least indications of improving thought and moral perceptions' (Hoover 1951, p. 173). A moral economy could be created through voluntary organizations without going to the extreme of national ownership and planning by the government. Still, Hoover let the Department of Commerce in the 1920s assist trade associations in developing their codes to eliminate unfair competition and had them sanctioned by the Federal Trade Commission (Rothbard 2000, p. 5331 n.).

At the same time, Hoover recognized that the government had to take charge of areas such as the operation of dams, the regulation of electricity generation and radio communication, and the mitigation of business cycles. Regarding business cycles, Hoover had formed a Committee on Business Cycles in 1921 with the aim of finding out what could be done to alleviate the social damage caused by recessions. In a report to Congress on the committee's findings Hoover wrote:

> The first strategic point of attack was that Government construction should be so regulated that it may be deferred in times of intense private construction and expedited in times of unemployment. The effect would be not only to secure more economical construction for the government but also to stabilize the construction industries and to considerably mitigate unemployment in periods of depression. (Hoover 1951, p. 174)

Hoover supported the policy of counter-cyclical government spending that Mitchell had described in his work (see Chapter 3).

Underlying Hoover's approach to industry and economics was a philosophy he set forth in 1922 in his book, *American Individualism*. The book reviewed the many social ideologies fighting for legitimacy in the US and Europe. To Hoover, the most fertile path for the US to follow was 'the ideals that constitute progressive individualism' (Hoover 1922, p. 8). Of course, he added, individualism alone had the potential to get out of hand and cause social damage. In the US that individualism was constrained by the ideals of equality of opportunity, an abhorrence of autocracy and a promotion of social justice that aimed at a fair division of the products of industry. As a result, he argued, the US had a singular social system that was not easily placed in categories such as capitalism or socialism. It was an effective system because it avoided the ills of both systems. Regarding socialism, Hoover was vehement in his denunciation of it, writing that its economic decisions would be made 'by a Tammany Hall or a Bolshevist party, or some other form of tyranny' (Hoover 1922, pp. 17–18).

The US also needed to avoid 'capitalism in the sense that a few men through unrestrained control of property determine the welfare of great numbers' (Hoover 1922, p. 18). The misuse of property rights by misguided individuals was being reduced, however, due to the growth of large corporations run by executives and owned by stockholders. Organizations such as trade associations, chambers of commerce and labour unions were springing up as 'mixtures of altruism and self interest' (Hoover 1922, p. 43). Individual self-interest as informed by moral and social responsibility such as Hoover saw possible in the US would offer a better way to ensure the type of cooperation he thought voluntary organizations would provide. In that way he hoped to formulate an economy that was open to competition but did not go to the extreme of having individuals wreak havoc on the market economy through manipulations of the marketplace. In doing so, he hoped to avoid the two extreme ideas 'that all human ills can be cured by government regulation' and 'that all regulation is a sin' (Hoover 1922, p. 49).

In charting this middle course, Hoover clearly did not care for government micro-management of business. We shall see in this and subsequent chapters that supporters of the moral economy continued to believe that the experience of the WIB in World War I showed the benefits of government planning of the economy. During the war the federal government took over the country's railroads and used them as part of its planning system. Hoover, however, found that the railroads 'had been thoroughly demoralized by the war and government operation' and their freight carrying capacity had been diminished (Hoover 1951, p. 63). Once the railroads were returned to private management they formed, with assistance from the Department of Commerce, associations to organize national shipping. As a result, their

productivity improved between 1919 when they operated under government management and 1926 when the railroad associations were fully
operative. In his memoirs Hoover drew the following lesson: 'It is an
interesting commentary upon government operation of the railroads that
their employees in that period had risen to a maximum of 2,000,000. By
1926, about 8 per cent fewer employees were handling a 20 to 30 per cent
greater volume of traffic' (Hoover 1951, p. 64).

In arguing this way Hoover can be seen as doubting that the moral
economy would be efficient. He went further than arguing for the inefficiency of national planning, however. In a speech in 1928 he warned:

> You cannot extend the mastery of the government over the daily working life of a
> people without at the same time making it the master of the people's souls and
> thoughts. ... Even if governmental conduct of business could give us more
> efficiency instead of less efficiency, the fundamental objection to it would
> remain unaltered and unabated. It would destroy political equality. It would
> increase rather than decrease abuse and corruption. It would stifle initiative and
> invention. (Hoover 1951, p. 203)

In short, on Hoover's account Bellamy's moral economy laid too much of a
burden on the moral behaviour of the persons who ran it. Government
operation of business and the economy gave government officials more
power than they could be trusted to take. And their use of that power could
subvert the process of creative destruction that had contributed to economic
growth.

FOSTER AND CATCHINGS DEFEND THE MARKET ECONOMY

In Chapter 4 we presented William T. Foster and Waddill Catchings as
providing an explanation of the business cycle on the basis of the problem
of 'underconsumption.' They remained staunch defenders of the market
economy, however, and in their books took their readers on a survey of the
economic economy of the US that touted its virtues. Foster and Catchings
were not about to overlook the benefits that the market economy brought to
human life. Moreover, they were critical of the alternatives to it in the form
of government regulation or socialism and discounted arguments over the
deficient morality of business (Foster and Catchings 1925, pp. 12, 16, 46,
64, 74, 170). Here is just one example of their comments on communism:

> Communism does away with prices and profits. It thereby disenfranchises
> consumers. As they can no longer elect their commercial representatives by

casting their dollar-votes, they have no effective means of indicating what they
want to have produced. This might not matter if the community had infinite
wealth. If there were no limit to the volume and variety of goods that could be
produced, everybody could call upon the State for everything he wanted. But
even under communism, wealth would be finite. Arbitrary limitation of production in certain directions would still be necessary in order that output could be
increased in other directions ... . Consequently, the State would have to ration
everything. (Foster and Catchings 1925, pp. 215–16)

The experiments in Russia under communism showed this point clearly,
because they had reduced total output in the economy by two-thirds,
causing severe rationing.

The US did not face such rationing because it functioned under a market
economy of money, prices and profits. Foster and Catchings noted that
profit-seeking had produced great wealth for humanity. To them, profits
were the compensation for the risks that businessmen took in setting up a
business, hiring workers, producing a product and trying to sell the product.
Oftentimes they failed and instead of profits they suffered losses. The
source of most risks was that the economy was always changing and the
changes were unpredictable. Those changes and the risks they brought were
due to the freedom of choice consumers had in how to spend their money.
Foster and Catchings described this problem as follows: 'This uncertainty is
due largely to three options enjoyed by the holder of money. He can decide
when he will buy, what he will buy, and where he will buy it (Foster and
Catchings 1925, p. 57). Because consumers had these options, businesses
had to win them over with advertising methods and product design. Critics
of the market economy considered these to be wastes, but Foster and
Catchings argued that they were necessary and the only way to eliminate
them was to eliminate consumer choice. They were wastes only if society
did not think consumer choice was valuable.

Because profits depended on the risk of whether or not a business could
satisfy consumer choice, high profits indicated that a business had undertaken a high risk to satisfy consumers with something new and consumers
had rewarded them; the process of creative destruction was not always
successful, which is why it paid large rewards when it was. Persons who
wanted to reduce profits had to find a way to reduce those risks. One way
government tried to reduce high profits was to regulate prices, but government was not 'qualified to take over the function of price' (Foster and
Catchings 1925, p. 74). Governments took this role in an effort to control
'unreasonable profits.' The concept of unreasonable profits was hard to
define, however, because defining it had to include a measure of the risk the
person making the profit had faced as well as the risk that changing

consumer tastes might turn that profit into a loss quickly, because consumers ultimately decided what prices business could charge. Consumers always had the option of not spending on a high-priced item, and when they exercised that option, profits would fall. Foster and Catchings wrote of businesses, 'They charge whatever consumers, competing for the same good, allow them to charge; and there is no other way of determining who is to get the goods. But if this is what we mean by profiteering, who among us shall cast the first stone' (Foster and Catchings 1925, p. 185).

Foster and Catchings could not find any standard of 'normal profits' by which to judge whether profits were reasonable or not. Instead, they pointed out that profits and losses varied considerably among businesses and over time. Because of this large variation in profits, they determined, 'The relative shares of capital and labor in the products of industry also vary widely from year to year' (Foster and Catchings 1925, p. 164). There was no set distribution of income in society and no way to determine if that distribution was fair. Efforts to settle the distribution of income by government regulation would not succeed, as the often 'ridiculous' decisions of the WIB in World War I demonstrated. Anyone who wanted to use the WIB as a model for national economic planning must recognize the problem such an effort faced. Foster and Catchings wrote, 'No Congress, no Cabinet, no commission – not all the public officials in the country put together, even if they gave all their time to the work – could possibly measure and meet the desires of one hundred million people as accurately and quickly as they are measured by the price system – a system, let us repeat, under which some large profits are unavoidable' (Foster and Catchings 1925, p. 213). Reformers and pundits might try to figure out ways to plan the economy for the common good, but it was 'some other man's freedom of choice they wish to curtail for the common good' (Foster and Catchings 1925, p. 214). Sumner's forgotten man had not been forgotten, at least not by Foster and Catchings.

Nor had they forgotten the price government paid for forgetting the forgotten man. Government efforts to control profits impaired the workings of the market economy by distorting the signals that profits and prices send about what consumers wanted. Once profits were made by business, the government had a say in how much of them a businessman could keep through taxes. Businessmen already paid a 'considerable' part of their profits in taxes, and because a large majority of society did not have a share in profits they could vote for even higher taxes on profits. Foster and Catchings added, however, that the majority refrained from taxing business heavily because they did 'not care to make themselves poorer merely for the sake of making the rich poorer' (Foster and Catchings 1925, p. 218).

Government should intervene in the economy to eliminate unscrupulous or illegal profit-making, but not to mitigate high but legal profits.

In the return to the normalcy of the 1920s the writings of Foster and Catchings proved to be very popular. Still, popular ideas did not deter Progressive pundits from thinking and writing about their own programmes. After this brief interlude of support for the market economy we now return to consideration of the moral economy.

REXFORD GUY TUGWELL FUSES MORALS AND MARKETS

Rexford Guy Tugwell (1891–1979) had a long career in government service as part of Franklin Roosevelt's Brains Trust and later as the appointed governor of Puerto Rico. Before that, during the 1920s, he was a professor of economics at Columbia University. In 1927 he made a study trip to the Soviet Union with a number of prominent economists and liked what he saw (Goldberg 2007, p. 102). More important here, in that year he published a study of the increased productivity of the US economy, *Industry's Coming of Age*. The book is especially interesting because Tugwell subtly revealed in it a philosophy of planning that would come to the forefront in his New Deal activities. Although he waited until the end of the book to state it plainly, we start with this statement about the effects of planning on those who participated in it:

> The main point in this to one who happens to be interested in a better moral world would seem to be that ... there would be a great strengthening of the bonds of identity among men and women engaged in common tasks. They would possess a new ability to regard industrial activity as a service to society ... . This merging of self in the group will come about just as rapidly as the social arrangements we make for industry will let it. And it will serve for the productive morality we spoke of earlier. (Tugwell 1927, p. 239)

The path that Tugwell took to get to this statement of the moral economy was complicated, however.

There were hints of it early on. In his 'Introduction' Tugwell gave a succinct statement of the problem he would address. The US economy was organizing into an efficient productive system, Tugwell called it a new industrial revolution, but few persons, including economists, understood how the system functioned. If society had any 'hope to subject industry to its uses' (Tugwell 1927, p. vii), it needed a better understanding of that system. The first part of attaining that understanding was the realization of how productive the industrial system had become. Tugwell presented a variety of data to demonstrate that the 1920s were the most prosperous decade ever in the US. Not every industry shared in the productivity gains, but they were areas that were ripe for improvement. However, the US had to be guarded against 'too great social optimism' because much needed to be done to arrange for 'coordination and mutual assistance in troubled times' (Tugwell 1927, p. 28).

Tugwell recognized that the increased productivity of the new industrial system, gave society the potential to solve many of the problems associated with poverty. Before discussing how the market economy could be modified to ensure that this potential was used effectively, Tugwell wrote at great length to review the theories that economists set forth to explain why the new industrial system was so productive. It was a comprehensive review that considered items ranging from the development of more standardized products to the increased female participation in the labour force. Here we focus on two items consistent with the theme of this book, business cycles and the fitness of businessmen to run industry.

The business cycle itself was a hindrance to increasing productivity but an enhanced ability to diminish those cycles aided productivity gains (Tugwell 1927, p. 89). Tugwell was not a business cycle theorist and relied on the works of Wesley Mitchell, Thorstein Veblen and Irving Fisher (see Chapters 3 and 4) in his survey of business cycles. To him, the academic study of business cycles by these and other economists had greatly increased the knowledge of business cycles, and large businesses that had to plan and coordinate the production and distribution of their products also found it necessary to understand how a business cycle could upset their plans. That knowledge was not complete, but 'we seem to have made some considerable progress toward correcting the swings of the rhythm and toward smoothing out the fluctuations in activity which are its worst social manifestations' (Tugwell 1927, p. 93) The Federal Reserve System was also doing a good job in controlling the money supply and credit in ways that kept prices stable, and if it continued that good job 'one of the worst features of the cycle will have been obviated' (Tugwell 1927, p. 95).

Despite such progress, in a later chapter Tugwell also included 'the persistence of depressions' as one of the 'barriers to productivity' (Tugwell 1927, p. 204). When a recession came about, it upset all of the careful plans that businesses had made. Even though the business cycle had been reduced, it still was there as part of the dynamic nature of the market economy. The problem, as Tugwell put it, was that 'we have no plan toward which we work.' He then added, 'Such a plan may in time come about by being built upon the smaller plans industries are beginning to make for themselves. When every industry shall have attained a definite program for a future period, it seems possible that some inter-industrial body may be set up to formulate a general plan. But this is in some far future' (Tugwell 1927, p. 207).

What about government programmes to coordinate and plan the economy and help smooth out the business cycle? Tugwell indicated that business efforts to coordinate with each other's plans had 'gone on entirely outside of government interferences' (Tugwell 1927, p. 97). Rather, businesses either gained control over the risk of relying on markets through horizontal combinations (buying up competitors) or vertical combinations (buying up suppliers); firms that could not achieve such integration formed 'trade associations of all kinds' (Tugwell 1927, p. 112). All of this contributed to what Tugwell called 'our voluntary industrial policy' (Tugwell 1927, p. 157).

The voluntary programmes that Tugwell highlighted took place because the persons in charge of business were becoming more effective at their jobs. This increase in effectiveness resulted from the developments in scientific management by Taylor and his associates and Tugwell gave a lengthy account of their activities. He believed that they had increased efficiency in the organization of business and in the planning of work and production (Tugwell 1927, p. 124). The educational system was also improving the ability of more persons to apply Taylor's principles. All of this meant that businessmen began 'to think of themselves in social terms – which means that what is socially good is good for the organization' (Tugwell 1927, p. 69). Tugwell referred to this new approach as the socialization of business and found that it produced the programmes of voluntary cooperation that he approved.

These voluntary programmes by business leaders were all to the good, but still they were not enough. Tugwell offered a series of policies for how to improve these voluntary programmes, including a recommendation:

> That the whole field of social, as against voluntary regulation, be studied, so that the controls of society can be applied at the places and at the times which are strategic. We linger in the past, with our clumsy governmental machinery for control hopelessly out of date. We muddle where we ought to clarify; we obstruct where we ought to encourage. Governmental controls ought to be brought to bear where voluntary ones break down. (Tugwell 1927, p. 224)

What were the sorts of things government should be doing? As a way of directing the economy for social results the government should take charge of the allocation of capital to areas where it would do the most good and it should control prices. According to Tugwell, the government was probably capable of doing more in terms of directing the economy as the experience of the WIB demonstrated (Tugwell 1927, p. 234). But allocating capital would be a good start, and 'price control is a necessary concomitant of any pecuniary system which may achieve socialization' (Tugwell 1927, p. 236). Too many sharp operators in business used price fluctuations to make private gains and thereby upset the plans of others. Once the government took over price controls, voluntary planning by business would be much more effective.

As another problem area in the economy, Tugwell highlighted the existence of poverty during the 1920s and counted it as a barrier to productivity because it hindered the effective use of all workers. In looking at what to do about poverty, he believed 'we have to take into account those forces in society which make for inequalities in the apportionment of incomes and for unwise uses of them' (Tugwell 1927, p. 217). Both issues related to the way the market economy used monetary incentives to motivate performance. At one time those incentives may have been useful, but the new industrial revolution had changed the way they worked. It was not wrong that humans would want to take care of themselves and those they loved, but now they needed to cooperate with each other instead of competing as in the olden days of the market economy. In those days, society took place on a smaller scale and people esteemed their neighbours who gave them quality goods and services at a reasonable price. They would not tolerate anyone who became wealthy 'at the general expense' by charging neighbours high prices. Instead, they held to 'the notion that great wealth must have been acquired dishonourably' (Tugwell 1927, p. 257).

In the new economy of the 1920s that notion lost its grip as many members of society emulated the wealthy person's consumption patterns and 'he incurs no neighborly disapproval with his wealth' (Tugwell 1927, p. 258). If the view of wealth had changed from negative to positive, however, it could be turned the other way. Tugwell put it this way, 'Some moral controls over the immense and increasing spending power of our age must be constructed' (Tugwell 1927, p. 260). One way to add those controls was to create a culture in the US where the wealthy were reviled for becoming wealthy 'at the general expense' while also boosting the public recognition of the virtue of work. Attacks on the morality of the wealthy have always been part of the advocacy of the moral economy.

Another difficulty with great wealth was that it led to wasteful consumption on a variety of superfluous items. Tugwell, however, saw the US economy as 'entering a period of slow income-leveling.' Such a 'movement toward greater equality' would reduce the tendency to use spending as a sign of prestige and would allow society the opportunity to make better use of economic production to meet the basic needs of more persons, that is, to eliminate poverty. The changes Tugwell hoped to see would move society to 'ordering affairs so that the greatest rewards should go to the greatest producers rather than to the shrewdest or luckiest bargainers' (Tugwell 1927, p. 248).

Because Tugwell did not specifically propose that government should develop programmes for class warfare by reviling the wealthy and re-distributing income, we are reluctant to infer that he would have supported them. Against this reluctance, we must add that Tugwell found the slogan, 'Keep the Government out of Business,' to be 'uncharacteristic of the American spirit in its very expression.' He found it puzzling that while citizens of the US thought of themselves 'as active and adventurous, as experimental and progressive' they did not want to use government to help in the 'most critical dilemmas of industrial life' (Tugwell 1927, p. 251). He added later in the book, 'We cannot treat either our morals or our industrial arrangements as absolute and expect to progress very rapidly ... . The real necessity is for fusion. And this fusion can be accomplished only on the basis of expediency' (Tugwell 1927, p. 262). Tugwell's opportunity to experiment on the basis of expediency would come within a decade. And while in 1927 he did not advocate government intervention in many areas where it would intervene during the New Deal, he did believe, 'Governmental controls ought to be brought to bear where voluntary ones break down' (Tugwell 1927, p. 224).

WALTER LIPPMANN UPDATES HIS VIEWS

In 1929 Walter Lippmann published another of his searching books analysing the status of civilization in the US, *A Preface to Morals*. The overall problem he was addressing, he began, was that many persons no longer believed in religion, with the result that they felt 'a vacancy in their lives' (Lippmann 1929 [1964], p. 3). The proximate cause of this losing of religious faith was that science had undermined its foundation by showing that nature had a rational and not a moral order. But science could not fill the 'vacancy' many were feeling, and Lippmann pondered over how to fill it with a moral humanism.

In doing so, he looked at how economic activity was changing the world through its use of science. As noted earlier, Lippmann had considered science to be the impetus for mastery, due to its discipline. Science became necessary in modern life, for it was the most creative element in that life. What it had created in the market economy was 'the machine process,' the building of an integrated system of economic production based on scientific technology. Just as Veblen had observed a quarter of a century earlier (see Chapter 3), Lippmann argued that this technology required 'a population which in some measure partakes of the spirit which created it' (Lippmann 1929 [1964], p. 225). Much of the upheaval of the last 75 years, he went on, had been a process for finding an industrial philosophy consistent with the demands of modern technology and the moral needs of human beings, that is, what we call the moral economy.

In that process many old ideas had been discarded and new ones tried and found wanting. Religion had tried to hold business and the acquisitive spirit it produced in check for nearly two millennia through moral precepts against business practices such as usury, but business had persevered and eventually succeeded. Business had carried the day by using Adam Smith's arguments in favour of the market economy, but the market economy did not fit in with modern technology (Lippmann 1929 [1964], p. 231).

When the government tried to regulate business its problem was in thinking that politicians and government officials would 'be wise enough and disinterested enough to make business men do what they would not otherwise do' (Lippmann 1929 [1964], p. 233). To some degree, the problem of government regulation was one of compliance. In the complex world of the machine process the government did not have the resources to enforce compliance with its laws and had to rely on voluntary compliance and the intentional reporting of offenders by innocent bystanders (Lippmann 1929 [1964], p. 259). Here Lippmann appears to have given up his earlier Progressive case for the efficacy of a scientific public administration. The problem for Lippmann was that no person or committee could monitor and regulate, much less control, the complex economy that the 1920s had produced.

His answer to the problem was that the leaders of industry were evolving their ideas towards what was needed to run that interconnected industrial system. They did this through their use of technical experts they hired in their firms as well as by their application of statistical methods to keep track of what the firm was doing. They also did this through the formation of trade associations that kept track of how their industry was doing. And they held conferences and established councils to share economic information and the knowledge of new business techniques with each other. Moreover, because the executives in charge of the large corporations of industrial society were not owners, and the owners (stockholders) were not managers, the acquisitive spirit of business leaders was atrophying. The leaders of business focused more on getting their job done than in wondering how to make more money from it. As a result, it was becoming difficult to determine whether these large corporations were 'public or private institutions' (Lippmann 1929 [1964], p. 241).

In making the case for this managerial capitalism, Lippmann exhibited an optimistic complacency typical of many pundits in the 1920s, who felt that the economic transformation and prosperity of that decade would go on forever. We now know that he was wrong, and that when managerial capitalism suffered a recession as severe as the market economy had experienced in the past, the only difference was that the higher integration of managerial capitalism meant that the recession would spread quickly and severely throughout the globe.

STUART CHASE FINDS WASTE IN THE MARKET ECONOMY

Stuart Chase (1888–1985) was a graduate of Harvard University with a broad interest in economics. Like many Progressive pundits he made a trip to the Soviet Union and expressed praise for what was taking place there. During the 1920s he wrote two influential books, *The Tragedy of Waste* (Chase 1925) and *Prosperity: Fact or Myth?* (Chase 1929). In these books he took an engineering perspective to the US economy to analyse how wasteful it was and how that waste contributed to the myth of prosperity in the 1920s. As evidence of how influential he was and by whom he might have been influenced, we cite the words of Rexford Tugwell: 'No writer on economic subjects has been able to command an audience nearly so big; and certainly no contemporary author is to be compared with him in this respect. Among other Americans, indeed, only two names come to mind – Edward Bellamy and Henry George' (Tugwell 1930, p. 418). Here was one of those rare occasions where a Progressive pundit not only mentioned Bellamy's name but used it to add lustre to the reputation of a Progressive compatriot. And he was right to do so.

We can see how right Tugwell was from considering Chase's concern with the relationship between waste and real as opposed to mythical prosperity, a concern he shared with Bellamy and Veblen. Our starting point is with his definition of waste as what society produces that is beyond basic human wants. 'A sound theory of waste,' he wrote, meant that 'necessities have right of way over luxuries' (Chase 1925, pp. 29–30). To make the distinction between necessities and luxuries more clear, he gave lists for both. Under necessities he listed food, shelter, clothing, education, recreation, government and community control, the safeguarding of health, religion and art forms. Regarding wastes in consumption, Chase came up with the military establishment, harmful drugs, commercialized vice and crime, adulterated products, speculation and gambling, quackery in medicine, super luxuries and their cheap imitation, fashions, commercialized recreation (spectator sports), perversions of professional services and advertising.

Proponents of the market economy such as Foster and Catchings would eschew this classification system on the grounds of the difficulty of making interpersonal utility comparisons. 'One man's meat is often another's poison' was how Chase used a popular aphorism to define the issue. But if that were the case, why not let consumers decide for themselves what a necessity was and what waste was? Chase's answers were that 'consumers are not educated for their protection against deleterious products and they have not equal purchasing strength in the market, and are thus led to buy cheap imitations of goods held by their economic superiors.' In addition, advertisers used methods of 'artificial stimulation' to lure in uneducated consumers and the number of products available to the consumer made it 'impossible for the consumer to test and value what he buys' (Chase 1925, p. 42). All of these factors led to wasteful consumption in items such as alcohol and tobacco that were beyond 'human want' (Chase 1925, p. 68).

Chase also found wastes in production stemming from the lack of coordination in production, excess plant capacity, duplication of services, restriction of output by business to keep prices high, lack of standardization, poor management, suppressed inventions, excessive selling costs, unemployment due to recessions, strikes and absenteeism, and the lost labour of 'the idle rich' and 'the hobo and bum' (Chase 1925, pp. 33–6). Some of these production wastes were being reduced through the work of Taylor and his followers, and Chase referred to this work throughout his book. To him, the issue of waste had 'become an engineering rather than a moral problem' (Chase 1925, p. 28). Later in the book he expanded on this idea, writing, 'There are today in America enough good engineers and enough good administrators to run a functional society, and to double and triple the standard of living' (Chase 1925, p. 277).

In his next book *Prosperity: Fact or Myth?* (Chase 1929) Chase was concerned with the question of whether the prosperity of the 1920s had been real or a myth. In terms of income per capita, there had been true gains in prosperity (Chase 1929, p. 32). The question, however, was how this prosperity had been distributed in society, as Chase recognized that some individuals, industries and regions of the country had prospered more than others. He found that farmers had not prospered, a large section of the middle class had not prospered, many regions of the country had not prospered, the coal, textile, shoe, shipbuilding and railroad industries had not prospered and the unskilled workers had not prospered (Chase 1929, p. 174). Who had prospered? Chase made that clear: 'The owning class was prosperous in 1922 and is still more prosperous to-day – absolutely and probably relatively' (Chase 1929, p. 178). To Chase, this was another case of the rich getting richer and at the expense of the other classes in society.

But there was another issue related to the 'owning class.' It controlled the industry of the country and dictated the terms over how that industry was used. The result was the wastes that Chase had found in his earlier book. In 1925 he had been optimistic about the way engineers could eliminate waste in production and consumption and had cheered efforts by engineers such as Hoover and the FAES group to study waste in industry. By 1929 he was more concerned with how 'the technician is constantly undone by the sales department' (Chase 1929, p. 187). Engineers wanted to produce human necessities as efficiently as possible, but for business prosperity to continue products had to be designed to appeal to uneducated consumers through fashion, style changes, annual models and advertising – wastes that prevented real prosperity from taking place. Chase expressed that status of engineers' efforts to bring about prosperity as follows: 'Prosperity in any deeper sense awaits the liberation of the engineer. ... A complicated technical structure should be run by engineers, not hucksters' (Chase 1929, p. 188).

Suppose engineers were put in charge, what would they have done to improve the economy and bring about prosperity? In 1929 Chase indicated that 'the technician is undone by failure to inaugurate a national system of super-management, whereby production might be articulated to consumptive needs' (Chase 1929, p. 187). To find an example of what he meant, we return to his 1925 study of waste. There he indicated that the best introduction to the problem of waste 'lies in an analysis of the war control of industry' (Chase 1925, p. 3). During World War I the US government had done an excellent job in planning the industrial production needed to equip its military. Chase described the results as follows: 'War control lifted the economic system of the country, stupefied by decades of profit-seeking, and hammered and pounded it into an intelligent mechanism for delivering goods and services according to the needs of the army and of the working population' (Chase 1925, p. 10). Yes, an advocate for the market economy might add, such an effort might have been effective, but that was because the needs of war were easy to identify, which made it easier to set priorities about what to produce. To argue this way plays right into Chase's hands, for that was why he went to such great lengths to identify basic human needs. Once they were identified, that made it easier to make plans about what to produce. He asked, 'Suppose that the war control of industry had been maintained to direct a war against poverty and low living standards' (Chase 1925, p. 16). Could we not have won that war as well?

To win it, Chase hypothesized 'an Industrial General Staff in its Washington headquarters' taking an inventory of productive capacity and determining how those resources compared to a survey of needs. Instead of those needs being defined in terms of war material, they would be organized in terms of housing, food, clothing, schools, roads and electric power (Chase 1925, p. 18). In fact, Chase added, the WIB had taken such an inventory of needs. Once the needs were defined, the Industrial General Staff could survey industry in terms of plant capacity and location, determine raw material and transportation requirements, and then set up a plan to produce what was necessary to meet basic human needs. That process would result in real prosperity, for Chase thought that engineering and planning effectively could 'double and triple the standard of living' (Chase 1925, p. 277).

Chase has returned us to the planned economy of Bellamy, only Chase did not indicate whether industry needed to be nationalized or just controlled by the Industrial General Staff. He was perhaps purposely vague because he was not optimistic that his scheme was socially feasible. He described the situation as follows: 'We have no illusion as to the immediate introduction of an economic system based on function rather than on property rights.' The Industrial General Staff might be 'an organ of the political government, a clearing house for producers and consumers co-operatives, a board of directors of a private holding company, a chamber of commerce of enlightened businessmen.' But it would not come to realization 'until the massed habits and folkways of the present generation have spent their course' (Chase 1925, p. 39). The ideology of the market economy still held sway in the US and Chase remained cautious about predicting its demise.

CONCLUSION

Chase's outlook on planning and what it would take to bring it about in the US represented the hopes of the three decades of thinking by Progressive pundits that we have surveyed in this and the previous chapter. What needed to be done was so obvious to them: replace the profit motive and all the wastes it created with a system of national planning by scientific experts to plan efficiently how to produce what was needed to meet basic human needs. In hoping for this world, they followed the ideas of Bellamy, at least by implication. Some of them, like Tugwell and Lippmann, indicated the social trends they thought were leading in the direction they hoped for, while others, like Chase, feared the 'folkways' of society that prized the market economy of property rights over the functionality of the moral economy were too strong to overcome.

Those 'folkways' were not immutable, however. In an event that surprised many Progressive pundits the economy produced a crisis that would be used to change the way everyone in the US thought about markets versus morals when the New Deal of Roosevelt came about in response to the crisis of the Great Depression, as we shall describe later. In the meantime, the Great Depression began under the presidency of Hoover, whom we have seen as sharing many of the ideas of the Progressive pundits. We shall examine in the next chapter how he deployed those ideas when the crisis came.

7.   The Great Depression

The economy of the US has always had business cycles of recession and recovery and they have always been tragedies in terms of human suffering and deprivation. Few of those economic cycles have warranted the designation of catastrophic. The Great Depression does warrant that designation. In the economy the recession began in August 1929 and lasted 43 months before hitting bottom in March 1933. By that time real gross national product (GNP) had fallen by 30 per cent and the unemployment rate reached 25 per cent. Real GNP did not reach its pre-depression level until 1937.

In this chapter we are concerned with the early phase of the depression, the economic decline of 1929 to 1933. Our focus is on what our representative groups of business leaders, politicians, pundits and economists had to say in these early years of crisis about what caused the depression and what should be done to turn the economy around. We must point out, however, that even with the advantage of hindsight, economic historians still debate what caused the Great Depression and perhaps the best explanation is that it was a perfect storm of many events. Among the explanations that economic historians have given for the Great Depression, the following have been widely scrutinized: a decline in business investment, turmoil in financial markets, poor policy by the Federal Reserve in contracting the money supply, the passage of the Smoot-Hawley Tariff, stickiness of wages, issues related to the gold standard, problems in banking that caused several waves of runs on banks, declines in personal consumption and weakening of the housing market (Rothbard 2000; Smiley 2003, pp. 11–70; Parker 2007, pp. 1–28). Many of these explanations were set forth by contemporary economists in the 1930s. The explanation that gained the greatest traction, however, was the decline in consumption, that is, the underconsumption problem that had been given great prominence by William T. Foster and Waddill Catchings.

HOOVER'S ECONOMIC POLICIES

As noted in Chapter 6, throughout the 1920s Herbert Hoover had championed the cause of voluntary cooperation among the major stakeholders in business to provide guidance to the market economy. In promoting this form of voluntary planning, Hoover hoped to avoid what he saw as the instability of the market economy and to prevent the growth of government controls. His initial step to head off the recession in 1929 was to set up a series of conferences at the White House to bring together the heads of leading industries in the US and enable them to take voluntary but organized action. The conferences took place in November 1929 and the industry leaders who attended agreed to maintain wages and to avoid laying off workers as a way to maintain consumption demand. Businesses stuck to this agreement for as long as possible, but during a period of deflation such as took place in the early 1930s, where prices fell by 25 per cent from 1930–33, maintaining wage rates meant that real wages rose. Eventually, businesses had to let go of workers and cut the wages of those they kept.

In addition to voluntary programmes, Hoover took governmental action. He created the Reconstruction Finance Corporation as a way for the federal government to help keep banks from failing with loans. The Federal Farm Board, formed in mid-1929, was given funds to make loans to farmers at low interest rates and to buy surplus production in agriculture. Hoover also tried to help the economy with tax cuts. For most of the 1920s, the federal government had experienced budget surpluses that it had used to retire debt from World War I. The budget remained in surplus in 1929 and Hoover and Congress used that surplus to pay for some tax cuts and to fund public works projects. By 1932, however, the federal government faced increasing budget deficits; Hoover and Congress increased income taxes and excise taxes on a variety of goods and services to get the budget back into balance (Rothbard 2000, pp. 4031–3). Hoover and the Congress also levied the Smoot-Hawley Tariff in 1930, raising the taxes on imports in an effort to keep wages and prices at higher levels; instead the tariff increases further diminished an already declining volume of world trade.

The brief survey of Hoover's policy, while not as comprehensive as Hoover deserves, is, we hope, sufficient to enable us to interpret it through our lens of markets and morals. As already indicated, Hoover tried to find a balance point between the two by using cooperation and guidance to supplement the market economy without going full-tilt into the moral economy of planning. The policies surveyed briefly above support this interpretation to some degree. For example, Hoover's advocacy of high wages and steady employment may have aimed at forestalling a recession, but Hoover characterized his approach as placing 'humanity over money' (Rothbard 2000, p. 4488). By securing promises from business leaders that they would maintain wages and employment, Hoover believed he had achieved his goal through voluntary cooperation. He also agreed that it was acceptable to spend a budget surplus on public works projects and tax reductions, but that it was immoral for the federal government to borrow and use deficit finance for the same purpose. Once the government had used up its surplus, it had done the best it could.

The real problem, however, was that no one anticipated that the recession that began in 1929 would last as long and be as severe as it turned out to be. As the Great Depression unfolded, all of our business leaders, politicians, pundits and economists would have to recalibrate their thinking as their perception of the extent of the problem altered as they gained additional information about it. In reviewing what they had to say, our emphasis is on those persons and ideas related to the ideal of the moral economy, especially its element of planning.

HOOVER DEFENDS HIS POLICIES

Having briefly summarized Hoover's policies to end the depression, we allow him to present those policies in his own words. Our sources for allowing Hoover to give his own accounting are his state of the union addresses, given annually during his term as president.

In his first state of the union address, given on 3 December 1929, Hoover was concerned about increased spending (Hoover 1929, pp. 50–52). Still, he was able to report that the projected federal budget for 1931 would be slightly lower than for 1930. He warned, however, that as Congress was taking on more responsibilities, the actual 1931 budget might go higher. He acknowledged that the federal government had to spend more for public welfare and added that it also needed to 'strive to find relief through some tax reduction. Every dollar returned fertilizes the soil of prosperity' (Hoover 1929, pp. 77–9). This fiscal policy was aided by the Federal Reserve's expansionary credit policy, and funds were flowing back into business. There might be 'a number of persons thrown temporarily out of employment,' but the outlook was good (Hoover 1929, pp. 114–16).

Despite that good outlook, business was not making use of the credit available to it and was pausing in its spending on investment. If nothing were done, the mild downturn might 'intensify into a depression with widespread unemployment and suffering.' To avoid that depression, Hoover pursued a programme of 'voluntary measures of cooperation' to ensure that 'wages and therefore consuming power shall not be reduced' (Hoover 1929, pp. 124–6). The cooperation included business, state and local governments and the federal government in maintaining wages, with an expectation that workers would keep spending and stimulate the economy. In holding this idea that steady wages were needed to maintain aggregate consumption,

Hoover was influenced by the underconsumption arguments of Foster and Catchings (see Chapter 4).

In his next state of the union address, on 2 December 1930, Hoover reported, 'During the past 12 months we have suffered with other nations from economic depression' (Hoover 1930, pp. 476–8). At this stage of the downturn Hoover insisted that it could not be 'cured by legislative action or executive pronouncement' (Hoover 1930, pp. 497–8). Recovery required the cooperation of all parts of the economy: business should improve its methods and help its workers; those with jobs should continue to spend and to help their less fortunate neighbours; and state and local governments should gear up for unemployment relief. The federal government's role consisted of organizing the voluntary programme of having business maintain wages and Hoover reported, 'The index of union wage scales shows them to be fully up to the level of any of the previous three years. In consequence the buying power of the country has been much larger than would otherwise have been the case' (Hoover 1930, pp. 510–11). The federal government had also expanded its public works spending and instead of public works showing a decline as they had in previous recessions, there had been an expansion of 'public construction to an amount even above that in the most prosperous year' with projected federal government spending on construction for 1931 doubling that of 1928 (Hoover 1930, p. 517). Private business had also expanded its construction. He added, 'The result of magnificent cooperation throughout the country has been that actual suffering has been kept to a minimum during the past 12 months, and our unemployment has been far less in proportion than in other large industrial countries' (Hoover 1930, pp. 522–3).

There were limits to federal government spending on construction, however. First, not all construction projects would contribute to the reduction of unemployment. Second, all government projects had to make economic sense and be technically efficient. Given these limits, Hoover advised, 'The volume of construction work in the Government is already at the maximum limit warranted by financial prudence. To increase taxation for the purposes of construction work defeats its own purpose, as such taxes directly diminish employment in private industry' (Hoover 1930, pp. 548–9). In addition, it took time to organize government construction projects because they were not, in recent terms, shovel-ready. They could do nothing to reduce unemployment in the short run. Hoover and his administration had got authorized public works projects up and running as fast as possible. The depression had also turned a federal government budget surplus into a deficit. Although Hoover admitted the necessity of this deficit, he added, 'I cannot emphasize too strongly the absolute necessity to defer any other plans for increase of Government expenditures' (Hoover 1930, pp. 599–602).

In his state of the union address on 8 December 1931 Hoover applauded the 'remarkable development of the sense of cooperation in the community' as a positive feature on an otherwise negative economy (Hoover 1931, pp. 676–9). The domestic economy showed signs of improvement and most of it was from private initiatives. Hoover noted, 'There has been the least possible Government entry into the economic field, and that only in temporary and emergency form' (Hoover 1931, pp. 721–3). That form included continued public works spending by the federal government and enlisting business in a cooperative effort to maintain as many jobs as possible through reductions in hours for each worker (Hoover 1931, p. 769).

To restore business confidence the federal government needed to take measures that helped the economy but did not compete with business. The first step was to rein in the large deficits due to the decline in tax collections and the increased spending caused by the depression, with the result that the deficit for the previous year had approached one billion dollars and the deficit for the present year was forecast at two billion dollars. Hoover went on,

> Several conclusions are inevitable. We must have insistent and determined reduction in Government expenses. We must face a temporary increase in taxes. Such an increase should not cover the whole of these deficits or it will retard recovery. We must partially finance the deficit by borrowing. (Hoover 1931, pp. 793–5)

Here we can see that Hoover was not completely doctrinaire about balancing the federal government budget, for he recognized that a deficit was aiding the recovery. He did, however, indicate that the tax increases should be planned to bring about a balanced budget by 1933. Perhaps he believed that the economy would recover by then. He also wanted the tax increases to expire in 1933 to give taxpayers and business confidence that the increases were truly temporary.

Hoover also recommended the creation of 'an emergency Reconstruction Corporation of the nature of the former War Finance Corporation' (Hoover 1931, p. 817). Here was an application of the World War I government apparatus that Hoover apparently approved and he believed that its existence alone would restore confidence. He anticipated that it would end its life within two years, once recovery of the economy took place. He also recommended revisions in the anti-trust laws but not a repeal of them. In some industries, especially in natural resources, 'destructive competition produces great wastes of these resources and brings great hardships upon operators, employees and the public' (Hoover 1931, pp. 845–9). There was good competition and bad competition and Hoover, who knew the difference, wanted to avoid the bad competition.

In his state of the union address on 6 December 1932 Hoover again applauded the community spirit of the people of the US in their voluntary efforts to meet the hardships being caused by the depression. Although the depression continued, he presented tables of 'current business indicators' to show the beginnings of a recovery (Hoover 1932, pp. 943–50). His confidence in the recovery showed in his writing, 'The measures and policies which have procured this turn toward recovery should be continued until the depression is passed, and then the emergency agencies should be promptly liquidated' (Hoover 1932, pp. 952–4). The Reconstruction Finance Corporation had been especially effective in helping the recovery through its expansion of credit.

Hoover's words indicated that he was not wedded to the market economy or balanced budgets to the extent he has been portrayed. In the case of the market economy he believed that it could lead to destructive competition and his programme of voluntary cooperation through trade associations aimed at avoiding it. He was also practical enough to understand that a balanced budget should be a long-term goal that would be reached once the economy recovered. Moreover, Hoover's words convey a sense of optimism that the recovery was imminent and this optimism led him to propose that all the government programmes he recommended, including budget deficits, were temporary, emergency measures that could be ended when the recovery came, perhaps in 1933, as he indicated in his 1932 state of the union address.

FOSTER AND CATCHINGS ON THE GREAT DEPRESSION

Foster and Catchings had created a stir in the 1920s with their theory that prosperity was always being blocked by too much savings in the economy. It should not surprise us that they used the same argument to explain the Great Depression. We see this in an article they published, 'Riotous saving,' in the November 1930 issue of *Atlantic Monthly*. In it they argued that the US had the highest standard of living in the world, as measured by the amount of consumption its citizens enjoyed, and the US economy kept increasing the amount of goods it produced. But that was the problem. Foster and Catchings wrote, 'We cannot keep producing more oranges or hats or anything else unless we can sell more. And we cannot sell more unless consumers buy more' (Foster and Catchings 1930b, p. 667). When business produced goods for sale they generated income. In order for that production to be continued, all the goods had to be sold.

Consumers, however, did not spend all of their income on consumption. They also saved. That was the reason for the depression taking place and for its continuing. Foster and Catchings wrote,

> If the people as a whole spend too little – which is the same as saying they save too much – they defeat the object of saving. That is what the people of the United States have been doing all year. Right now, large income receivers are trying to save more money than this country as a whole can possibly save to any advantage. For saved money is of no use *to the country as a whole* until it is invested. (Foster and Catchings 1930, pp. 667–8, emphasis in original)

Investment, however, would not take place so long as consumption was being cut back in favour of savings.

During a period of depression individuals saved for a 'rainy day,' that is, they became cautious and increased their savings in case an emergency came along such as losing their jobs. Those savings might be beneficial for the individual who had them but they were bad for the economy as a whole. The tradition of thrift in the US had termed extravagant spending as riotous living. Foster and Catchings turned the tables by calling the extra thrift of the depression 'riotous saving' (Foster and Catchings 1930b, p. 668). The country needed more extravagant spenders. If the affluent wanted 'to help their country, the best thing they can do, right now, is to spend more money' (Foster and Catchings 1930b, p. 670).

Foster and Catchings repeated their argument in two other articles, 'Must we reduce our standard of living?' in the February 1931 issue of *The Forum* and 'In the day of adversity' in the July 1931 issue of *Atlantic Monthly*. In the first article they argued against the idea that the US needed a programme of austerity and debt reduction to get out of the depression. Proponents of austerity argued 'that a country cannot save too much,' whereas Foster and Catchings believed, 'Right now, the United States is saving too much' (Foster and Catchings 1931a, p. 75). The second article pointed out that there were two ways to solve the problem of not enough consumption: consume more or produce less. More consumption was the best approach, because 'by producing less – by keeping production down to demand – we can stabilize poverty' (Foster and Catchings 1931b, p. 103).

In these articles Foster and Catchings had used a programme of exhortation to end the depression, that is, they strongly encouraged their readers to

spend! They also recognized that the federal government could take measures to help the economy and outlined these in a January 1930 article in the
Review of Reviews. Titled 'Mr. Hoover's road to prosperity,' the article
reviewed the policies the president was pursuing to end the decline in the
economy. Foster and Catchings observed, 'For the first time in our history, a
President of the United States is taking aggressive leadership in guiding
private business through a crisis' (Foster and Catchings 1930a, p. 50).
Previously, presidents had considered economic downturns to be inevitable
and had done nothing about them. Hoover was doing something, and his
policies were sound.

The point of those policies was to keep consumption at high levels.
Business was ready to follow Hoover's leadership by maintaining wages at
their level before the downturn, because he had been making plans with
them for over a year about what to do if a downturn came. In addition,
Foster and Catchings added, 'the President acted promptly for the purpose
of stimulating construction activities, public and private, thus sustaining
payrolls, employment, and consumer spending.' Hoover's opponents
labelled his programme wasteful spending, but Foster and Catchings indicated that Hoover was being very 'prudent.' He was calling for governments
at all levels 'to hasten construction of public buildings which were declared
necessary long before the crash in the stock market' (Foster and Catchings
1930a, p. 51). Here was the policy Wesley Mitchell had championed, timing
public works spending with the business cycle. Moreover, Foster and
Catchings recognized what John Maynard Keynes would later make famous
as the multiplier effect (see Chapter 12), pointing out 'that expansion of
construction adds to the demand for cement, steel, glass, lumber, and
hundreds of other commodities – trucks, tools, architect's plans and all the
rest' (Foster and Catchings 1930a, p. 52). Private sector jobs would be
created by government spending.

Foster and Catchings then gave an analysis of the conditions in early
1930 that tells us that they, along with many others including Hoover, had
not recognized how severe the downturn would become. They pointed out
that Hoover had mapped out a programme for spending over $8 billion on
construction in 1930. Was that enough spending? Foster and Catchings
answered, 'In the depths of a depression, it would not be. Under present
conditions, however, there is a statistical basis for believing that these
projected expenditures will prevent a major depression' (Foster and Catchings 1930a, p. 52). While these words may seem foolish to us now, we must
remember that few persons have been able to accurately forecast the
severity of an economic downturn, then or now.

JOHN MAURICE CLARK SUPPORTS PUBLIC WORKS

As described in Chapter 4, John Maurice Clark used his accelerator to explain how business investment decisions could be mistimed in terms of how they impacted the economy, with investment increasing during a boom when it was not needed to stimulate the economy and decreasing during a recession when it was needed. The same pattern would hold true of public works, because governments would see declining tax receipts during a recession and thus have to cut back on their projects, even as the economy might need them.

At the 1930 meetings of the American Economic Association (AEA), a roundtable discussion on public works gave Clark an opportunity to express his views on how the federal government could use 'the timing of public works in the attempt to mitigate cyclical fluctuations of unemployment' (Wolman et al. 1930, p. 17). In presenting his analysis, Clark first made it clear that Hoover's policies up to that time were 'a great experiment in constructive industrial statesmanship of a promising and novel sort' (Wolman et al. 1930, p. 15). Clark, however, believed that they needed to be better planned by deciding what type of agency was needed to carry out the policies and whether the spending would be based on a planned reserve of funds, set aside for use in a recession.

In terms of what type of agency was needed, Clark indicated that any coordinating body for spending on public works had to be part of the federal government. Only the federal government had the interests of the entire country in its sights. But that federal agency had to be supplemented by 'industrial councils' from private business, which still had important contributions to make through its investment in new construction, as well as by another body to represent state and local governments. A paramount criterion for any overarching agency was that 'Co-operation of the states and of private industry must necessarily be voluntary' (Wolman et al. 1930, p. 16).

Regarding the need for a planned reserve of funds to pay for the public works projects, Clark noted that this meant some projects would have to be held off until the economic circumstance of a recession called for them. That might not always be a fruitful way to plan government work, because holding back work might increase its cost. Without a planned reserve, however, the government would have to borrow to pay for public works projects during a recession. Clark raised the issue of what is now called 'crowding out,' whereby government borrowing might push up interest rates. He was confident that 'elasticity in the credit mechanism' would avoid the problem (Wolman et al. 1930, p. 18). More important was finding forecasting signals to alert the planning agency that a recession was coming and it was thus time for action, not an easy task as Clark admitted (Wolman et al. 1930, p. 19). Still, there was not too much danger of unnecessary programmes being undertaken from a false signal of a recession, because 'they are not likely to be carried far nor to do any positive harm' (Wolman et al. 1930, p. 19).

Clark was putting a great deal of faith in the ability of the government agency in charge of public works planning to avoid the problem of 'moral hazard.' He recognized this faith, asking, 'Even under present conditions, can we trust a political organization always to keep these strangely assorting ways of promoting prosperity each in its proper place?' Doing so would 'require more than ordinary political intelligence,' but 'we have something more at present in the White House' (Wolman et al. 1930, p. 20). Clark's belief in the ability of federal government planning by the Hoover administration to keep spending in check indicated that economists who were not wedded to the market economy, such as Clark, saw virtue in what Hoover was doing.

ECONOMISTS DISCUSS THE DEPRESSION

Public works were not the only component of Hoover's anti-depression policies and economists took those other policies under consideration. At its annual meeting for 1931 the AEA held a discussion on 'The Business Depression of Nineteen Hundred Thirty.' While the participants were supposed to be discussing papers that had been presented by Joseph Schumpeter, among others, they spent more time presenting their own views.

For example, Arthur B. Adams found that the depression resulted from 'a relative shortage of consumers' purchasing power' (AEA 1931, p. 183). While this argument resembled that presented earlier by Foster and Catchings, Adams attributed reduced consumption not to savings but consumers' incomes not keeping pace with prices of consumer goods. During the 1920s many industries had modernized with mass production technology through 'the displacement of labor by machinery.' Even though wages had increased during the decade, employment had decreased. The result was that the distribution of income had tilted away from wage-earners and towards property-owners. Consumer demand had been sustained for a period from the rise of consumer credit, a high level of production taking place in capital goods, foreign demand and spending from gains made in the stock market. By the fall of 1929 'these artificial supports of the market for consumers' goods' had declined, causing the downturn (AEA 1931, p. 184).

The usual implication of a reduced consumer demand was lower prices. Adams, however, found the price system to be distorted, which added to the problem of the depression. Large companies had been able to keep their prices stable 'through monopolies, cartels, and trade associations,' while other segments of the economy such as farmers had experienced large price declines for their products. Economists were arguing that wages needed to decline to end the depression, but Adams did not accept that unemployment 'would be relieved materially by lowering wages' (AEA 1931, p. 186).

The issues of wages and the depression formed the focus of Carter Goodrich's comments at the discussion panel. Goodrich also disparaged the view that wage reductions were the key to ending the depression. First, he pointed out that labour was bearing a heavy burden of the depression through unemployment that sharply reduced the total income of workers as a group. Second, employers in the US seemed to have determined to keep wages steady, perhaps because they had recognized the importance of being on good terms with their workers. Third, he doubted that wage reductions would generate the desired effect of increasing employment. Economists who argued that wages must fall typically recognized that the depression was so severe that business would not borrow money even if the interest rate fell to zero. What they needed to do, Goodrich argued, was to apply the same logic to labour and understand that 'there are many employers who would not now hire additional labor if it were offered for next to nothing' (AEA 1931, p. 190).

Another discussant, Willard L. Thorp, returned to the issue of uneven price declines among various industries. He pointed out that some industries had been able to take joint action to raise prices slightly and other industries were asking 'that the antitrust laws be relaxed in order that they may legally and publicly stabilize their industries' (AEA 1931, p. 196). Thorp objected to this idea because, while its proponents were vague about what they meant by stabilization, they probably meant price stabilization even though that would create large fluctuations in output and employment. He then raised the issue of 'central control and planning' as a solution to the depressed economy but considered that 'there seems to be almost a taboo against suggesting that the only way to eliminate the business cycle may be by definite modification of the present freedom of enterprise' (AEA 1931, p. 197).

Thorp may well have had a point regarding economists and national planning. We saw in Chapter 3 that none of our business cycle theorists with a moral economy perspective made a categorical advocacy for planning. Thorstein Veblen had argued that the industrial system might evolve towards a Bellamy-like system of planning, under the right circumstances, but remained aloof about recommending that it should. Wesley Mitchell attributed the business cycle to the lack of coordination in the economy at the national level, but also questioned whether the federal government had the ability to supply that coordination. Perhaps there was a taboo on the subject. If so, the Great Depression caused it to be broken.

GERARD SWOPE OFFERS A PLAN

Gerard Swope (1872–1957) earned his degree in electrical engineering from the Massachusetts Institute of Technology in 1895. He took a job in the electrical industry and wound up serving as president of General Electric in 1922–39 and 1942–44. During World War I he joined the US army and went to work in its procurement division, where he became an assistant to General Hugh S. Johnson at the time when Johnson was the army's procurement representative to the WIB.

In 1931 at a meeting of the National Electrical Manufacturers Association he offered what became known as the Swope Plan as a way to end the depression through planning. The germ of the plan was to take voluntary trade associations and make them mandatory under federal government supervision. As a starting point, Swope recommended that all businesses with more than 50 employees and engaged in interstate commerce form a trade association. The trade associations would set standards for ethical behaviour, accounting methods and industry practices including product standardization. They would also engage in 'stabilization of prices ... to promote stabilization of employment' (Swope 1931). Trade associations were already performing much of this work but the Swope Plan would allow them to accomplish even more.

The interest of the public in this industry-wide organization would be safeguarded by its being supervised by the Federal Trade Commission, an agency in the Commerce Department or a new federal government agency. All companies in an industry that met the basic requirements of 50 employees and engagement in interstate commerce could choose to join as soon as the new organization took effect, 'but shall be required to do so within three years unless the time is extended by the federal supervisory body' (Swope 1931). New companies formed in the industry had the same option to join once they were organized with mandatory membership taking place after three years. Each trade association would form a 'General Board of Administration' with nine members – three from the trade association, three from the ranks of employees and three appointed by the federal supervisory agency to represent the public. The General Board would supervise the 'individual company Boards of Administration' (Swope 1931).

The General Board would also administer the other parts of the Swope Plan related to taking care of workers. Swope proposed a number of items that had long been held dear by Progressives and forward-looking managers: a workmen's compensation programme, life and disability insurance, pensions and unemployment insurance. The insurance plans and the pensions would be funded jointly by workers and employers at a set per cent of wages, with a ceiling on the amount of wages used as a basis. The pension plan would be portable, allowing workers to move from job to job; the retirement age was fixed at 70 years. Unemployment insurance would start to pay two weeks after the worker was laid off at a rate of 50 per cent of the worker's average pay, with a cap to avoid being too generous to high-income workers. Payments would be made for up to ten weeks in any year, and workers forced to take part-time jobs could collect unemployment insurance to make up the difference with their full-time pay. Trade associations and company boards of administration would manage these programmes, under the supervision of the General Board and the federal supervisory agency (Swope 1931).

The overall aim of the Swope Plan was to control competition. Trade associations had previously organized their industries to coordinate many industry activities, but their impact had apparently been limited. To some extent that may have been due to their voluntary nature. Firms that did not join the association might act as 'free riders,' gaining from the work of the association while not joining in all its programmes. For example, firms in the association might all agree to provide pensions to their workers, but this might give them a higher cost structure compared to firms not in the association. Similarly, members of the association might agree to 'price standards' and their necessary production quotas, only to see non-member firms take away their market share.

The Swope Plan generated a great deal of interest among business leaders and pundits. It was endorsed by the US Chamber of Commerce, and the Chamber's president, Henry Harriman, wrote that those who did not go along with the plan would be 'roped and branded and made to run with the herd' (Rothbard 2000, pp. 3922–5). While not as severe as Bellamy's constraint that 'A man able to do duty, and persistently refusing, is sentenced to solitary imprisonment on bread and water till he consents' (Bellamy 1888 [1926], p. 128), it was close enough to be worrisome. Never a fan of Hoover, Murray Rothbard credits him for not supporting the Swope Plan and criticizing it as fascism, even though he had been advised that failure to support it would cost him the support of business in the 1932 election (Rothbard 2000, pp. 3965, 5517 n.).

ECONOMISTS DISCUSS PLANNING

From 17 October 1931 to 21 May 1932 the National Broadcast Company presented a series of radio lectures on the 'Economic Aspect of the Depression,' given by a group of well-known economists. The lectures covered a range of topics from the tariff to agriculture. Here we are concerned with the lectures that dealt with national economic planning.

One of those lectures, 'Forward planning of public works to stabilize employment,' was modest enough. We have seen in Chapter 3 that the idea of using public works to counter both a boom and a recession had been mentioned several times by Wesley Mitchell. The lecturer, Otto T. Mallery, had been a long-time advocate of public works and had served as secretary of the Public Works Committee during the 1921 Presidential Conference on Unemployment called by Hoover as Secretary of Commerce. Hoover credited Mallery for the public works section of the Employment Stabilization Act of 1931 (Rothbard 2000, pp. 2847–50, 3747–9).

In his lecture Mallery compared public works spending to the gyroscopic stabilizers on a ship that could 'prevent millions of men from being rolled out of their jobs every five or ten years by economic storms like the present' (Mallery 1932, p. 87). The construction industry was an important component of the economy and public works projects could offset the severe decline that had taken place in it during the depression. The majority of public works projects, however, were undertaken by state and local governments. Mallery rated the federal government as contributing 20 per cent of all public works during the Great Depression. This was a doubling of its share of projects, but still indicated how much more state and local governments contributed. The problem was that these projects were not planned. Mallery noted, 'Public works cannot be quickly improvised and expanded after bad times have arrived. An absolute essential is advance planning over at least a six-year period' (Mallery 1932, p. 89). With a plan of projects in place, it would be easy to speed up some projects during a recession and employ labour unemployed in the private construction sector. To fund the six-year plan, governments should sell long-term bonds to provide a reservoir of funds ready to be used during a recession, when it would be difficult to get the money from tax collections.

Moreover, Mallery argued that the wages paid to workers on public works projects would have a large simulative impact on the overall economy. Using the concept that Keynes later called the multiplier (see Chapter 12), Mallery said,

> You have heard people say that public works helps only the construction labourer. Are they not mistaken? Does it not help the storekeeper and the factory

worker? The public works worker spends his wages with the storekeeper. His wages also create a demand for shoes and stockings, as one example, and send factory workers back to the factory to make more shoes and stockings. The wages of shoe and stocking workers create a demand for more milk, garments, radios, and everything else. (Mallery 1932, pp. 91–2)

The increased demand from public works projects would spread throughout the economy creating new jobs in other industries and generating a multiple of income from the spending. Once good times returned and jobs grew in private construction, government could cut back on public works projects. With a six-year plan of public works projects, government could be ready to move projects forward when they were needed to stabilize the economy.

In a later broadcast Rexford G. Tugwell argued in favour of an expanded version of planning in his lecture, 'Responsibility and economic distress.' We have seen in Chapter 6 that Tugwell had argued in favour of some form of planning during the 1920s. In his radio talk he repeated the same idea that the market economy was outmoded. Neither business nor government was responsible for the Great Depression, but the real problem was, 'We make no attempt at control or direction' (Tugwell 1932, p. 131). When competition produced more output than could be sold for a profit, businesses retrenched and that caused a recession. Hard times resulted from the way the US organized its economy. Tugwell said, 'We ought not to be surprised if we get what we have prepared for. The problem we have before us is to devise a set of institutions which provide for order and regularity rather than waste and periodic failure' (Tugwell 1932, p. 132).

In his earlier writing Tugwell had recognized that business did a great deal of planning in large firms and through trade associations and referred to it as voluntary planning. He had then argued, 'Governmental controls ought to be brought to bear where voluntary ones break down' (Tugwell 1927, p. 224). Since he had concluded that voluntary planning had broken down, Tugwell put the burden for planning on government. As he put it, 'We have to start by admitting that there is only one agency whose scope is wide enough to cover all business and all interests, which represents all of us, and to which we can safely intrust the necessary power: this is the federal government' (Tugwell 1932, p. 132). To bring about federal government planning it would be necessary to change national law, including the Constitution, but once that was done, the federal government would be able to plan by forecasting 'the needs of consumers for goods rather than the need of business men for profits' and to make sure 'that these needs shall be met' (Tugwell 1932, p. 133). Because scientific management had improved the way businesses were run and because businessmen were willing to participate in planning their own industries, the first steps towards planning had been taken. Businessmen and the public, however, typically opposed 'the suggestion of federal control' over business. They did so from a distrust of government, but Tugwell argued that the federal government 'might perform quite differently if it had so vital a task of supervision' (Tugwell 1932, p. 135).

Tugwell did not give details of how the federal government would accomplish its planning, but later lecturers in the radio broadcast series offered examples of government planning. George Soule's lecture, 'The idea of planning,' referred listeners back to the WIB as an example of what the federal government could do (Soule 1932a, pp. 143–4). Lewis Lorwin described 'Planning in Western Europe' as a model to follow; he recognized that Soviet Russia was making strides in national planning, but it was too dramatic a change for the US to contemplate. Instead, it could use the examples of Germany, France and Italy, and Lorwin especially referenced fascism in Italy as 'developing a new economic structure which may serve as a foundation for a national planned economy' (Lorwin 1932, p. 152). Colston Ware gave a lecture on 'Planning in Russia' that directly drew lessons from the Soviet experience (Ware 1932, pp. 156–65), which Stacy May's talk on 'Federal planning' continued by citing a character from a Russian schoolbook who asserted, 'We have a plan ... . In America they work without a plan' (May 1932, p. 175).

A more trenchant analysis of national economic planning was presented by Sumner Slichter, who spoke on 'The limitations of planning.' He began by arguing that the market economy was not working very well, adding, 'We have created the kind of economic system which cannot be trusted to run itself' with the result that we had 'to experiment with methods of controlling industrial activities' (Slichter 1932, p. 185). The federal government had already taken steps towards this control through the Interstate Commerce Commission, the Federal Reserve, the Federal Farm Board and other agencies. Many were proposing the creation of a National Economic Council of experts to make recommendations for improving the economic system. Slichter warned, however, 'The ideal of an industrial system kept stable and free from depression by the guidance of experts is attractive, but our experience with industrial control should prevent us from expecting too much. ... This does not mean that national planning is not worth attempting, but it does remind us that much of the planning in existence today is bad' (Slichter 1932, p. 186).

There were two features of economic planning that Slichter addressed, planning in individual industries and national planning by the proposed National Economic Council. He agreed that organizations to plan individual industries were needed. But neither state legislatures nor Congress had the knowledge or time to regulate those industries. Plans proposed by industry organizations, moreover, could make the depression worse. Trade associations that existed typically tried to get the members of their industry to maintain existing prices when a recession started, but this merely put off the necessary price changes in the industry and came at the expense of reduced production and unemployment (Slichter 1932, p. 188). If a way to overcome this obstacle was not found, planning by industry members would be severely limited.

The proposed National Economic Council also had limits on what it could achieve. It would make mistakes, no matter how competent its members were. Existing federal government agencies had made many mistakes, such as the Federal Reserve cutting its discount rate in 1927 and the Federal Farm Board advising farmers to 'hold their wheat' in the fall of 1929. Slichter noted, 'The fact that the experts were wrong simply illustrates the difficulty of making correct decisions' (Slichter 1932, p. 189). Moreover, recommendations of the Council would 'often be defeated by the opposition of special interests' (Slichter 1932, p. 190). In planning the national economy a National Economic Council would have to make decisions about which industries to contract and which to expand, by the allocation of capital, and those that were cut would not blandly accept its decisions. Rather, they would fight against them (Slichter 1932, p. 192). Few persons in the US had the expertise to directly challenge the experts of such a National Economic Council, but that would not keep them from ignoring these experts as much as possible.

Having set forth these limitations on planning, Slichter insisted that they did not imply 'that an Economic Council would be undesirable.' Rather, he went on, 'We are compelled to make a choice between two basic economic policies – either we may let events in the world of industry take their course without attempting to control them or we may face facts frankly, study them with care and discrimination, and endeavour, in some degree, to determine our economic fate' (Slichter 1932, p. 195). Slichter favoured the latter course but only if the US went further than any democracy had in being able to look objectively at economic conditions and see them from the perspective of the whole nation and not from the viewpoint of a special interest. A National Economic Council, if it did nothing else, would be a way to raise the economic intelligence of the US to a point where an unbiased consideration of the national economic interest would be possible.

GEORGE SOULE AND THE PLANNED SOCIETY

The idea of a national planning organization received further attention from George Soule (1888–1970). Soule was concerned about the lack of coordination that existed in the market economy and his book, *A Planned Society*, reflected many of the issues we have covered in this book, such as the instability of the market economy, the importance of Frederick W. Taylor and scientific management in organizing managerial capitalism, and the salience of the WIB as a model for a planned society. Soule was unabashed in relying on Karl Marx for an analysis of the problems of the market economy and in seeing the Soviet Union as offering a practical approach to planning.

Soule went a bit further than most advocates for planning. Using the WIB as his model, he considered how it could lead to successful planning in peacetime. In looking for his answer, Soule considered the ideas of Stuart Chase and Gerard Swope, among others. He criticized Swope for doing little more than establishing industry cartels and for not providing an overall coordination of all industries. Then he proposed his solution: 'There is needed a National Economic Board at the top, representing the whole public.' The board would coordinate industry, raise the lowest incomes, direct investment and identify troubled industries. Industries would be given time to make up their own plans but if they did not the board would do it for them. To ensure that the board worked effectively and for the common good, Soule added, it 'should be composed, not of bargaining representatives of various interests, but of qualified experts representing the nation as a whole' (Soule 1932b, p. 252). These experts would include economists, statisticians, engineers and accountants. They would be supported by government appropriation and appointed by the president and confirmed by the Senate.

This board would have a great deal of power and Soule did not find that troubling. He noted that during World War I the federal government did many things that would have been 'constitutionally difficult in peace time,' with the president having the ability to act almost as a dictator. But the WIB had not needed to act as a dictatorship because there was national agreement on its objectives. Furthermore, the objectives had been clearly defined in terms of what needed to be produced and the federal government held in its hands sufficient purchasing power to bring about adherence to its plans by the way it spent the money it had. In addition, the federal government had used its price-fixing powers to set prices in the economy at a level that gave business profits but kept prices low enough to satisfy consumers, thus keeping the distribution of income on a reasonable basis (Soule 1932b, pp. 194–6).

As for the issue of federal government officials serving the interest of the nation as a whole, Soule argued that the government was no less efficient than a large corporation and could be relied on to operate a National Economic Board for national planning (Soule 1932b, p. 259). Soule then asked and answered the ultimate question every advocate for planning must address. He wrote:

> Would planning of the sort here suggested be voluntary or compulsory? Would it require a dictatorship or would it not? The answer cannot be given, at the beginning. First you create a National Board, with power to accumulate the necessary facts, to lay down the outlines of a national plan. This Board has not, at the beginning, to impose a new organization or a production schedule on industry. (Soule 1932b, p. 261)

If industry did not go along with what the board recommended, however, the board would go to Congress for legislation to make its recommendations legal and compulsory. The result would be 'an attempt to apply a scientific, experimental method to the solution of the question of how much compulsion it is necessary to exercise over business in effectuating national planning.' While the outcome of the experiment could not be predicted, Soule indicated that it did not preclude 'complete socialization' along the lines sought by socialists nor did it commit to 'public ownership' (Soule 1932b, p. 262). One could not predict where an experiment with planning would end up. What mattered was to make a start.

STUART CHASE OFFERS A NEW DEAL

In 1932 Stuart Chase, whom we saw in Chapter 6 advocating economic planning as a way to use the economy to meet the basic needs of all human beings, offered an updated version of his ideas with the suggestive title, *A New Deal* (Chase 1932). Chase used the Soviet Union as an example of what national economic planning could produce, although he stopped short of recommending that the US follow the path to communism. Chase did believe that economic recovery from the depression would require 'the drastic and progressive revision of the economic structure [while] avoiding an utter break with the past' (Chase 1932, p. 173).

As an important part of that past, the US economy had solved the problem of production through the application of science and technology to mass production industries of the market economy. What the US had not yet done was solve the problem of distribution. The problem of distribution was that it involved money-making. As a result, the market economy existed to further the gains of business instead of providing the necessities of life for humans. The bias towards business ultimately created monopoly firms controlling supply tightly to extort higher prices alongside wasteful competition that needlessly duplicated production facilities and created a need for useless products sold by deceptive advertising (Chase 1932, p. 18).

From this result it followed that the US had a dual economy with one part that was run under 'collectivism' and another part that remained individualistic and competitive. The collective sector consisted of government at all levels, large corporations, trade associations, labour unions and cooperatives. The competitive sector held retail stores, wholesale outlets, banks, agriculture and new products. The trend was towards greater collectivism, however, and the market economy was in decline. But collectiveness had not yet developed so far that the entire economy had become coordinated. The market economy was ending, but its replacement had not yet emerged (Chase 1932, pp. 44–64).

Chase then tied his view of the market economy to the business cycle (Chase 1932, pp. 116–35). There were a variety of causes for the business cycle, but they all boiled down to one. Chase wrote, 'The primary cause is neglect of the mechanism; the failure to control it from the top.' As a result, the decentralized market economy was outmoded and 'a new deal is in order' (Chase 1932, pp. 135–6).

In looking at Chase's new deal, we must recall that he was interested in engineering and to him engineering meant that all processes had to be set up, regulated and monitored. The ideal of the market economy to him meant the existence of 'a self generating perpetual-motive machine' (Chase 1932, p. 151), that is, a technical impossibility. Machines not properly regulated and monitored will periodically break down. The problem for the US was that there was no leadership to regulate and monitor the market economy. The WIB had been a school for such leadership but it had shut down before that leadership had learned its lessons. From whence would that new leadership emerge and how would it function?

To Chase, it was clear that the Great Depression called for 'drastic change in our economic system' and that change had to be in the direction of collectivism (Chase 1932, p. 153). The US was at a crossroads where it could go down three paths, a violent revolution such as took place with the communism of the Soviet Union, a coup of business interests such as led to the fascism of Mussolini or a new system that used the basic laws and traditions of the US but in a new way (Chase 1932, pp. 153–72). The track of the third path was being laid by science, and Chase praised the efforts of Frederick W. Taylor and engineers for bringing about a 'scientific attitude in industry' (Chase 1932, p. 177). He liked the idea of 'the scientific attitude as dictator of economic conditions' (Chase 1932, p. 179). Under a scientific attitude, he went on, the role of profits in an economy could be expanded. Under the current business approach profits were a gain for selling something, no matter how useful. In a broader approach, such as in the Soviet Gosplan, they were becoming a tool for determining if a factory was adhering to the overall plan. Such social profits could be turned over to the federal government, but would be just as effective an incentive as private profits. Under a system of managerial capitalism with salaried managers it did not matter to those managers who paid their salaries and they would function just as efficiently under government ownership as under private ownership (Chase 1932, p. 185).

Chase argued in favour of national economic planning in a chapter titled 'Control from the top.' He wrote, 'The drive of collectivism leads toward control from the top' (Chase 1932, p. 213). Control from the top required a General Staff of planners with overall responsibility for the economy and subordinated committees for specific industries. Chase's proposal drew heavily on the WIB and the Soviet system and resembled many of the features of Edward Bellamy's moral economy. Still, areas of the economy where competition remained effective would not need to be part of the planning system – that would be an issue for the General Staff to decide just as it would decide which new inventions were useful and when to introduce them (Chase 1932, pp. 215–24).

More important, a public works programme would be part of the overall plan. To Chase, public works were needed where private investment could not or would not undertake the project. He provided a simple slogan for public works: 'When prices begin to fall, borrow and extend public works; when they begin to rise, retrench' (Chase 1932, p. 227). Such decisions would be a vital part of the system of planning that Chase espoused and he had no qualms about admitting his system was 'frankly aimed at the destruction of capitalism, specifically in its most evil sense of ruthless expansionism' (Chase 1932, p. 240).

Here we might ask how Chase would have answered an obvious question: Under your system of planning how do we check the 'ruthless expansionism' of the government? Chase admitted that he was not very good at politics and the answer he gave to this question certainly indicated his naiveté, for his answer rested on a comparison with the Soviet Union. We let him speak for himself as he answered the question of how economic changes took place in the planning system of the Soviet Union:

> They happen principally by virtue of edicts pronounced by Comrade Stalin … . But back of the edict is the will of the Central Executive Committee of the Communist Party, and back of that the majority opinion of the Party itself, which

> elects the Central Committee and tolerates Stalin … . If Comrade Stalin should
> continue to displease this majority, his days would be numbered. (Chase 1932,
> pp. 243–4)

The people of the Soviet Union thus exercised control over the government
and the technical experts in the government exercised control over the
leaders, with the overall economy being run in the interests of all persons.
There is no need to give further details about the folly of this analogy or of
its applicability to the US. Suffice it to say, Chase did apply it to the US. He
concluded, 'Why should the Russians have all the fun of remaking a
world?' (Chase 1932, p. 252).

CANDIDATE ROOSEVELT ADVOCATES PLANNING

Franklin Delano Roosevelt (1882–1945) was the consummate politician,
and we will have more to say about him in later chapters of this work. What
made him such a great political figure was his ability to speak directly to
voters in a way that apparently heartened them. Here we focus on one of his
speeches given in Atlanta, GA, where he advocated planning.

The speech, on 22 May 1932, was a commencement address at Oglethorpe University, in Atlanta. In it Roosevelt started with commonplace
observations of how much the economy had changed since 1928, when the
graduates had entered college. Then he offered a statement that might have
startled some of them:

> As you have viewed this world of which you are about to become a more active
> part, I have no doubt that you have been impressed by its chaos, its lack of plan.
> Perhaps some of you have used stronger language. And stronger language is
> justified. Even had you been graduating, instead of matriculating, in these
> rose-colored days of 1928, you would, I believe, have perceived this condition.
> For beneath all the happy optimism of those days there existed lack of plan and a
> great waste. (Roosevelt 1932a)

As examples of this lack of plan, Roosevelt turned to higher education
where colleges and universities contributed to an oversupply of teachers and
lawyers, demonstrating that 'foresight and planning have been notable for
their complete absence' (Roosevelt 1932a).

If we looked at the history of industrial development in the US, according
to Roosevelt, we would recognize how haphazard and wasteful it had been.
With its focus on individualism, the US economy had a system where many
businesses failed in order that a few would succeed and become highly
profitable, where many firms duplicated what other firms did with no

advantage to society and where industrial plant and equipment was scrapped even when it was still productive. Much of this waste, Roosevelt believed, 'could have been prevented by greater foresight and by a larger measure of social planning' (Roosevelt 1932a). Instead, what planning took place was done by business organized for its own interest and not the good of society. This lack of planning had led to too many investments in superfluous factories, with the resulting oversupply of goods. It was 'the same story as the thoughtless turning out of too many school teachers and too many lawyers' (Roosevelt 1932a).

Now that the economy had reached this state of oversupply, many persons counselled that the government should do nothing to address the situation. Roosevelt disagreed and hinted at the need for more public works and bluntly stated that there was a need for the redistribution of income in order to increase consumer demand. But the biggest need was for the country's leaders to 'recognize the vital necessity of planning for definite objectives.' Once those objectives were established, then it would be possible to find the means to plan for them. He said, 'When the Nation becomes substantially united in favor of planning the broad objectives of civilization, then true leadership must unite thought behind definite methods.' The nation wanted bold experimentation to find the right methods of planning and such experimentation meant that it was necessary 'to take a method and try it: If it fails, admit it frankly and try another' (Roosevelt 1932a).

In pushing for this experimental approach, Roosevelt harkened back to the views of Walter Lippmann as presented in Chapter 5. There we saw that Lippmann had argued that social programmes should always proceed through experimentation, and we shall see shortly that Lippmann took great interest in Roosevelt's speech. Roosevelt, however, did not consistently push for his programme of planning. Instead, he often settled for a more typical stump speech where he paraded the virtues of fiscal prudence. For example, in the speech he gave in Atlanta on 24 October 1932 Roosevelt insisted 'that even in hard times it is possible to have a balanced budget … by cutting expenditures rather than by loading the people with more taxation' (Roosevelt 1932b). In this way, Roosevelt portrayed himself as a fiscal conservative compared to Hoover. The tone of this speech lacked the boldness of the first Atlanta speech with its call for planning in the national interest.

WALTER LIPPMANN MODERATES HIS SUPPORT FOR PLANNING

In previous chapters we presented Walter Lippmann as an influential pundit. By the 1930s his influence had been extended by his being a regular contributor to the New York *Herald Tribune*. As a testimony to his influence, his articles from 1931–32 were immediately collected and published in book form (Lippmann 1932).

Like many other supporters of planning, Lippmann accepted the value of public works projects as a way to stabilize the economy. What mattered was that it should be the right type of public works. To him, public works projects should include bridges, tunnels and highways from which tolls would be collected and slums replaced with higher-quality public housing that would earn rent. Another prudent approach was using the Reconstruction Finance Corporation to lend money to businesses that would be in a position to repay the loans with interest (Lippmann 1932, pp. 80–81).

In opposition to many advocates of the moral economy of planning, Lippmann criticized efforts by Hoover to maintain wage rates. In part, the maintenance of wage rates was misdirected; keeping hourly wages at high levels did no good to workers who had their hours reduced or were laid off. But the real problem was that wages represented a cost of business and Lippmann questioned 'whether American industry can revive at a lower price level while the costs of production remain at the boom level' (Lippmann 1932, p. 35). The problem, as he saw it, was that the Hoover policy aimed at partial deflation when what was needed was either a policy of complete deflation or a policy of inflation (Lippmann 1932, p. 14).

What about a system of planning such as Lippmann had espoused in his younger days (see Chapter 5)? Lippmann still believed that the US was at the beginning of a new epoch. Having solved the problem of production, the US needed to solve 'the problem of the management of plenty' (Lippmann 1932, p. 3). The era of plenty had been based on the acquisitive instinct of human beings. The Russian system held 'the premise that the acquisitive motive shall be outlawed' but Lippmann demurred because the Russian experiment showed that the wealth produced under the impetus of the acquisitive instinct would not be sustained using 'cooperative motives' (Lippmann 1932, p. 3). The market economy was outmoded and the US was only beginning to find ways to replace it. One possible replacement, he noted, was a proposal for a revival of the WIB to plan the economy. Lippmann remained sceptical of this revival because neither Congress nor the citizenry were ready to trust their lives to a small committee of planners when there was not a wartime emergency (Lippmann 1932, p. 32).

Lippmann did, however, support the proposal for planning set forth by Gerard Swope. On Lippmann's account, Swope had proposed that the firms in the electrical products industry take measures to sustain employment or offer assistance to unemployed workers. The problem with the plan was that it was illegal and required changes in existing laws as well as in the Constitution. The direct value of Swope's proposal was that it made clear that 'our laws commit and condemn us to an uncoordinated, disorderly individualism which inevitably produces alternating periods of boom and depression. Any serious attempt by a whole industry to substitute coopera-tive planning involves the risk of prosecution under the anti-trust laws' (Lippmann 1932, p. 38). Still, the Swope Plan had merit. Indeed, Lippmann reached the inescapable conclusion that any plan 'to stabilize industry would require ultimately a Federal control of prices,' for there could be no 'industrial planning without a highly centralized control of production and prices' (Lippmann 1932, pp. 39–40).

Lippmann found an advocate for such industrial planning in Roosevelt's candidacy. Lippmann started as a critic of the Roosevelt campaign as trying to please too many voters with too many promises. Then he made a startling commentary: 'In taking his stand in favor of what Mr. Stuart Chase and Mr. George Soule and others are calling a Planned Society, Governor Roosevelt has sought to identify himself with the aspirations and necessities of the time we live in' (Lippmann 1932, p. 330). Lippmann was referring to the speech in Atlanta at Oglethorpe University where Roosevelt had advocated national planning. According to Lippmann, however, the real issue was whether Roosevelt understood planning. A planned society required a planning apparatus to put the plan into effect and Roosevelt had not identified what that apparatus would be. Nor did he address how planning would deal with the sacrifice of individual choice that his speech implied would have to take place under planning (Lippmann 1932, p. 332).

To highlight the issue he was raising, Lippmann turned to Roosevelt's speech. As an example of problems caused by the lack of planning, Roosevelt had pointed out that colleges were graduating more teachers than the country needed in schools, adding that someone needed to tell college students that teaching was not a viable career option as a way to get them to pursue another career. Lippmann objected to this approach. If planning was to reduce the oversupply of teachers it must do something to make it hard for students to enter teachers' colleges, by raising requirements or setting quotas. That type of planning would be easy compared to planning for the oversupply of 'miners, shopkeepers, stenographers, wheat farmers and the rest.' It would not do to tell them how to gain a livelihood, but would require that 'a public agency decide that for them' (Lippmann 1932, p. 333).

Lippmann doubted that either Roosevelt or the country were ready for this degree of planning.

CONCLUSION

When the economy began its decline in 1929, President Hoover took measures to arrest that decline, including fiscal stimulus and exhorting business to hold the line on wages and employment. Hoover very likely believed that the business cycle would be as short-lived as the previous recessions during the 1920s. His policies to make it even shorter were unprecedented in the US. The crux of those policies was to solve the problem of underconsumption. When the economy worsened instead into the crisis of the Great Depression, our sample of politicians, business leaders, economists and pundits turned their attention to planning. This chapter has set forth several views on the need for national economic planning, from the Swope Plan to the ideas of Soule and Chase. Even a cautious advocate for the market economy, Sumner Slichter, became a reluctant supporter of giving planning a try.

Surprisingly, Lippmann, with a track record of support for planning, had become sceptical about its use. According to him and other opponents of planning such as Hoover, the problem with the programmes being put forth by advocates for planning was that they confused engineering and politics and thus believed that a human society would be easy to plan. In engineering the objective to be solved was easy to define as a technical issue of inanimate objects and to solve by manipulating them. For Lippmann, however, in 'a human society it is the objectives which divide men into parties, sects, classes and nations.' That was why in Russia and in Italy planning was being undertaken by leaders who did 'not tolerate differences of opinion about objectives.' Where differences of opinion were tolerated, Lippmann wrote, 'a planned society in the full sense of the word is impossible' (Lippmann 1932, p. 334). The WIB was often put forward as a model for national planning, but as was the case with engineering, the objective of the plan was easy to define and public support for the plan was readily won. Whether Roosevelt could produce such a planned society with a toleration of differences of opinion was something Lippmann would have to see to believe.

According to Chase and advocates of planning, in the US the market economy suffered from the lack of coordination that full collectivism could bring. As one example, Chase argued that in the Soviet Union under the five-year plan the leaders planned just enough shoe factories to meet the needs of the people, while in the US shoe factories kept being built even though everyone already had shoes (Chase 1932, p. 77). Such over-building was common in the US and led to wasted resources and a supply of goods that could not all be bought. In contrast, Chase reminded his readers of the WIB that had operated 'to the extremes of collectivism' (Chase 1932, p. 84). His new deal for society would require broad social agreement that planning methods to end the depression and eliminate poverty by focusing on the production of necessities were the moral equivalent of war.

8. Franklin Delano Roosevelt and the moral economy

More than any president, Franklin Delano Roosevelt led the way in moving the US towards the moral economy and his rhetoric often took the moral high ground regarding the defects of the market economy. In his first inaugural address, for example, Roosevelt forcibly declaimed, 'The money changers have fled from their high seats in the temple of our civilization. We may now restore that temple to the ancient truths. The measure of the restoration lies in the extent to which we apply social values more noble than mere monetary profit' (Roosevelt 1933a, p. 3).

In making this call for a moral economy, he used an appeal that Edward Bellamy would have appreciated:

> If I read the temper of our people correctly, we now realize as we have never realized before our interdependence on each other; that we can not merely take but we must give as well; that if we are to go forward, we must move as a trained and loyal army willing to sacrifice for the good of a common discipline, because without such discipline no progress is made, no leadership becomes effective. We are, I know, ready and willing to submit our lives and property to such discipline, because it makes possible a leadership which aims at a larger good. (Roosevelt 1933a, pp. 6–7)

As noted in Chapter 2, Bellamy had indicated that his cooperative commonwealth would operate through mutual cooperation and function as an army with all the discipline that entailed to produce what we have called a moral economy.

What type of moral economy was Roosevelt calling for? What did Roosevelt know about economics and the economy? For starters, let us recall that the chief features of the moral economy proposed by Bellamy and championed by Progressives were government stewardship of all of industry, industrial planning by the leaders of each industry to determine how much to produce and what price to charge and national planning by a council of industrial leaders. We shall see in the rest of this book that many of these ingredients of Bellamy's moral economy were part of the ethos of the New Deal. In the next five chapters we intend to reach a better understanding of the Roosevelt New Deal through an analysis of how his policies, the National Industrial Recovery Act (NIRA) and government spending programmes, were viewed by a selected group of his contemporaries among economists, pundits, politicians and business leaders. Our goal is to recreate the debate over the New Deal that took place throughout the 1930s to shed light on just what the New Deal meant to insightful thinkers at the time it was being put into place. In this chapter we explain how Roosevelt might have come to favour those policies.

ROOSEVELT'S ECONOMIC THOUGHT

The literature on Roosevelt's thought and character is voluminous and far-ranging, as befits the complex nature of his personality to which all writers on his life attest. He was an astute and wily politician deft at playing his friends and opponents against each other. His oratorical style was especially suited for conveying his ideas to the public through the mass medium of radio. But how much did he know about economics?

Daniel Fusfeld has given us a lengthy study of Roosevelt's experiences in studying economics and applying it to social problems (Fusfeld 1956). He finds that Roosevelt had studied economics in his student days; he had taken a course in economics at Groton School, a feat rarely accomplished by high school students today, and he stayed at Harvard University for a year of graduate work specializing in economics. This means that he had probably taken more courses in economics than any president before him and perhaps most of the presidents who came after him. Fusfeld does not mention whether or not Roosevelt had read Bellamy. He entered Groton just after Bellamy's period of influence, but Bellamy's ideas could well have been part of the background noise of his life.

The economics Roosevelt learned was not entirely in tune with the market economy. First, we shall see that the economics he studied at Groton contained a higher moral content than proponents of the market economy would be comfortable with. Second, as Fusfeld points out, Roosevelt's family background, being from the agrarian gentry with its spirit of *noblesse oblige* and its lack of contact with modern industry, made him more susceptible to the moral content of the economics he studied (Fusfeld 1956, pp. 7, 11). Moreover, Roosevelt came of age during the Progressive Era and the economics he learned was greatly influenced by Progressive thinking.

The course he took at Groton, in 1896, contained a discussion of the main economic issues of the time, the gold standard, tariffs and labour unions. Its methodology was that of classical economics, especially as presented by John Stuart Mill (Fusfeld 1956, pp. 17–20). Classical economics of which

Mill's works were a culmination focused on the production of the goods and services society needed and the distribution of income. Mill had argued that while the laws of production were determined by the application of science and were thus unalterable, the laws of distribution were social constructs, to use the modern term, and could be altered by reform. Moreover, Mill's works often carried a patina of morality. He used morally weighted terms such as 'productive consumption' to distinguish between the necessities of workers and the extravagances of the wealthy and supported higher taxes on the wealthy (Stabile 1996, pp. 65–6).

Despite this moral tone, Mill insisted that '*Laisser-faire*, in short, should be the general practice: every departure from it, unless required by some great good, is a certain evil' (Mill 1848 [1969], p. 950). In holding this principle Mill wanted to avoid a parental state where the working poor became dependent on the government. Instead, Mill argued that workers could help themselves get higher wages through the formation of labour unions, making him the first well-known economist to investigate the nature of unions and to wish to see them strengthened as a social institution. He opposed government interference in the form of laws against unions as a way to keep wages low. Mill wrote, 'If it were possible for the working classes, by combining among themselves, to raise or keep up the general level of wages, it needs hardly be said that this would be a thing not to be punished, but to be welcomed and rejoiced at' (Mill 1848 [1969], pp. 933–4).

Economists typically argue that unions cannot raise the level of wages above the market wage rate without causing unemployment or reducing the wages of other workers. Mill argued that workers might be underpaid and the anti-union laws of his day very likely kept wages lower than the market level. To him, workers were at a disadvantage in negotiating with employers over wage rates and they needed to organize unions to get the wages the market economy accorded them. He also anticipated that unions would help workers develop their capability for acting democratically, with high moral character, in their efforts to attain justice. Once the relationship between workers and employers became based on justice, society would be elevated in its morality. Mill confessed that he did not think that the market economy with its 'struggling to get on' was 'the most desirable lot of human kind.' Rather, he wanted a society of well-paid workers and few if any wealthy employers, so that everyone had the leisure 'to cultivate freely the graces of life' (Mill 1848 [1969], pp. 748–51). He called that society the 'stationary state' and in it the pace of economic change, as determined by technological innovation, would be slowed if not completely halted. Mill's stationary state, however, would moderate what Joseph Schumpeter called the process of creative destruction (see Chapter 4). To ensure 'social justice' for those harmed by innovation, the moral economy might have to end the process of creative destruction or at least control it.

We do not know the extent of Mill's influence on Roosevelt, but Mill's ideas regarding unions became generally accepted by Progressives in the US in the early twentieth century. Certainly Mill's ideas about unions and the way they could help workers enhance their moral capabilities fit in well with the spirit of *noblesse oblige* that Roosevelt maintained and probably enhanced in his years at Groton. And Roosevelt would certainly agree with Mill that laissez-faire economics could be supplanted in the name of a greater social good.

In his second year at Harvard in 1901 Roosevelt took the standard introductory course in economics. It also relied heavily on Mill, and the instructor included the idea that the market economy through competition was the best way to satisfy the needs of the community (Fusfeld 1956, p. 23). During his graduate year at Harvard, however, Roosevelt took courses in the economics of transportation and the economics of corporations (Fusfeld 1956, p. 25). At this time, the early 1900s, the growth of big business through the corporate system and the methods of finance had become an issue of concern to Progressive reformers and the courses Roosevelt took would have analysed this issue. The lesson Progressives gleaned from their analysis was that the large corporation had replaced competition with managerial planning and market power and it was no longer clear that competitive forces of the market economy set prices effectively. In that case government might do a better job than the market economy. Certainly it was doing that job through the regulation of railroads, something Roosevelt learned in his course on the economics of transportation. His instructor in the economics of corporations, William Z. Ripley, had written a book published a year after Roosevelt took his course, arguing that with all corporations there was a need for 'a strong and steady administrative control through some permanent board or commission' once it was clear that competition did not exist (Fusfeld 1956, p. 28). In short, Roosevelt's study in economics was not a theoretical overview of the merits of the market economy. Rather, he learned that government regulation in the economy was often desirable.

ROOSEVELT, POLITICS AND ECONOMICS

After attending law school at Columbia University and passing the bar exam, Roosevelt began his political career, using his cousin Theodore Roosevelt as a role model. Theodore Roosevelt's view of the role of the federal government was that the president had a duty to broaden his influence and to use that influence to ensure the welfare of all members of the US society (Roosevelt 1916, p. 371). The government would act as agent in turning the market economy into a moral economy where businesses would behave properly by serving the public interest. It would also end the 'crass inequality in the bargaining relation between the employer and the individual employee standing alone.' This imbalance of power would be remedied by workers forming unions to bargain collectively. To Theodore Roosevelt, workers 'were forced to cooperate to secure not only their economic, but their simple human rights' (Roosevelt 1916, pp. 486–7). He believed that the interests of employers and workers could be harmonized. It was thus appropriate to enact laws, such as minimum wage laws and insurance of workers 'against the ills of industrial life,' as part of an advocacy of 'political and industrial democracy' that would secure fair treatment for workers (Roosevelt 1916, pp. 497–9). To him, the days of the market economy were over, and the federal government could intervene in the economy to eliminate bad behaviour by business and by unions. We already saw in Chapter 3 that he did intervene in the economy to end the Panic of 1907.

This early influence of Theodore Roosevelt's progressive thinking brought Franklin Roosevelt to a community approach to economics, which we can see in a speech he made in 1912:

> The right of any individual to work or not as he sees fit, to live to a great extent where and how he sees fit is not sufficient. ... To put it another way, competition has been shown to be useful up to a certain point and no further. Cooperation must begin where competition leaves off and cooperation is as good a word for the new theory as any other. (Cited in Fusfeld 1956, p. 49)

This call for cooperation was a hallmark of the moral economy and a key ingredient of Progressive thinking. This speech indicated Roosevelt's acceptance of planning.

Fusfeld points out that Roosevelt's interest in planning came from his political work regarding agricultural reform and resource conservation. Roosevelt believed that the preservation of an agrarian society and the conservation of natural resources meant that the government would soon be telling 'a man how many trees he must cut' and eventually would 'compel every farmer to till his land or raise more beef or horses' (cited in Fusfeld 1956, p. 50). Another element in Roosevelt's interest in planning may have come from the WIB that planned production for World War I and served as a model of economic planning for Progressives, who wanted it to continue in the post-war economy. One of his earliest political positions at the national level was service in the administration of Woodrow Wilson as Assistant

Secretary of the Navy. In this position he would have seen the WIB in action and he did work with the War Labor Board. He also had experience with the government, advising business what it needed to produce in the way of naval equipment. He did not believe that the government should produce its own defence material, but did feel that it could tell business what to produce.

By the 1920s Roosevelt had developed a consistent policy focus of government intervention in the economy and one such policy, which he recommended for the Democratic Party platform in 1920, is especially germane to the content of this book. Roosevelt at this time set forth a policy of deficit spending during a recession by favouring the sale of 'Prosperity Bonds,' short-term loans that the president could use 'whenever he declares a state of acute industrial depression to exist.' The proceeds would fund public works projects that would be a 'constructive preventative for acute depression' (Fusfeld 1956, p. 75). Here Roosevelt was in tune with the idea of Progressive business cycle theorists such as Wesley Mitchell, who saw government public works projects as a potential antidote to recessions (see Chapter 3). Herbert Hoover supported this policy too (see Chapter 6).

The 1920s also saw Roosevelt becoming engaged with another Progressive idea of the 1920s, the growth of trade associations, a policy also encouraged by Hoover. As described in Chapter 6, Hoover hoped to nurture a new economy from voluntary cooperation by business through the activities of trade associations. In the early 1920s, Fusfeld reports, Roosevelt worked with Hoover to form a trade association, the American Construction Council, to bring stability to the chaotic construction industry. Hoover believed that the Council should be voluntary and Roosevelt apparently agreed. By 1928, while president of the Council, Roosevelt took a more aggressive approach towards industry planning, writing, 'Muddling through has been the characteristic method employed by the construction industry in the last few years. There has been no system, no cooperation, *no intensive national planning*' (cited in Fusfeld 1956, p. 103, emphasis in original). He believed that this 'intensive national planning' in the construction industry had to be brought about through voluntary cooperation by all segments of the industry. Roosevelt recognized that this type of planning might go too far and violate the anti-trust laws; he insisted that public-spirited businessmen could keep their planning within the law (Fusfeld 1956, pp. 107–8).

Thus, by the 1920s, Roosevelt had set forth two approaches to ending recessions that his New Deal would try in fighting the Great Depression. First, he proposed temporary deficit spending on public works projects as a way to increase consumer spending through the hiring of workers to complete public works projects. Roosevelt's deficit spending plan was consistent with what business cycle theorists in the US had argued. It was also consistent with what the Hoover administration was doing in the early 1930s. Second, he believed that planning by industry trade associations would stabilize each industry. In his early advocacy of this approach he felt that the planning should be undertaken on a voluntary basis, much as Hoover had argued, in a way that served 'to limit the freedom of action of each man and business group within the industry for the common interest of all' (Fusfeld 1956, p. 243). That would be the goal of the NIRA.

By the time of the election campaign of 1932, as noted in the last chapter, Roosevelt took a mixed view of planning. In a speech on 22 May 1932, at the commencement ceremony at Oglethorpe University in Atlanta, GA, Roosevelt said, 'As you have viewed this world of which you are about to become a more active part, I have no doubt that you have been impressed by its chaos, its lack of plan' (Roosevelt 1932a). With regard to this lack of planning, he added, the nation wanted bold experimentation to find the right methods of planning and such experimentation meant that it was necessary 'to take a method and try it: If it fails, admit it frankly and try another' (Roosevelt 1932a). The speech caused an uproar, however, and on the subsequent few occasions when he mentioned planning in his speeches, Roosevelt included a responsibility for the federal government 'to apply restraint' to business that did not cooperate and to 'protect the public interest' (Fusfeld 1956, p. 243). As Fusfeld concludes, this meant that Roosevelt would retain the market economy but would supplement its activities by governmental action (Fusfeld 1956, p. 251). In this way he could combine the market economy with the moral economy.

In presenting this overview of Roosevelt's economic thinking we must make clear that he was not an economist. Rather, he was an economics major of sorts who continued to read in the discipline throughout his life, but it is doubtful he kept abreast of advances in economic theory. He did have an advisor who was economist, however, and it is to him we now turn.

REXFORD GUY TUGWELL AND THE BRAINS TRUST

One of the enduring legends of the New Deal is that it was the work of Roosevelt's Brains Trust, his intellectual advisers. The core of this group consisted of three professors from Columbia University: Raymond Moley, a political science professor; Adolph Berle, a law professor; and Rexford Guy Tugwell, whom we met in Chapter 6 as an economist who had supported national economic planning in the 1920s. The main function of the group was to advise Roosevelt during his campaigns for the nomination and for the presidency in the general election, as Tugwell made clear in his lengthy memoir of his role in the Brains Trust (Tugwell 1968, p. xxx).

Our focus here is on Tugwell, because he was Roosevelt's chief economics adviser and tutor during the period of the Brains Trust. In his economic thinking Tugwell was a member of the Institutional School of economics, who gained their inspiration from Thorstein Veblen, Wesley C. Mitchell and John Maurice Clark. A theme among Institutionalists was that the market economy no longer operated effectively, assuming it ever had, and must be supplemented by government. Not all Institutionalists were as vocal in their support for national economic planning as Tugwell was.

Tugwell made this support clear in his memoir, calling himself 'a planner, a collectivist, even if only an academic one' (Tugwell 1968, p. xxviii). He tried to turn his academic planning into real planning through his influence on Roosevelt, but admitted that he failed. In his memoirs he asked if Roosevelt had thought it politically feasible to start the transition of the US 'into a collective economy with all its necessary appurtenances, would he have chosen this course?' Tugwell had felt that during the campaign seasons of 1932 there were times when Roosevelt seemed to be answering yes, but ultimately Roosevelt backed off from national economic planning with its goal of bringing about 'co-operation in the public interest' (Tugwell 1968, p. xxiv). For this reason Tugwell believed that the New Deal did little more than continue and extend Hoover's economic policies.

Tugwell considered himself to be a radical from the younger group of Progressives who clustered around such leaders as Walter Lippmann. Those radical Progressives espoused the spirit of collectiveness and were leery of Roosevelt as a potential president. To them, Roosevelt was an intellectual lightweight who would say what was needed to win votes but who could not be relied upon to pursue a true radical Progressivism in the critical moment the Great Depression offered (Tugwell 1968, pp. 64, 119, 123, 126, 160, 269). The chief difference was that Roosevelt was an old-time Progressive who wanted to end corruption in politics and business while Tugwell and his colleagues were new-school Progressives who believed in scientific management, efficiency and planning.

Despite his own misgivings about Roosevelt, Tugwell found that his tutee did have a grasp of the basic ideas of economics. In his early discussions with Roosevelt about economics Tugwell explained to him that thanks to scientific management and Frederick W. Taylor's influence (see Chapter 5), industry had become much more productive. The problem was that business had a much harder time selling the extra items efficiency had produced. The reason was underconsumption, where effective demand had not kept pace with the vastly increased supply (Tugwell 1968, pp. 23–4). The solution Tugwell offered was that of getting people to 'work together, in concert, with an equitable mutual arrangement ... for the continuation of productivity' (Tugwell 1968, p. 44). Roosevelt resisted this solution most of the time, according to Tugwell, but Tugwell did record one paragraph he was able to insert into a Roosevelt campaign speech that rested on this approach. Tugwell recorded it as follows:

> I am not speaking of an economic life completely planned and regimented. I am speaking of the necessity that there be a real community of interests, not only among the sections of this great country, but among its economic units and various groups in these units; that there be common participation ... planned on the basis of a shared common life. (Cited in Tugwell 1968, p. 48)

Tugwell took no credit for Roosevelt's speech at Oglethorpe University where he made his clearest statement in support of national economic planning, but he did take heart from it as indicative that his tutelage of Roosevelt was working (Tugwell 1968, pp. 104, 123, 126).

In that tutelage Tugwell explained to Roosevelt that 'the price system actually was a system' (Tugwell 1968, p. 81). Prices were a way to gauge the interconnections among all the segments of the economy. Efforts to regulate one price in this system would cause all other prices to respond to the regulated price in ways that were not predictable. A policy for establishing farm prices at a particular level would create changes in all other prices. A market-oriented economist would have argued that efforts to regulate one price were bound to fail and it was best to leave the market economy alone; once the government regulated one price and did not get the result it wanted it would have to extend that regulation to other prices. Eventually it would wind up regulating all prices. Tugwell did not have this market orientation but he agreed with its conclusion. Thus, he tutored Roosevelt that what was needed was the regulation of all prices through planning. In making this case Tugwell referred to the Swope Plan (see Chapter 7) and reminded Roosevelt that he had proposed much the same ideas in his work with the American Construction Council (Tugwell 1968, p. 100). According to Tugwell, a key problem in pursuing these policies for planning was the anti-trust laws, which aimed at keeping competition alive and thus allowing it to be a negative influence on overall economic performance (Tugwell 1968, pp. 100, 129). In place of anti-trust, Tugwell proposed a policy of 'price-fixing in the public interest' (Tugwell 1968, p. 99).

Tugwell, however, did not find his pupil to be advanced enough to follow his reasoning. He expressed his fears to his fellow Progressives as follows:

> I told them that Roosevelt still listened when I argued for a collectivized progressivism, even sometimes mentioned it himself. But I had to admit that I was not happy. Collectivization, I kept saying, would have to include some

device for management – that is, for determining what, in the public interest, industries must do. (Tugwell 1968, p. 306)

Tugwell insisted that the country would never move towards such a policy unless Roosevelt made it a part of his presidential campaign, that he had to make more speeches like the one at Oglethorpe University where he had promoted the cause of national planning. Instead, he felt, Roosevelt had given up on the ideas of the Oglethorpe speech.

Tugwell went on to give Roosevelt's explanation of the political problems inherent to his difficulty in making planning a key ingredient of his campaign. To do so, Roosevelt looked back at Woodrow Wilson's experience in passing the Federal Reserve Act. The problem in getting the Act passed was that Progressives were strong individualists, each of whom had their own solution to resolve any social issue. As a result, they could not agree on the details of any policy and considered compromise a bad word. Meanwhile, conservatives were concerned with the much easier task of keeping a new policy from being enacted and this made them much more unified than Progressives. Looking at all the Progressive members in the Democratic Party in 1932, Roosevelt found even less unity than Wilson had worked with two decades earlier. Tugwell admitted that he attained a better appreciation for the political problems Roosevelt would face as president (Tugwell 1968, p. 308). Still, Roosevelt was now head of the party and its old guard was committed to him. What he needed to do was win over the Progressives with radical ideas that the old guard was in no position to challenge. To help him in developing those ideas, Tugwell drafted a proposal for an Economic Council with a programme of, among other things, 'planning the national output of staple goods, agricultural and manufacturing' along with 'estimating the future needs of the population' for items of consumption (Tugwell 1968, p. 526).

If we use Tugwell's proposed Economic Council as a standard for planning, we shall see in later chapters that the New Deal never lived up to it. The Roosevelt administration's one foray into planning, the NIRA, never went to the extent of planning national output to a level consistent with the consumption needs of the population. While this type of planning reminds us of Bellamy's moral economy, we must also recall that Bellamy insisted that government own all of the means of production; he had argued that the people of the US would realize that they could take over large firms and run them through a planning system as he devised it. From Roosevelt's perspective, and Tugwell might have reluctantly agreed, the people of the US had not come to the realization that Bellamy ascribed to them. Consequently, Roosevelt and the New Deal would have to settle for the middle ground of combining markets with morals in the hopes they could avoid the wasteland where moral imperative became moral hazard.

CONCLUSION

We have seen in this chapter that Roosevelt had a better understanding of economics, especially the economics of the moral economy, than most politicians of his day. He was sure that government intervention in the economy was needed, not just during a recession but at all times, a point he had gained from his training in economics. Whether that intervention involved national economic planning remained uncertain, but Roosevelt hinted that planning by the government could be an effective social reform. This was his chief difference with Hoover. Hoover wanted to undertake government intervention to solve an economic crisis; Roosevelt used an economic crisis to justify government intervention. The electorate sided with Roosevelt and we have been on the road to the moral economy ever since.

As a candidate for the presidency, Roosevelt was in a strong position. The economic decline of 1929 to 1933 caught everyone by surprise, even though Hoover took unprecedented measures to arrest it. Hoover's background of government service in humanitarian causes had convinced him that government intervention in the economy during a recession was the right thing to do. But his measures had not worked, and his failure gave Roosevelt the opportunity to appeal to voters by promising a variety of policies, including his reference to planning in several speeches.

In the rest of this book we shall investigate what politicians, business leaders, economists and pundits thought and wrote about Roosevelt's efforts to end the Great Depression through planning and government spending. The closest the New Deal came to adopting a system of national planning that the moral economy requires was with the NIRA and the next three chapters consider the NIRA from the perspectives of advocates of the moral economy and the proponents of the market economy. In these chapters we shall be looking at components of the New Deal most directly concerned with the overriding goal of ending the Great Depression by planning.

9. The National Industrial Recovery Act: moral economy perspectives

As we have indicated in earlier chapters, the idea of national economic planning had been around in the US from at least the time of Edward Bellamy. It had been discussed by pundits such as Walter Lippmann and Stuart Chase, hinted at by business cycle economists such as Thorstein Veblen and Wesley C. Mitchell, proposed by the businessman Gerard Swope and used by the federal government's WIB in World War I. In the depths of the Great Depression national economic planning was clearly on the agenda. To give one example, in 1932 the peak association of business, the US Chamber of Commerce, published an article in its journal, *Nation's Business* ('A panorama of economic planning,' 1932, pp. 29–32), that surveyed a variety of programmes for national planning from the Swope Plan to Chase's proposals.

The New Deal responded to this call for planning with the NIRA to be administered by a National Recovery Administration (NRA). While we might look backward to Bellamy for the germ of the idea motivating the NRA, the NIRA had more in common with the WIB than with Bellamy's moral economy. The NRA borrowed its symbol of compliance, the 'Blue Eagle,' from a similar symbol used by the WIB and Hugh S. Johnson, who had served for a time as the army's liaison to the WIB and was head of the NRA. In this chapter we present the interpretations of the NIRA and NRA provided by advocates of the moral economy. First, we give a brief description of the programme.

THE NATIONAL INDUSTRIAL RECOVERY ACT

The NIRA was passed by Congress on 16 June1933 to devise a set of industry codes for business behaviour to eliminate what was thought to be the ruinous effects of excessive price competition. The key to the codes was for businesses to be able to establish an industry standard of fair competition, including the setting of wages and prices; while this goal was reminiscent of Herbert Hoover's attempts to have industry trade associations plan production and price levels on a voluntary basis, the NIRA gave them a bit more power, a point Hoover often made (Hoover 1951, p. 173 n.). The NIRA called for a sharing of the authority for the codes among business, labour, consumers and the government. Here was the Progressive Era's vision of democratic planning and the moral economy, with labour being represented by democratic unions and the rest of society being represented by government officials at the NRA. Both government and labour could thus serve as a countervailing power to business and promote plans that took care of the problem of underconsumption that was given primacy as a cause for the Great Depression.

Regarding labour, for example, Section 7A of the NIRA strengthened the right of labour to organize unions and Section 7B aimed at eliminating the practice of wage-cutting. One of the hallmarks of Hoover's efforts to end the depression was to get businesses to agree to hold wages steady on a voluntary basis in order to maintain a high level of consumer spending. The New Deal was a bit more forceful in its efforts to keep wages steady. The industry codes for labour established under the NIRA usually contained provisions establishing minimum wages for the industry, maximum hours of work (a 40-hour week was typical) and the prohibition of child labour. The codes, however, varied depending on the industry and its geographic location – industries in the South had a lower minimum wage.

ROOSEVELT EXPLAINS THE NIRA

President Roosevelt, in his Fireside Chat radio broadcast of 7 May 1933, explained the overall problem that faced all sectors of the US economy, agriculture, labour and business – underconsumption. Regarding manufacturing business, for example, he said, 'We have found our factories able to turn out more goods than we could possibly consume.' The same problem existed with farmers, who produced more crops than could be consumed, especially by low-wage workers. He added, 'All of this has been caused in large part by a complete lack of planning' with the result that everyone in the US had been wrongly persuaded that the economy could keep producing more each year and 'some magician would find ways and means for that increased output to be consumed with reasonable profit to the producer' (Roosevelt 1933b, pp. 118–26).

The magician, of course, was the market economy. The market economy, however, has never guaranteed that everything can be sold at a 'reasonable profit.' Rather, it only says that if you want to sell more you must lower the price and if that lower price does not work or even if it does but only at low or negative profits, then the producers have made a mistake, which the market was ruthlessly correcting. Instead of the market, Roosevelt's approach was to form a partnership with the producers, not in sharing profits, but 'a partnership in planning.' As an example, he considered the cotton manufacturing industry. In that industry 90 per cent of businesses would agree to higher wages, reduced hours for labour and reduced output. The problem was that an 'unfair ten percent' would not make the same agreement and the 'fair ninety percent' would have to go along with them. The government, he went on, 'ought to have the right,' through the partnership in planning, to enlist the help of the 'fair ninety percent' to persuade the 'unfair ten percent' to agree to arrange better forms of competition. Whatever agreements they reached, Roosevelt assured the US public, would not be at odds with the anti-trust laws. Those laws, he concluded, 'were never intended to encourage the kind of unfair competition that results in long hours, starvation wages and overproduction' (Roosevelt 1933b, pp. 131–41. The market economy produced too many bad (immoral) outcomes and needed the guidance if not the planning of the moral economy headed by the federal government.

In his next Fireside Chat on 24 July 1933, Roosevelt made this clear when he told his audience that the idea underlying the NIRA went 'back to the basic idea of society and of the nation itself that people acting in a group can accomplish things which no individual acting alone could even hope to bring about' (Roosevelt 1933c, pp. 239–41). What businesses could accomplish by acting together was the key to getting the economy moving again and Roosevelt was confident of success. He spoke, 'the agreements already approved, or about to be passed on, prove that the plan does raise wages, and that it does put people back to work' (Roosevelt 1933c, pp. 278–80). The moral economy would be a robust economy thanks to the NIRA.

THE SWARTHMORE CONFERENCE REVIEWS THE NIRA

From October through December 1933, Swarthmore College hosted a series of lectures on the New Deal and its recovery programme. The lectures were published as a book, *America's Recovery Program*, edited by Clair Wilcox, Herbert F. Fraser and Patrick Murphy Maling. The lecturers themselves were drawn from business, government and academia and we shall start with the 'Introduction' by the editors.

Writing in the early days of the New Deal (the 'Introduction' was dated 1 March 1934), the editors took a sympathetic attitude towards its programmes, noting that the Roosevelt administration had achieved 'many of the things which progressives have striven for a generation to achieve' such as child labour laws, minimum wages, unemployment relief, securities regulation and public works (Wilcox et al. 1934 [1970], p. 8). In this way the New Deal had ended some immoral practices that were part of the market economy and had protected the working poor. The editors questioned, however, whether these programmes had done anything to help the economy recover. While they felt that some of the New Deal programmes were bringing about recovery, they indicated that there were 'other elements in the program which seem to impede rather than promote a revival of business.' In that vein, they continued, 'We do not look upon the National Industrial Recovery Act, despite its name, as a recovery device' (Wilcox et al. 1934 [1970], p. 9). The recovery element of the NIRA was based on the idea that it would bring about increased employment at higher wages and thus restore the purchasing power of consumers. Instead, many employers violated the labour codes of the NIRA and used the industrial codes to reduce production and raise prices, thereby keeping inefficient businesses alive when they should have become bankrupt. By raising prices and reducing wages and making consumption more difficult, the NIRA hindered economic expansion and the editors concluded that the NRA's recovery programme would have been more effective had it not initiated the NIRA (Wilcox et al. 1934 [1970], pp. 10–11).

A more positive view of the New Deal's reforms was presented by Rexford Tugwell. As a member of the Brains Trust, he had done his part in getting Roosevelt elected. After the election, Tugwell became Assistant Secretary of Agriculture. With his background, he was a key lecturer in the Swarthmore series. He began his lecture by depicting how agriculture had been hit hard by the Great Depression. For the previous two decades productivity gains in agriculture meant that agriculture had become able to supply more food than the economy demanded at prices that gave farmers an acceptable living. The Great Depression, by further reducing the demand for food, made the plight of the farmer even worse.

Tugwell ascribed the farmers' plight to circumstances where 'our national policy, ever since the war, has been in drift' (Tugwell 1934 [1970], p. 48). Previous administrations had tried to increase prices without placing limits on supply, which only added to the total output. Meanwhile, during the 1920s efficiency in farming from technological innovation had improved even more. Tugwell recognized the destruction part of the process of creative destruction by noting that 'Fewer farmers are therefore needed today, to produce enough food for all of us, than ever before' (Tugwell 1934 [1970], p. 51).

The problem for farmers was that in a market economy one farmer could enhance his income by increasing his production to sell more units of a crop at an existing price level. When all farmers tried this approach the aggregate increase in output caused prices to fall and farm incomes declined. Economists refer to this phenomenon as the Fallacy of Composition. The market solution was to let enough farmers go broke to reduce the level of supply to be consistent with demand, just as in business some firms would go bankrupt during a recession. That solution would let the destruction phase of creative destruction run its course until only the most efficient farmers and business firms remained. The theory of the depression that influenced the New Deal, however, was underconsumption. The NIRA aimed at cooperative effort by industry firms to eliminate the overproduction through price-fixing and production quotas while the higher wages the NIRA anticipated would reduce the underconsumption.

There were too many farmers to organize them under the NIRA, however. Consequently, the Agricultural Adjustment Act (AAA) used taxes on processing and direct payments to farmers to reduce production (Tugwell 1934 [1970], p. 65). In his lecture at Swarthmore College Tugwell did not mention the NIRA. In his memoir, *Roosevelt's Revolution*, Tugwell wrote that under the NIRA, 'The proposed reorganization of industry was conceived as a companion to the AAA.' Just as the AAA had brought about cooperation among farmers, the NIRA would attain an industrial policy through the cooperation of all its components by 'the making of agreements to eliminate unfair practices among competitors' (Tugwell 1977, p. 80).

In addition to helping farmers, the New Deal also aimed at improving conditions for labour. Leo Wolman (1890–1961), a professor at Columbia University and the chairman of the Labor Advisory Board of the NRA, gave one of the lectures at Swarthmore College, titled 'Labor under the NRA.' To him, the NIRA had been intended to help create a better economic situation for workers by shortening the work week and thereby causing more workers to be hired and increasing the wages of those workers to stimulate consumption and bring about a recovery (Wolman 1934 [1970], p. 89). This intention was simple enough to state but it had not been so simple to implement. As expected, the problems of implementing the codes resulted from a process where 'the creation of a vast machinery of social reform and economic reorganization' would inevitably overlook problems that would only be discovered from operational experience. Wolman pointed to the labour codes of the textile industry as an example. There, once the minimum wages and maximum hours for workers and machinery were set, the issue arose of the intensity of work. In textile production the machinery had set the pace and during the depression the pace had increased through what was known as a stretch-out. To address the stretch-out 'a national system of industrial relations boards in the cotton textile industry' was formed. Wolman considered it to be 'one of the most significant experiments in industrial relations' to exist in the US (Wolman 1934 [1970], p. 91).

The NIRA was also changing the attitude of labour unions in the US. Labour unions had long opposed any government establishment of wages, including the minimum wage, especially when it was applied to skilled workers. Union leaders soon recognized 'that the support of the Government as an ally in the making of labor provision was a powerful force not to be rejected' (Wolman 1934 [1970], p. 95). Unions especially valued the provisions of Section 7A of the NIRA, which gave workers 'the right [to] organize and bargain collectively through representatives of their own choosing' (Wolman 1934 [1970], p. 97). With Section 7A behind them, unions increased their membership by over one million workers during the early days of the NIRA and a system developed whereby unions held organizational elections under the supervision of the NRA (Wolman 1934 [1970], pp. 98–100). Labour was being brought into the moral economy through the efforts of the NRA on Wolman's account.

Business leaders, at least in the time of the New Deal, were not prolific writers on economic affairs. The Swarthmore College lectures, however, gave one businessman, Herbert J. Tily, the president of the Strawbridge and Clothier department store and president of the National Retail Council, an opportunity to give his views on the NRA. Tily began with the following analogy to explain his experiences. 'I assumed a Bellamy-like character and projected a possible future for merchandising.' As with Bellamy, Tily saw that future as 'the correcting of all the evils and unethical practices with which the retail craft had been plagued in the past' (Tily 1934 [1970], p. 193). A more moral economy was what the future held and the NRA was helping to bring it about.

The source of the unethical behaviour that Tily wanted to end was, in his words, 'competitive acquisitiveness.' Business had made a mess of the economy through its 'competitive acquisitiveness' and it was time to 'codify our actions' to find out 'if we cannot control human nature' (Tily 1934 [1970], pp. 194–5). The approach of the NRA was to let businesses cooperate in setting up rules to compete fairly. The reliance on business cooperation was important, moreover, for the approach of the NRA in the writing of codes was an effort 'to give business and industry a mandate to control itself and thus eliminate the very real hazards of political control.' Indeed, Tily held the hope that over time 'federal regulation of business will change in inverse ratio to the wise control of business by business men' (Tily 1934 [1970], p. 196). By eliminating unfair practices, the NRA was bringing about a new approach that was 'an attempt to regulate by mutual agreement, by mutual understanding, business practices which have gotten us into a sorry mess' (Tily 1934 [1970], p. 204).

The series of lectures that took place at Swarthmore College gave an opportunity for a number of individuals from the Roosevelt administration with expertise about the NIRA to give their accounts of its working. John Dickinson, Assistant Secretary of Commerce, used his opportunity to defend the NIRA as a crucial part of the New Deal recovery programme in a lecture titled 'The recovery program.' He began his defence by taking the offence against the market economy. To him, the economy of the US in the early twentieth century had become populated by the business firm 'of very considerable size' (Dickinson 1934 [1970], p. 28). These large firms had, in effect, although Dickinson did not use this phrase, become too big to fail. He put it this way, 'Under conditions today the prospect of toppling giants is so fraught with menace throughout the whole system that men shun automatic adjustments bought at such a price' (Dickinson 1934 [1970], pp. 29–30). The recovery programme of the New Deal had to accept that these large firms could not be allowed to disappear, for their collapse would place the entire economic system at risk.

The recovery programme, however, also recognized that it had to save those large firms without changing 'the major outline of the so-called capitalist economy' (Dickinson 1934 [1970], p. 32). Within this context the main purpose of the NIRA was to increase the ability of the workers in industry to purchase the products that industry produced and thereby prevent the failure of the large firms that made up the consumer products segments of the economy. The revival of consumer purchases would cause firms to increase their capital goods purchases and revive the capital goods industries. Since this would be a slow process, the NIRA had to be supplemented by public works projects that would also stimulate consumption spending (Dickinson 1934 [1970], pp. 37–9).

Dickinson made it clear, moreover, that he believed that those who saw the NIRA 'as embodying the principles of economic planning' were wrong. To him, the term planning was becoming a banal expression used to frighten the public with the idea that 'a planned society is but a utopia, an idle dream.' If planning was considered as having a general idea of social goals based on social values and a 'common public purpose,' then it was feasible (Dickinson 1934 [1970], pp. 41–2). It was also, Dickinson added, the type of planning the New Deal was using. Under the leadership of Roosevelt, he argued, 'all groups and classes have been stirred to a recognition of the common national interest.' As a result, they were all cooperating in the New Deal programme of economic recovery (Dickinson 1934 [1970], p. 42). To the extent that the NIRA added to this common set of goals, it was a feasible and acceptable form of planning.

One of the longest lectures given in the series at Swarthmore College was made by Alexander Sachs, who had been the chief and organizer of the Division of Economic Research and Planning at the NRA. Within a context of economic planning he argued that the NRA had two responsibilities of giving workers 'a more fair wage return' and 'to prevent unfair competition' (Sachs 1934 [1970], p. 128).

Sachs quoted President Roosevelt's words on signing the NIRA in regard to this moral element: 'Its goal is the assurance of a reasonable profit to industry and living wages for labor' (Sachs 1934 [1970], p. 130). In reaching that goal the NRA was to engage in 'industrial planning towards an economic constitutional code.' According to Sachs, the policy section of the NIRA had defined planning as 'the promotion of the organization of industry for cooperative action to eliminate unfair competitive practices, to use to the fullest the present productive capacity and generally to rehabilitate industry' through the development of the industry codes (Sachs 1934 [1970], p. 153). This type of planning, he went on, needed 'no change in the economic motivation of business men, only the enlightening of their self-interest.' It was a polar opposite from the type of planning that some individuals – Sachs especially mentioned Tugwell – thought would have to be done by the federal government through a top-down approach. In summing up the issue, Sachs spoke as follows: 'Can capitalism plan and still be capitalism?' Businessmen thought it could but advocates of 'planned collectivism like Professor Tugwell, have emphatically denied it' (Sachs 1934 [1970], p. 181).

To Sachs, the type of collectivist planning advocated by Tugwell would not work and he based his view on a surprising source, Joseph Stalin. According to Sachs, Stalin had analysed the inefficiency of the Soviet Union's economy as resulting from 'equal wages,' 'bureaucratic management' and the 'uneconomic size of the governmental combines' (Sachs 1934 [1970], pp. 185–6). The US under the NIRA avoided these inefficiencies in planning by seeking cooperation among all members of society. Here Sachs added to the view that the NIRA sought a middle ground between the market economy and the moral economy that has been attributed to the New Deal. Moreover, he offered a standard of how to assess that middle ground, noting: 'The test of economic planning is in its success in hindering the hindrance to free and rational economic human action' (Sachs 1934 [1970], p. 189). The moral economy of the NRA and the New Deal would allow human action to be free as long as that action was rationally guided by enlightened self-interest.

GEORGE SOULE LOOKS FOR A REVOLUTION

George Soule (1887–1970) was an economist and editor of *The New Republic* whose thoughts ranged far beyond the issues that concerned most practitioners of the dismal science. By 1934 his thinking led him to consider the prospects for a revolution in the US and he described those prospects in a book, *The Coming American Revolution*. In it he first noted that many were calling Roosevelt's first 100 days a revolution. He went to great lengths, however, to show that those persons characterizing the New Deal as a revolution were using the term revolution in an uninformed way. To Soule, a revolution required two important conditions: 'The old ruling classes are unable, because of their own weakness, to carry on successfully' and 'The rising classes have already achieved substantial power' (Soule 1934, p. 69).

Were those two conditions being met in the US in the 1930s? The market economy was in trouble, Soule had no doubt (Soule 1934, p. 87). Changes in technology brought about increased production, but since the returns that came from increased production went to the capitalists, unless they spent all their profits, the economy would falter through reduced demand. As long as the maldistribution of income persisted and technological change continued, there would exist 'a growing incompetence of the ruling classes to deal with the situation in which they find themselves' (Soule 1934, p. 147). Soule found Hoover to have been an agent of the old ruling class, which was why his policies had not been successful (Soule 1934, pp. 161–3). This finding satisfied Soule's first condition for a revolution.

Soule was certain the economy needed to be changed, because he clearly saw, as did so many others, the end of the market economy. One potential method of change was planning (Soule 1934, p. 199). Planning, however, was inconsistent with the market economy, and the Roosevelt's New Deal had not overcome this inconsistency. Soule admitted that its programmes had been misinterpreted by its opponents. Conservatives believed that 'a small group of professors who had been to Russia and wanted to destroy capitalism' organized into a Brains Trust and put Roosevelt up as a dictator to run the economy. Liberals saw Roosevelt as 'the instrument of a capitalist plot to establish a fascist dictatorship' through the NIRA. The Brains Trust theory was true in the sense that Roosevelt had turned to experts for advice, but that only showed the beginnings 'of the rise to power of a new class' and indicated 'a shift in class power' (Soule 1934, pp. 206–7). The 'new class' of experts was divided over what to do to end the depression, however, and Soule's second condition for revolution was not met.

Regarding specific programmes, Soule found the NIRA to be neither planning nor the product of a Brains Trust. Rather, it came from the US Chamber of Commerce and 'from Gerard Swope ... and from other powerful industrialists' (Soule 1934, pp. 215–16). When the NIRA came into effect, the idea that it was a partnership among business, labour and consumers translated into a system where 'business ran the show, labor got consideration only when it could create enough disturbance, and consumers had no vote and little voice' (Soule 1934, pp. 224–6). There was no overall planning of industry under the NIRA and 'you could look in vain in Washington for a board of experts' geared up to evaluate the outcomes produced by the NIRA (Soule 1934, p. 229).

Soule evaluated the NIRA as a failure in attaining its goals. He provided data to show that production in the economy declined right after the NRA began to function (Soule 1934, p. 253). Rather than industrial planning, the NIRA had resulted in contradictory policies in the New Deal because the NRA-sanctioned price increases offset gains farmers might have had from the AAA. Planning was essential for the revolutionary change Soule believed the economy needed (Soule 1934, p. 279) and the NIRA had not brought this change about.

JOHN MAURICE CLARK, PLANNING AND THE NIRA

As described in previous chapters, for over a decade before the New Deal John Maurice Clark had been an advocate for national economic planning, based on the problems caused by two economic concepts he had devised: the accelerator and overhead costs. In the early 1930s he had refined his view of planning in a book, *Strategic Factors in Business Cycles* (Clark 1934a). His goal was to identify the forces within an economic downturn that were strategic in two senses – they had a strong influence over the other economic factors in the downturn in a way that could govern the outcome of the downturn and they were susceptible to manipulation by human action (Clark 1934a, pp. 6–7).

Clark then pinpointed the strategic factors that had brought about the Great Depression and reached a strong conclusion, 'The study of the special features of the present depression seems to indicate that it may have extended past the point at which the usual forces of automatic recovery can be expected to come into operation' (Clark 1934a, pp. 121–2). In short, the market forces underlying Say's Law that proponents of the market economy believed would bring about the end of the depression could not be hoped for and 'a search for more powerful and positive measures was urgently indicated' (Clark 1934a, p. 122). Unemployment would remain as an ongoing problem and the government should engage in 'long-range planning' to solve the problem (Clark 1934a, pp. 122–3).

To give his own suggestions of how to solve the Great Depression, Clark introduced the idea of a 'balanced economy.' A balanced economy meant that all the productive capabilities of the economy were in tune with the needs of society (Clark 1934a, p. 131). A proper balance had to exist between the prices of inputs, including labour, and the prices of final products as well as between the level of savings and the amount of investment. Clark summed up the problem as follows: 'It appears that balance in the full sense is an unattained ideal, equivalent among other things to economic stabilization. A tolerable working approximation to balance calls for a much greater degree of stability than we actually have' (Clark 1934a, p. 158).

Clark's solution for this lack of consistent stability in economic variables was to identify the strategic factors in the beginning of a recession and manage those that were susceptible to human control. He believed that stabilization would be attained, 'If producers learn to look at the matter collectively and see that their present behaviour is contrary to their joint interests, as tending to produce booms and depressions' (Clark 1934a, p. 195). What was needed was a way to organize industry so that joint interests could overcome individual interests. Clark wondered if this type of joint interest could be established 'without going so far as to make the system of private enterprise impossible.' The only way to find out was by experimentation that might set off an evolutionary process leading to 'a system decidedly different from private enterprise as we now understand it' (Clark 1934a, p. 197).

Armed with this approach, Clark conducted an early review of the NRA in his March 1934 article, 'Economics and the National Recovery Administration,' published in the *American Economic Review*. Clark reviewed the main features of the NIRA and the objectives behind it. He quoted President Roosevelt as stating the aims of the NIRA as follows: 'Industry has long insisted that, given the right to act in unison, it could do much for the general good which has hitherto been unlawful. From today it has that right' (Clark 1934b, p. 12). Clark listed the NRA's objectives and categorized them as having a short-run aim of ending the depression and a long-run aim of ensuring a stable economy with enduring prosperity. One criticism of the NRA was that it focused on the long-run goals and was therefore hampering recovery. Clark disagreed with this criticism because the revival that was concomitant with the NRA's early days had been too rapid to be sustained regardless of what the NRA did (Clark 1934b, pp. 12–18). Clark did see its efforts to limit production as contrary to a recovery, however. He was also concerned about efforts to protect inefficient firms through setting prices at levels that made them profitable (Clark 1934b, pp. 20–21). The problem was that the philosophy of cooperation of the NRA had to 'be converted from a mere philosophy into an organized interest, wide enough to include those who contribute and those who benefit, on a basis somewhat more solid than mutual expressions of good will' (Clark 1934b, pp. 23–4). Until it could accomplish this general cooperation, the NRA was only a step in the direction needed to foster the moral economy of national planning.

WESLEY C. MITCHELL EVOLVES TOWARDS PLANNING

In Chapter 3 we featured Wesley C. Mitchell as the pre-eminent business cycle theorist in the US. In his writings on business cycles he set as a cause of business cycles a market economy based on profits. To him, business cycles arose from the problem of coordinating the production activities of all businesses. Until that problem was solved, Mitchell supported government efforts to offset a downturn by spending on public works to get the economy started.

By the 1930s and the Great Depression, Mitchell published two articles on how government planning was growing in popularity in the US. One article, 'The social sciences and planning' was published in the 18 January 1935 issue of *Science*. Mitchell began the article by asserting that many individuals in the US had the notion that economics presented a strong case against national economic planning. This notion had originated from the way the market economy was presented in England by Adam Smith. Smith's success was widespread to the point 'that for two generations the British government planned to have no plan' (Mitchell 1935, p. 55). That situation did not last, however. Mitchell noted, 'The frequent recurrence of economic crises and depressions is evidence that the automatic functioning of our business system is defective' (Mitchell 1935, p. 57). This dilemma implied that government intervention was necessary to control business cycles.

The Great Depression was bringing a new era for planning to solve the business cycle. The Roosevelt New Deal was starting down that path and other countries, Japan, Germany, Italy and Russia, were undertaking even bolder steps towards national economic planning. The US needed to become bolder as well because planning that solved one problem did not take into account the way all parts of society were connected with each other. Moreover, the way the New Deal planned to meet an emergency was ineffective because it did not take the time to carefully think through its plans. These defects of planning in the US made it possible for critics to 'make out a strong case against much if not most of the national planning we have done in this country.' But, Mitchell argued, it was useless to oppose planning. Private citizens and the government would always try to devise plans to solve social problems and to handle national emergencies. He added, 'The course of wisdom is not to oppose national planning, but to make that planning more intelligent.' The need was palpable, 'for national planning of some sort, or rather of many sorts, we are certain to have' (Mitchell 1935, p. 60).

Mitchell offered a second article on planning, 'Intelligence and the guidance of economic evolution,' in the November 1936 issue of *Scientific Monthly*. In it he observed that there was a growing use of government intervention in the economy and he found that government intervention came about from the success of the market economy; it had produced prosperity by becoming interconnected. But this interconnected economy meant that each person's actions had a greater impact on other persons than ever before and everyone became concerned to have rules that limited what individuals could do that harmed others (Mitchell 1936, p. 457). This trend towards government intervention and planning was a process to be studied but not to be deplored. As scientists, economists should not try to 'pronounce a verdict that laissez-faire is better than governmental regulation, or that governmental regulation is better than laissez-faire.' The wiser course was to find 'choices among the indefinitely numerous possible mixtures of private enterprise and governmental regulation' (Mitchell 1936, p. 461). That was the approach the New Deal was following, and Mitchell admitted that it would not be easy. He wrote, regarding the New Deal's effort at national planning:

> To design an efficient National Industrial Recovery Act is vastly more difficult than to design an efficient bridge across the Golden Gate. The one task we essayed in a fine frenzy of good intentions and rushed it through in short order; the other we performed deliberately after elaborate study of the geological as well as the mechanical factors involved. (Mitchell 1936, p. 463)

The problem was that in the US the federal government in establishing the NIRA had relied heavily on its experiences with the WIB. Those experiences, Mitchell pointed out, were not helpful because during a wartime emergency social goals were easy to determine and translate into a simple mission that could readily be accomplished.

During peacetime social goals were not as easily ascertained, which meant that national planning would be more difficult. All the factors that made for a good plan had to be studied in light of the conflicting goals that any society would have. Mitchell described the problem this way: 'In a democratic country, national planners would have to serve as an agency for accomplishing what the majority desired' (Mitchell 1936, p. 465). Social scientists could help solve the problem by studying how to determine what would best serve the majority. If they did not solve this problem, the US would either be stuck with piecemeal and poorly designed planning such as the NIRA or it might move towards the type of planning represented by communism or fascism. Mitchell hoped it would use its intelligence to develop a planning process that would avoid these alternatives.

THE US CHAMBER OF COMMERCE WORKS WITH THE NIRA

The US Chamber of Commerce is an overarching association of business with a role of providing a national perspective on business, government and the economy. Local chambers of commerce had existed since the earliest days of the US as a country. The national organization, a federation of local chambers of commerce, was formed in 1912. It established its own journal, *Nation's Business*, to set forth a business perspective on a variety of issues. From that perspective, it looked favourably on the NIRA, as long as the NIRA was committed to a policy of business self-regulation.

We can see this business attitude in an article in *Nation's Business* in June 1933 titled 'Business agrees to regulate itself.' The article was a summary of proposals made at the annual meeting of the US Chamber of Commerce. The article summed up the proposals as indicating, 'Business has reasserted its right to govern itself through its own organizations subject to the approval of the government.' What the proposals at the meeting had in mind was that trade associations in collaboration with government and labour would set up fair practices for each industry; this was a policy the Chamber had long espoused and it was consistent with the voluntary planning promoted by Herbert Hoover. If the New Deal would follow these proposals, business would accept its policies. What motivated business towards this type of voluntary planning was that in the previous four years it had learned 'a bitter lesson in the evils of unrestricted competition with lowering wages and salaries and disappearing profits.' Under this type of unrestricted competition businesses had 'sought always to grow larger without proper understanding of the present and future needs of the nation' (*Nation's Business* 1933, pp. 13–14).

In its next issue *Nation's Business* expanded on its views of the NIRA, calling it 'the boldest of a series of bold, swift measures to start economic restoration.' The article, written by Morris Edwards, made it clear what business believed was the deal the NIRA offered it with its title, 'The truce on the Sherman Law.' Edwards outlined the deal business was making as follows:

> If business men will agree, voluntarily if possible, by compulsion if necessary, to put men back to work and raise wages, the Government will do two things. It will refrain for the time being from any more drastic form of control to achieve these ends. Furthermore, it will sanction a control over factors affecting prices to a degree sufficient not only to finance such employment and wage increases but to permit resumption of reasonable profits and dividends. (Edwards 1933, p. 13)

Business could achieve the collaboration needed for maintaining prices with impunity from anti-trust prosecution in return for 'the partial relinquishment of control over management policies' not to the government but to 'a group of proprietors among whom he has one voice' (Edwards 1933, p. 13).

In pointing out the deal business was making with the NIRA, Edwards indicated that the main reason for the NIRA programme was 'to restore normal consumer purchasing power by putting men back to work and raising wages.' Business was ready to agree with this reason. Edwards also had praise for the NRA, warning business leaders that they should not try to sidestep the codes set forth under the NIRA. NRA administrators had 'experience with this sort of thing in the War Industries Board' and were fully capable of dealing with businesses that did not comply with the NRA codes. In addition, the government had a 'big stick' in the form of its authority 'to formulate and promulgate its own code for an industry, if that industry did not move voluntarily' (Edwards 1933, pp. 13–15). Businesses needed to work towards voluntary cooperation was the message.

To bring about this voluntary cooperation, *Nation's Business* gave an example of how the NIRA worked with an article in January 1934, 'Putting a code to work.' The article was written by Wilson Compton, who was counsellor to the Lumber Code Authority. It outlined what Compton considered the desperate need of the lumber industry 'for just the things the NIRA seemed to promise, that is, planned and orderly production, rationalization of prices, steady employment, elimination of "sweat shop" wages and "sweat shop" competition.' The lack of control in the lumber industry had led to overproduction and a waste of a precious natural forest resource. The code permitted a system of balanced production and forest preservation. There were difficulties in getting the code approved by the industry, however. The establishment of production quotas for individual firms meant that some of them had to reduce their output just when they were getting back to normal operations, which caused resentment among those hurt by the quotas. But the industry overall was in favour of the NIRA over 'the old, mad cut-throat system' (Compton 1934, pp. 41–2).

A representative from the retail trade, Benjamin H. Namm of the Namm Stores in Brooklyn, NY, also defended the NIRA's elimination of unfair competition in an article in *Nation's Business* in April 1934, "The war on cut-throat prices.' Namm identified three types of unfair competition in the retail industry, loss leaders, destructive advertising and selling below cost. The retailers who wrote the NIRA code for retailing overwhelmingly favoured the ban of these practices. Namm added that none of the practices aimed at price-fixing, but wanted to ensure that no retailer could abuse his competitors by selling at prices below the labour cost of producing the items being sold. The codes of fair competition would not eliminate competition but would save 'retailing from those who seem willing to destroy it for their own ends' (Namm 1934, pp. 60–61).

In terms of our theme of a moral economy, the business perspective presented in *Nation's Business* took a half-way approach. Some features of the New Deal and the NIRA that eliminated what some business leaders considered to be immoral practices such as unfair competition were generally acceptable as long as business was allowed to write the codes that eliminated them and as long as voluntary cooperation was at least tried before resort was made to compulsion.

HERBERT HOOVER CRITICIZES THE NIRA

For a plain-spoken engineer, Herbert Hoover somehow lent himself readily to myth-making. It was his opponents who created the myths and made them stick. The most important of these myths was that he favoured the market economy, and we hope we have allowed Hoover to debunk this myth in writing about him in Chapter 6. Hoover consistently sought a moral economy that was somewhere between unbridled capitalism and socialism. He initiated many of the programmes of the New Deal but he did so with a different theory of government and business. The government could nurture cooperation among business, labour and consumers but it should not force it upon them.

Hoover expanded on the problems of involuntary cooperation in the form of the NIRA in response to a press inquiry on 15 May 1935. He made it clear that the best policy would be to abolish the NRA. He wrote,

> The whole idea of ruling business through code authorities with delegated powers of law is un-American in principle and a proved failure in practice. The codes are retarding recovery. They are a cloak for conspiracy against the public interest. They are and will continue to be a weapon of bureaucracy, a device for intimidation of decent citizens. (Hoover 1938, p. 45)

On Hoover's account, the NRA had sent a bureaucratic army to every locality in the country to pressure the population. They did more than that, he went on: 'People have been sent to jail, but far more have been threatened by jail' (Hoover 1938, p. 46). The codes were overwhelming small business and 'preventing new enterprise' (Hoover 1938, p. 47). Some businesses that had gained from the NRA codes wanted them perpetuated, but they did not realize how dependent they would become on the government if the NRA continued.

Hoover was especially adamant about the negative impact of the New Deal and the NIRA on the economy and for society. In 1934 he published a book, *The Challenge to Liberty*, to continue his attack on Roosevelt's policies. He did not place the New Deal in any of the systems of communism or fascism but created a new one, Regimentation, to define its policies. Under the NIRA, he insisted, 'the application of Regimentation to business has made great strides.' Hoover admitted that the NIRA had eliminated child labour, sweatshops and unethical business practices. But it had done so at the price of creating 'National Regimentation.' This national Regimentation had taken place through the centralization of power in the hands of the president. It expanded in the NRA with its 'coercive cooperation' over all of the economy. In addition, the codes imposed heavy costs and minimum prices that harmed small businesses. Hoover then concluded, 'The whole thesis behind this program is the very theory that man is but the pawn of the state' (Hoover 1934, pp. 83–8).

In another speech, 'Are our national problems being solved?,' given in Fort Wayne, IN on 6 April 1934, Hoover went further in his attribution of centralized authority as a goal of the New Deal. He told his audience, 'Today we have before us the full import of the NRA. It was framed on the exact pattern of Mr. Mussolini' (Hoover 1938, p. 154). Indeed, Hoover added in another speech that the NIRA had the potential to change the US 'into a Fascist state' (Hoover 1938, p. 170). By making this criticism Hoover tells us that drawing the line between the moral economy and the market economy is not easy. Both he and Roosevelt tried to draw the line that created the mixed economy that combined morals and markets. Moreover, the lines they drew were closer to each other than they were to earlier places where the line had been drawn. Many of Roosevelt's policies were like Hoover's but with some extensions and it was these extensions that Hoover criticized. Hoover, however, was not the only politician to level criticisms against Roosevelt and the New Deal as fascist, and we now turn to another politician who took the same attitude. Only he was a member of the president's party.

HUEY LONG OPPOSES THE NIRA

Huey Long (1893–1935) has often been called a classic populist politician, more in the line of William Jennings Bryan than Progressives like Theodore Roosevelt and Woodrow Wilson. He used his populist policies to win election as governor of Louisiana and, in 1932, as senator from that state. His overarching policy, the solution of all economic problems, was the redistribution of income by taxing the rich and giving the proceeds to the poor, a policy of equality that was always a part of the moral economy.

He thought he had an ally in his policy in Roosevelt. As a result, he saw Roosevelt's other policies as a distraction from the promise of income redistribution. He thus felt he had to criticize those policies and in the case of the NIRA he was unsparing in his attacks. In a speech in the Senate on 1 March 1934 he said, 'If the NRA has done any good, I can put it all in my eye without having it hurt. All I can see that the NRA has done is to put the little man out of business,' adding, 'he has to hire a Philadelphia lawyer to tell him what is in the code; and by the time he learns what the code is, he is in jail or out of business' (Long 1985, p. 44).

Long went further in his criticism of the NIRA in another speech in the Senate, 'Our blundering government,' on 12 March 1935. According to Long, when the NRA started up,

> They had parades and Fascist signs just as Hitler, and Mussolini. They started the dictatorship here to regiment business and labor much more than anyone did in Germany or Italy. The only difference was the sign. Italy's sign was a black shirt. Germany's sign of the Fascist was a swastika. So in America they sidetracked the Stars and Stripes, and the sign of the Blue Eagle was used instead. (Long 1985, p. 85)

Once in place, the NRA set up rules for every industry, and businesses that did not comply found their owners being sent to jail. Long offered the story of 'A little fellow who pressed pants' being sent to jail 'because he charged 5 cents under the price set in the rule book.' The codes were complex and Long indicated that even he, as a trained lawyer, could not understand them. The Roosevelt administration continued to perpetuate 'a high-handed, tyrannical, outrageous system of government' (Long 1985, pp. 85–6). When two politicians as different in temperament and policy prescriptions as Long and Hoover agree on an issue as contentious as the NIRA, the political world has entered into strange territory. Even stranger, a defence of Roosevelt from these charges was made by a socialist politician, Norman Thomas.

NORMAN THOMAS: CAPITALISM, FASCISM AND THE NIRA

Norman Thomas (1884–1968) ran for president of the US six times. That he was never successful was likely due to his running on the Socialist Party ticket with a platform to establish a cooperative commonwealth. In 1934 he published a book, *The Choice Before Us*, to explain a world in which socialism was not the only 'ism' then being proposed to cure the ills of the Great Depression. His overarching concern was with the rise of fascism in Italy and Germany and the possibility that fascism was an alternative to socialism.

As was common during the early years of the Great Depression, Thomas saw it as the end of the market economy. On his account, the market economy had changed from one of small producers to a reliance on large corporations using the technology of mass production to produce the goods and services society needed. It was a system run by engineers and other experts but controlled by managers who operated on behalf of absentee owners. That system had collapsed through the production of too much capital and the resulting overproduction (Thomas 1934 [1970], p. 11).

One approach to recovery was fascism. The form it took was state capitalism, where 'the power of the state is used to stabilize the maximum amount of private ownership and the operation of the system for the profit of private owners.' The old individualistic capitalism of the market economy was gone, for 'the state is supreme and dictatorial' (Thomas 1934 [1970], p. 43). In Germany the Nazis' total rule of the economy was abhorrent to Thomas because he feared it would become permanent. He was more optimistic about the dictatorship of Stalin under the communist system of the Soviet Union, interpreting it as 'a temporary dictatorship for a transitional period' (Thomas 1934 [1970], pp. 45, 67).

To Thomas, the New Deal represented a new economic order that had started with Hoover's policies, but it was 'not Fascism, at least not yet, and emphatically not Socialism or Communism' (Thomas 1934 [1970], p. 83). Roosevelt's policies were being characterized as a revolution but to Thomas it was 'a revolution from laissez faire to state capitalism' (Thomas 1934 [1970], p. 92). Now Thomas had also called fascism state capitalism. The difference was that the powers Roosevelt had used in bringing about this state capitalism had been 'democratically granted and kept under sufficient democratic control' with the result that they did not 'amount to setting up a dictatorship' (Thomas 1934 [1970], p. 94). As for the NIRA, Thomas found that business had welcomed it because its labour provisions were less onerous than they might have been and it allowed them to form trade associations without being prosecuted under the anti-trust laws. Labour also favoured the NIRA because it believed the NIRA gave workers a better chance to organize unions to engage in collective bargaining. The NIRA had not lived up to its promise of recovery, however. The ultimate flaw in the NIRA was that it had done nothing to alter the distribution of income towards greater equality, which Thomas saw as 'the root of our trouble (Thomas 1934 [1970], p. 104).

The key to this flaw was that the NIRA was not socialism and thus could not attain a systematic programme of planning. Thomas noted, 'It is hard to plan for what you do not own or to bring order into an industry, the moving power in which is a desire to make profit' (Thomas 1934 [1970], p. 104). As a result, the NIRA had to side with business in its pursuit of profits, and businessmen who were 'at first suspicious of the codes ... came to love them best' (Thomas 1934 [1970], p. 105 n.). Business appreciated the advantages the NIRA had for it and would have preferred the Swope Plan, which Thomas characterized as 'business fascism.' In a democracy such as the US the 'producing masses' were able to prevent 'a government by big business and for big business ... with scarcely more than veto power reserved to the government' (Thomas 1934 [1970], p. 129). Given the limited success of business in getting all it wanted, what did the future hold? Regarding the New Deal, Thomas saw the possibility of its expansion over time. He explained, 'They will increase social control, they will protect the underdog, they will stabilize business, and yet somehow or other preserve individual initiative, private profit, and the rights of the little man. Theirs will be an American plan, a capitalist collectivism' (Thomas 1934 [1970], p. 164). Roosevelt may have unintentionally aided the conditions that might lead to fascism, but 'his success lies in the success of his own New Deal without Fascism' (Thomas 1934 [1970], p. 164).

Thomas, however, believed that the New Deal could not succeed. It was trying to solve what Marxists would call a contradiction of capitalism by endeavouring to develop a system of planned capitalism. Planning was not compatible with the market economy and its pursuit of profit, nor could policies such as the New Deal represented save the market economy from its ultimate demise. Sooner or later the Roosevelt experiments with their benign form of 'state capitalism' would incur the wrath of the workers who were not being benefited. Then the only issue would be if a demagogue was able to sway those workers to 'an American adaptation of measures already used in Italy and Germany' (Thomas 1934 [1970], p. 189) or whether workers would have the wisdom to move forward to the moral economy of the 'cooperative commonwealth' (Thomas 1934 [1970], pp. 200–205).

HUGH S. JOHNSON MAKES HIS CASE FOR THE NIRA

General Hugh S. Johnson (1881–1942) had a long career of military service. A West Point graduate, he rose to the rank of general and was the army's liaison to the WIB in World War I. He also found the time to complete law school. On retiring from the army he became a business associate of Bernard Baruch. With this multi-faceted background he was as qualified as anyone in the US to serve as head of the NRA. He was appointed to that position at the start of the NRA in 1933, serving until his resignation in September 1934. He was energetic in his work with the NIRA and equally energetic in making the case for that work in a book and numerous articles in the press.

One example of his writing is an article, 'Administration of NRA,' in the *Saturday Evening Post* of 14 June 1934. In his article Johnson focused on the rapid work the NRA had done in getting its early codes in place. In its first year of operation the NRA had negotiated over 450 codes of fair competition and contributed to the recovery of the economy as part of the president's 'balanced and comprehensive plan of attacking every particularly depressed element in our national economy.' He added, 'No recovery in the history of business cycles has been so rapid and conditions today are better than at any time since December 1930' (Johnson 1934, pp. 10–11).

Johnson indicated that this recovery had included improved working conditions for labour. The NRA had abolished sweatshops and eliminated child labour, and its labour policies with their encouragement of collective bargaining had brought about increased wages with reduced hours although Johnson admitted that some of these gains had come at the cost of labour strife. In another area the NRA was hearing complaints from the owners of small businesses and taking steps to address them. All in all, the NRA had produced a 'national cooperative effort toward a safer economy' (Johnson 1934, p. 89).

Critics had insisted that the NRA had legalized price-fixing and nurtured monopolies. Johnson insisted with equal strength that the NRA codes did the reverse, arguing that the price stability the codes sought was beneficial to all business whereas it was 'price cutting … by large companies that tends toward monopoly.' The NRA did not 'favor price fixing except in an emergency,' but it did try to eradicate 'destructive price slashing.' The NRA had written numerous codes in its first year and that work was just about completed. In writing those codes it had favoured no groups, as many had alleged. Once the codes were completed, which would happen very soon, Johnson concluded, the NRA would 'demonstrate to the country real compliance and real results from all of the existing codes' (Johnson 1934, p. 92).

Johnson continued his case for the NRA in another article in the *Saturday Evening Post* of 19 January 1935, 'The Blue Eagle from egg to earth.' Written after his resignation from the NRA, Johnson was particularly eager to defend his policies. The criticisms of the NRA resulted from its being part of a new philosophy of government and the economy. Indeed, Johnson 'regarded NRA as a holy cause.' As would any devotee of a new philosophy, he was hurt from being misunderstood especially in light of all the good he was doing by bringing the order of government to the chaos of the market economy, making it possible for all sectors of the economy 'to act in unison.' This united effort was a new approach to economic thinking and it caused discontentment among the old-style business leaders who were used to having their way (Johnson 1935a, pp. 6–7). Johnson gave two examples of how his efforts to provide common policies proved contentious.

The first example came under the goal of trying to improve the purchasing power of labour. One way to create more opportunities for labour was to diminish the introduction of labour-saving technology. Labour-saving machines lowered the employment and income of workers as a group, reducing their purchasing power. Johnson added, in the long run holding back the use of new technology 'opposes the irresistible march of human progress.' Johnson recognized the power of creative destruction, but he wanted that power to be controlled. Consequently, the NRA held a position 'that some regulation of new labor-saving devices is advisable.' That position did not mean that new methods of production should be prohibited, but that the government and the industry code authority could postpone their introduction if they 'would do more harm than good' (Johnson 1935a, p. 70).

Johnson's second example dealt with the level of wages and efforts to ensure that workers earned a living wage. The philosophy of President Roosevelt on this issue was that 'no industry which depends for existence on less than living wages has a right to continue to exist.' When the NRA took this philosophy as its marching orders and forced sweatshops to pay a living wage, the operators of those sweatshops said 'that NRA oppresses them.' They became its enemies. Johnson was willing to have his legacy stand on his rooting out these low-wage industries, even though consumers might benefit from them, because in addition to living wages being in his marching order from the president, 'they were also my convictions' (Johnson 1935a, p. 72).

While Johnson did not propose national economic planning to ensure a living wage, he believed that there had to be a national policy controlling all business to avoid wage differentials in one part of the country from undercutting living wages in another and to keep 'adroit manufacturers' from 'moving their plants to places where human labor can be exploited without great capital cost' (Johnson 1935b, p. 448). Government ownership of productive resources was not as necessary to the moral economy as Bellamy had thought; government control over business could serve just as well.

THE NATION SWITCHES SIDES ON THE NIRA

Founded in 1865, *The Nation* is one of the oldest weekly magazines in the US. Its speciality is the political scene, which would make it an obvious place to find views on the New Deal. It typically supported Roosevelt and his programmes but not unabashedly. We see this in its coverage of the NIRA, which it first supported and then criticized.

Support for the NIRA can be found in a regular column, 'Issues and Men,' on 3 January 1934, by Oswald Garrison Villard. Titled 'The gifts of the New Deal,' the column took heart in 'the great things that have been accomplished by the NRA.' The NRA had brought a change in the federal government from being pro-business to stressing 'the welfare and the progress of the plain people of the United States.' It had also launched 'the beginning of national planning of industry.' In accomplishing these important changes, the NRA had awakened the 'American people ... to new ideas and the necessity for new economic readjustments and beliefs' (*The Nation* 1934, p. 8). Another article in that issue by Paul Y. Anderson wrote as favourably about 'New Year's gifts for the NRA' (Anderson 1934, p. 17).

The Nation did not accept the gifts of the NRA unequivocally, however. The issue of consumer input in the NRA codes was raised in an unsigned editorial, 'Bombs bursting in air,' on 30 May 1934. The noted attorney, Clarence Darrow, had been asked by the president to analyse the NRA. His report urged the president to establish a planned economy that rested on 'socialized ownership and control, since only by collective ownership can the inevitable conflict of separately owned units for the market be eliminated in favor of planned production.' This was Bellamyism and the editorial added, 'with this conclusion we agree' ('Bombs bursting in air,' 1934, p. 606). Another editorial on 5 September 1934, aimed at 'Saving the good in the NRA.' The NRA was undergoing reorganization and it was important to retain its good features. 'The good in the NRA,' the editorial noted, 'was in the protection it promises labor.' The bad parts were the help it gave business through 'price-fixing and the evasion of the anti-trust laws.' The editorial saw these features as a political deal the NRA had made with business, that is, business would accept collective bargaining in return for protection from the anti-trust laws. *The Nation* thought it a bad deal that hurt consumers and hampered the recovery of the economy. 'If the continuation of the NRA means the perpetuation of this bargain,' the editorial indicated, 'we should advocate scrapping it altogether' ('Saving the good in the NRA,' 1934, p. 256).

The attack on the NIRA continued in *The Nation* on 10 April 1935 in an article, 'NRA – haven for cake-eaters,' by Paul W. Ward. The cake-eaters

Ward referred to were businessmen, because the NRA let them have their cake, price-fixing, and eat it too in the form of profits. The bill for reorganizing the NRA had been made public and it did nothing to curb businesses' ability to fix prices. Nor did it do anything to tilt the balance of power in writing codes from business to labour and consumers. Ward believed that the formulators of the NRA had accepted the argument that businesses that paid low wages would increase them if their competition was forced to raise their wages and had assumed that there was such a thing as 'fair competition.' These views had been proved wrong, and 'the New Deal ended so far as the NRA was concerned' when its first code was put in place in the textile industry. Ward described the outcome from that code as follows: 'The public, told that no industry deserved to exist that could not pay "a decent living wage," had been led to expect that a minimum wage meant a minimum wage.' Instead, workers were paid less that the code standards and offered a lower number of hours per week, while textile prices increased (Ward 1935, pp. 412–13).

FATHER CHARLES COUGHLIN AND THE NATIONAL UNION FOR SOCIAL JUSTICE

Father Charles E. Coughlin (1891–1979) was a controversial figure during the Great Depression. A Roman Catholic priest from Detroit, MI, he pioneered the methods now used by talk radio hosts, starting his radio broadcasts in 1926. He was bombastic and while he did not take telephone calls on the air, he did read letters from his listeners and respond to them on the air. The key to all his talk was his advocacy of social justice as presented by Pope Leo XIII in his encyclical *Rerum Novarum*, and he used his standard of social justice, we would call it the moral economy, to judge what politicians and the economy were providing for the US.

In the early 1930s he thought he heard a kindred voice in Roosevelt and became an early supporter of the New Deal. Coughlin, however, was not a devoted follower of anything but his own views of social justice. He wished for the success of the New Deal and believed that it had two years to prove itself by addressing the issue of 'why there is want in the midst of plenty' (Coughlin 1934). Coughlin had his own answer to this question. As did many other persons, Coughlin saw the problem of the Great Depression as one of underconsumption. Science and technology had created the means to produce everything society needed; the problem was that the distribution of the income was skewed towards the wealthy and the rest of society did not have enough income to purchase everything that was produced. The appropriate solution to the Great Depression was 'a just and living annual wage for all citizens who care to earn their own livelihood' (Coughlin 1934).

The living wage is a key ingredient of any programme for a moral economy. Coughlin was an advocate for a living wage for workers, following the writings of another Catholic priest, Monsignor John A. Ryan (Stabile 2008, p. 2). The living wage, however, was needed for economic as well as for moral reasons. Coughlin saw the problem of unemployment as being created when workers were paid low wages while they worked and then were laid off until the products they produced were sold. The idea of a living wage meant that 'a new annual wage scale must be adopted,' one that led to a 'new era where henceforth our problem shall be one of distribution of the profits not only to the owners and stockholders but also to the laborers and mechanics, enabling all to live prosperously even when the wheels of industry have ceased operating.' In making this argument Coughlin wanted to persuade the business leaders in charge of the economy 'to cooperate with the Government as it will move, we hope, towards the shortening of hours for all engaged in mass production activity and towards an annual wage system that is just and equitable' (Coughlin 1934).

The leaders of industry should cooperate with the New Deal in solving the unemployment problem. They needed to understand that they had a moral obligation to not use their ownership of productive property 'to the detriment of the common good.' In coming to this understanding, they should accept that their capitalist beliefs were outdated. Against them came the 'clarion call of communism' but something between capitalism and communism was required so the people of the US would not have 'to surrender our rights to life, to liberty and to the cherished bonds of family to communism' (Coughlin 1934).

To find that moral economy in between capitalism and communism Coughlin asked his listeners to form a National Union for Social Justice. He then outlined 'the principles of social justice' the US should try to establish. It was a long list and included: a living wage; nationalization of public resources, 'which by their very nature are too important to be held in the control of private individuals'; private ownership of the rest of property with control of it 'for the public good'; the right of workers to form unions under the protection of the government; a broader tax base centred on the principle of 'ability to pay' with tax cuts for workers; and a preference for 'the sanctity of human rights to the sanctity of property rights' (Coughlin 1934). These items we have listed would be consistent with the organization of Bellamy's moral economy, except Bellamy would have argued that all resources were public resources.

Because he thought that Roosevelt had heeded his call for social justice, Coughlin had supported him in the election of 1932. He coined the slogan 'Roosevelt or ruin' as part of his support, but his support for Roosevelt gradually dwindled when Roosevelt consistently followed what Coughlin viewed as unsound policies. He indicated that he could not 'praise policies like NRA when criticism is required' (Coughlin 1935). Never a whole-hearted supporter of the NIRA, he had written to Roosevelt that the 'NIRA alone cannot break the depression' and that while the 'NIRA shares work' it also 'shares prosperity along with poverty.' He had hoped that the NIRA would have served to help labour by maintaining wages and controlling prices, but a large number of letters from his radio audience told him that they 'have not much faith in the National Recovery Act' (Tull 1965, pp. 38–9). Coughlin was especially concerned that business influence in the NRA had kept wages low and allowed for price-fixing in most industries, with the result that wage increases lagged behind price increases. The NRA had not prevented business from exploiting its workers.

The point for Coughlin was that the NRA was not the moral economy of social justice that he had called for. It had not delivered on the promise of according workers a living wage and had not abandoned the primacy of profits over people. Consequently, Coughlin changed his praise of Roosevelt in a radio address on 19 June 1936 to 'Roosevelt and ruin.' He spoke as follows, 'It is not pleasant for me who coined the phrase "Roosevelt or ruin" … to admit that "Roosevelt and ruin" is the order of the day' (Coughlin 1936).

Coughlin would later become even more harsh in his criticism of Roosevelt, writing to his friend, Mayor Frank Murphy of Detroit, 'I sincerely feel that Mr. Roosevelt is a socialist of the radical type.' He added that while the New Deal talked of 'the splendid program of Christian justice' it was partly caught in 'the red mud of Soviet Communism' (quoted in Fried 1999, pp. 114–15). By the late 1930s, however, Coughlin, starting with the Spanish Civil War, began to see fascism as the one implacable foe of communism and began espousing Nazi propaganda on his radio programme. Eventually his superiors in the Church halted his political activities in 1942 (Fried 1999, p. 211).

THE NEW REPUBLIC DOUBTS THE NIRA

The New Republic was formed in 1914 by Herbert Croly and Walter Lippmann, two luminaries of the Progressive movement, to serve as a voice for Progressive thinking and it continued that voice throughout the New Deal. In serving that function, however, it did not slavishly follow the line set down by President Roosevelt and the Democratic Party. We see this independent thinking in its doubtful attitude towards the NIRA and the NRA. For example, in an editorial on 20 March 1935, 'What to do with the N.R.A.,' the editors stated quite clearly, 'After two years of trial, the N.R.A. has, on the whole, failed in its major purpose' (*The New Republic* 1935, p. 144).

That major purpose had been to increase production in the economy and bring about an economic recovery and it had not come close to being attained. The NRA had made some progress in getting wages increased and working hours reduced, but these results had not improved the economy. *The New Republic* set the cause for this negative outcome on business. It had used the NIRA to fix prices and restrict output, which should not have been unexpected. The basic error of the NRA program was its assumption that a partnership among business, labour, consumers and the government could effectively manage industry. Instead, business became 'the senior partner' and used its seniority 'to safeguard its share at the expense of the other partners' ('What to do with the NIRA,' 1935, p. 145). *The New Republic* doubted that this outcome could be changed as long as the US had a market economy, because the capitalists would always be able to exercise more influence over the government than any other group. The NIRA was doomed to failure until 'industry is socialized.' Meanwhile, the NRA could serve 'to train the personnel that will be needed for the planned society' ('What to do with the NIRA,' 1935, p. 146).

The New Republic continued its ambivalent attitude towards the NIRA in an editorial, 'Experts judge the NRA,' on 1 May 1935. The editorial was a review of a Brookings Study of the NIRA (see Chapter 10). The study's negative findings led *The New Republic* to the conclusion,

> The only way out of this mess is to back off and begin again. Mr. Roosevelt was once praised for his readiness to regard his measures as experiments, which he would abandon if they did not work. Here is one that has been weighed and found wanting by laboratory experts. (*The New Republic* 1935, p. 327)

Given how central the ability of the government to organize industrial production was to the overall objective of the New Deal of bringing about a recovery, a new version of the NRA was essential. The other spending programs of the New Deal as part of its policy of pump priming could not work with an ineffective NRA. Moreover, as another article, 'NIRA chiselers and sculptors,' in *The New Republic* of 5 June 1935, argued, the Roosevelt administration should not expect any help from business in reforming the NRA (Richards 1935, pp. 92–5).

CONCLUSION

In this chapter we have presented the views that advocates for a moral economy took of the NIRA and the NRA. Our categorization of those advocates has been broad, ranging from businessmen who wanted fair competition to proponents of national economic planning and government ownership. As a result, their views of the NIRA and the NRA were highly diverse and as some of the advocates for a moral economy indicated, the NIRA and the NRA were not what they meant by a moral economy. They saw the NIRA and the NRA codes as falling well short of the planning that Progressives had looked for to solve the lack of morality they saw in the market economy. Other advocates for the moral economy thought the NIRA and the NRA were a first step in planning, a tentative step that would eventually lead to more effective planning if not outright government ownership of the means of production.

Amidst the diversity of views by advocates of the moral economy, Roosevelt believed that he was trying to find a middle ground by travelling down a practical path. He took many parts of the economy as he found them but tried to get them to work together to solve the presumed problem of the Great Depression, underconsumption, in a way that gave business reasonable profits, labour a living wage and consumers fair prices through competition that was moral. To do so, however, he took Hoover's strategy of voluntary cooperation in planning by trade associations a step further by adding government and labour as additional elements to the planning process. Members of the Roosevelt administration we have included in this chapter, such as Johnson, Tugwell, Sachs and Dickinson, generally agreed with this vision of the NIRA and NRA. Hoover, however, decried the extra step as too much government intervention, calling it Regimentation.

Long-time proponents of planning, such as Clark and Mitchell, believed that the NIRA and NRA needed that extra step as a way to begin the difficult process of learning how to plan. They believed that planning was inevitable as a solution to the problem of business cycles but that planning itself would not be easy. Careful thought must go into any system of planning that the government initiated and they faulted the NIRA and NRA for being implemented hastily. Thomas agreed that the New Deal had created a system of democratic state capitalism where popularly elected leaders controlled business in the public interest and that this approach would ultimately lead to the full adoption of a cooperative commonwealth with government ownership of the means of production – Bellamy's moral economy. Soule followed a similar line by arguing that a revolutionary change was in process but it still lacked the commitment of a new class of experts for it to begin the transition to a moral economy. Still, the NRA was proving to be a training ground for that new class of experts.

Not all advocates for the moral economy were optimistic about the trends being set in place by the NIRA and the NRA. Pundits at *The Nation* and *The New Republic* along with Coughlin believed that business had gained too much power through its use of the writing of the NRA codes to serve its interests. To some extent, business advocates for the moral economy agreed with this attribution of their power. They believed that the NIRA gave them a chance to create a more moral economy by regulating themselves. One business leader, Herbert Tily, had argued that over time 'federal regulation of business will change in inverse ratio to the wise control of business by business men' (Tily 1934 [1970], p. 196). In line with this argument the US Chamber of Commerce held, 'Business has reasserted its right to govern itself through its own organizations subject to the approval of the government' ('Business agrees to regulate itself,' 1933, pp. 13–14). If this was the New Deal business was being offered, they were for it. We shall see in Chapter 10 that business control over the NRA codes was ultimately viewed by advocates of the market economy as their fatal flaw.

Although there was not an agreement among supporters of the moral economy as to the effectiveness of the NIRA, there was recognition by some, such as Wolman, that it had brought about a needed change in the way labour was treated. The NIRA brought about the beginning of a way for unions to be organized legally under government auspices; this approach also altered the attitude unions had towards government from an enemy that sided with business to an ally. The NRA codes regarding labour also reduced child labour and put minimum wages and maximum hours of work on the political agenda of the moral economy. Through codes that limited the introduction and use of labour-saving machinery, however, they slowed up the pace of creative destruction – a desirable policy according to Johnson.

That policy reflected a singular contradiction in the NIRA that was not much noted by advocates for the moral economy. By branding labour-saving machinery as immoral, they could feel that they were solving the problem of underconsumption. The dilemma with this feeling was that the prohibition of new methods of production, along with all the other approaches developed in the NRA codes, as Wilcox, Fraser and Malin observed, had apparently served 'to impede rather than promote a revival of business.' In that vein, they continued, 'We do not look upon the National Industrial Recovery Act, despite its name, as a recovery device' (Wilcox et al. 1934 [1970], p. 9).

10. The National Industrial Recovery Act: market economy perspectives

Supporters of the market economy are typically characterized as true believers in laissez-faire, the theory of economics that argues that all government intervention in the economy will cause harm. Market economists, however, admit that some government activities are necessary for the market economy to function. Adam Smith, for example, recognized that the government needed to provide a system of laws and police and courts to see that those laws were enforced. More surprising, Smith wanted the government to offer free education to the poor. In both cases he recognized that humans would often yield to the temptation to behave improperly. A criminal justice system and better education would reduce improper behaviour. The question market economy advocates asked of the NIRA was whether it was a law that enforced proper behaviour or an illegitimate government intervention in the economy.

In this chapter we look at what proponents of the market economy had to say about the NIRA and the NRA. Like Smith, they had no doubt that businesses would be tempted to eschew the benefits to society of competition and get together to fix prices and wages and use the government to help them. We saw in the last chapter that advocates of a moral economy felt that business had too much influence in the NRA codes. Market economists would not have been surprised. But they worried even more over how the New Deal programs were transforming government and politics in the US.

SUMNER SLICHTER SEEKS A BALANCED ECONOMY

Sumner Slichter (1892–1969), professor of economics at Harvard University, had called for experimentation in planning during the early years of the depression, as described in Chapter 7. In June 1933 he gave a series of lectures at Utah State Agricultural College, which he revised and published as a book in late 1934. In the book he looked not for planning but for ways to achieve balance in the economy. The experiments with planning by the New Deal, such as the NIRA, had not been satisfactory to him.

The difficulty as Slichter saw it was that 'the problem of achieving stability under capitalism is a problem of stabilizing the prospects for profit' (Slichter 1934, p. iii). Unless businesses' outlook for future profit improved, no effort to revive the economy could succeed. Since profits depended on how selling prices related to costs, the Roosevelt administration's efforts to enhance consumer purchasing power with higher wages were misguided. Business needed an approach that adjusted costs and prices in a way that improved the profit outlook. Instead, Roosevelt and the New Deal were hindering the outlook for profits by making the economy reliant on government policy. This created a new problem, Slichter wrote, 'As the question of what the government is going to do or not do becomes increasingly important in the calculations of business men, political uncertainties will add to the army of unemployed by causing business managers to defer commitments' (Slichter 1934, p. 6). Government intervention added to businesses' uncertainty.

To Slichter, the market economy had an emphasis on growth and change because the process of creative destruction gave businesses incentives to enhance their profits through innovation 'regardless of the effects it produces upon the community.' It then became necessary to balance creative destruction with stability (Slichter 1934, p. 1). The market economy used prices to attain that balance but could produce recurrent imbalances. To Slichter, recurrent imbalances indicated that 'prices do not move promptly enough to eliminate maladjustments before the maladjustments themselves produce new maladjustments' (Slichter 1934, p. 8).

Slichter provided his readers with a lengthy account of how the problem of sluggish price changes could cause the economy to stay unbalanced. Price flexibility was an essential element in attaining balance and a recovery. When the market economy was out of balance because the prices of consumer goods were falling, flexibility in the costs of production, including wages, was necessary. But wages and prices had to fall in a balanced way. Uncontrolled deflation threatened the solvency of businesses. Anti-deflation policies, however, were equally a threat when they raised the wrong prices. From this perspective, Slichter found the NIRA to have been 'a monumental mistake as a recovery measure because it was based upon two great fallacies: (1) that a revival can be produced by raising rather than lowering the cost of doing business and (2) that the cure for a deflation that has been concentrated upon agriculture is to raise the wages of industrial workers and the prices of industrial products' (Slichter 1934, p. 38).

To bring home the inadequacy he saw in the NIRA, Slichter considered its policies to control investment. Many thought the depression had been caused by excessive investment in productive capacity, leading to a problem of overproduction. A few of the NRA codes authorized limits on increases in productive capacity. If these codified limits took place in only a few industries that would cause little damage to the economy. But when restrictions on investment became widespread, 'serious trouble would result' (Slichter 1934, pp. 42–3). Moreover, there was talk of going beyond the NIRA to create a Capital Issues Board to allocate capital to different industries. To do so, Slichter continued, such a board 'would soon find itself passing on the merits of hundreds of individual issues – a stupendous task and one which would impose on the Board an impossible responsibility' (Slichter 1934, p. 65). The board would be lobbied heavily by business firms for funds to increase their capacity and for the denial of funds to competing firms.

From his pinpointing the problems of controlling investment, Slichter expanded his inquiry into the prospects of national economic planning, an idea he believed had 'captured the popular imagination' (Slichter 1934, p. 155). He defined a planned economy as 'one in which production is guided by plans instead of by prices – in which plans replace markets as the immediate determinants of what shall be produced and in what quantities.' He thought the idea of planning was becoming popular because under the market economy everything depended on business making profits and it shocked the popular mind to find that millions were unemployed when 'business men fail to discover enough new ways of making money.' The question was whether planning required the end of private enterprise. Slichter noted, 'The socialists believe it would, and I think they are correct' (Slichter 1934, p. 156).

Slichter's agreement with socialists on this issue represented his view that national economic planning and private enterprise were incompatible. National planning meant that a National Planning Board would set production quotas for each industry; in doing so it would also have to establish prices for each industry to ensure most businesses made a profit. If the board had an accurate forecast of the demand for all the products being produced, its plans might work out. The problem was, as Slichter stated, 'The planners would be unable to control demand and often would fail to predict it accurately' (Slichter 1934, p. 157). If its estimate of demand for any product turned out to be wrong, plans might have to be revised in terms of the production and prices of that industry, but that would upset the plans of all the other industries. An alternative would be to have that industry make excessive gains or losses by staying with the plan but eventually production in the industry would have to be changed, which would require that production in all other industries would have to be altered as well. The same problem would occur when the National Planning Board had decided how to allocate capital.

Slichter then turned to the NIRA, which he characterized as being 'often described as representing the introduction of national planning into American industry' (Slichter 1934, p. 169). Slichter believed that many of the NRA codes were adding complexity to the problem of attaining a balanced economy. First, the codes would discourage innovation; businesses were always trying to protect themselves from the competition brought about by innovation. Unless the government took steps to prevent this process of protection, innovation would be much more limited. Slichter wrote, 'One makes this prediction with even greater assurance because many provisions which discourage innovation have already found their way into the codes. Indeed the codes have indicated beyond a shadow of a doubt that trade associations are quite as ready as trade unions to place restrictions on innovations' (Slichter 1934, pp. 170–71).

A second problem the NRA codes caused was their effort to abolish price-cutting. Price-cutting often resulted from cost-cutting and the NRA codes were 'delaying the transmission of savings caused by technological changes to the consumers in the form of lower prices' (Slichter 1934, p. 174). The third problem being caused by the NRA codes was that they were adding to unemployment. When consumer demand fell, as it did during the depression, 'either prices must fall or production and employment must drop.' Instead, the codes, Slichter concluded, 'are likely to aggravate the severity of depressions by increasing the tendency for the prices of many non-agricultural products to become inflexible' (Slichter 1934, p. 175). The NIRA was encouraging inflexible prices and thus hindering balance in the economy.

Slichter questioned the wisdom of government interference in the economy but believed that 'a continuation of the trend is inevitable' because the market economy had not worked well and 'the community was bound to insist on trying something else' (Slichter 1934, p. 183). This trend posed a new set of problems from the changed relationship between government and business; Slichter restated his view that when government took charge of economic policy, business would hold off on its plans until it saw what the government was going to do (Slichter 1934, p. 183). In a democracy government policies must be in accord with the interests of voters and to please enough voters, politicians had to make compromises. These compromises caused dissatisfaction among voters who then sought a change of policy. Policies would always be changing and efforts to control business would be ineffective unless 'the administration of basic policies is in the hands of experts who are left considerable discretion over what they do and do not do' (Slichter 1934, p. 184).

Starting with Bellamy's moral economy, proponents of planning recognized the need to take politics out of planning through the use of scientific experts who made decisions based on their judgement of the needs of the overall economy and society. Individuals such as William Graham Sumner doubted whether such experts could be found. Slichter doubted that they would be used, even if they were found. Arguing in a way that anticipated the ideas of Mancur Olsen (Olsen 1965), Slichter pointed out that the call for action by government in the economy usually came from special interest groups. The action these groups sought might actually be harmful to the rest of society, 'for one of the simplest ways of promoting the interest of a small group is to permit it to exploit the rest of the community.' Since the gain to the special interest group was concentrated, while the costs were spread over the whole of society, making each individual's costs low, few persons had an incentive to fight special interest programmes. As a result, Slichter argued, 'politicians find that a convenient way to build up majorities is to sacrifice the interests of the unorganized general public in order to confer favors on many small groups' (Slichter 1934, pp. 184–5).

The upshot of the process would be a poor policy and the entire New Deal fit this picture according to Slichter, who characterized it as 'a series of self-defeating attempts to confer favors on too many special groups' (Slichter 1934, p. 185). That was why he found its efforts at bringing about recovery to have been a failure. It was also why he felt safe 'in predicting that the government as now organized is not capable of formulating a policy of intervention which will be satisfactory in the long run' (Slichter 1934, p. 187). To maintain a successful programme of intervention in the market economy, government had to appreciate 'the crucial importance of profits under a system of capitalism.' That appreciation would be hard to come by because other interest groups – Slichter referred to workers and farmers – were not 'likely to find that the stabilization of profits is of special concern to them' (Slichter 1934, p. 198).

Slichter's dour outlook on the future of government intervention points to a problem of going halfway to a moral economy. In a moral economy everyone takes or is compelled to take the community's interest as paramount and all decisions can be made with the general welfare in mind. In the mixed economy, where there is government intervention, unless someone is in charge who takes the general welfare as paramount and who can impose acceptance of the plans for maximizing the general welfare on all the disparate groups that comprise society, the moral economy will be difficult to achieve and moral imperatives will turn into moral hazards.

HARVARD ECONOMISTS DEFEND THE MARKET ECONOMY

In much of our study of the Progressive Era and the New Deal our attention has been focused on advocates of the moral economy over the market economy. We must be sceptical, however, in inferring that the views of those advocates were widely accepted in the economics profession. To bolster this scepticism, we now turn to a series of essays on the New Deal policies produced by economists from the Harvard University economics department in 1934 with the title, *The Economics of the Recovery Program*.

The lead essay by Joseph Schumpeter asked, 'Can we learn from past experience?' As described in Chapter 4, Schumpeter had used the process of creative destruction to explain economic development. Innovations in the form of new products or new methods of production had a twofold impact on the structure of the economy: they created new industries and destroyed older ones. Schumpeter placed these newer and more productive ways of producing 'at the bottom of the recurrent troubles of the capitalist system,' adding that they were temporary. He continued,

> They are the means to reconstruct each time the economic system on a more efficient plan. But they inflict losses while they last, drive firms into bankruptcy court, throw people out of employment, before the ground is clear and the way paved for new achievement of the kind which has created modern civilization. (Schumpeter 1934 [1968], p. 13)

This process would take place regardless of the errors of businessmen or of their moral behaviour. Errors and immoral behaviour did not cause depressions, the process of creative destruction did.

Schumpeter doubted that the government could do much to mitigate the losses inflicted by creative destruction and what it did was detrimental to ending a depression. He reviewed several depressions of the nineteenth century and drew his lessons from them. First, while the market economy was not perfect, one of its traits was that it was sensitive to political interference. Schumpeter observed, 'Nothing prevents recovery as effectively as fear of political action' (Schumpeter 1934 [1968], p. 4). Second, the process of creative destruction must be allowed to run its course. It was within the ability of government to provide relief to the needy during a depression, but 'the inaction of the government, however reprehensible on humanitarian grounds' was the best way to bring about a recovery (Schumpeter 1934 [1968], p. 7). During the Great Depression, as distinct from earlier depressions, Schumpeter insisted, 'non-economic causes play the dominant role in its drama' (Schumpeter 1934 [1968], p. 15). It was political action in the form of a recovery programme that prolonged the depression.

Schumpeter did not mention specific examples of the types of political actions that prolonged the depression, but he probably had policies like the NIRA in mind. For example, the NRA codes, by fixing prices and establishing quotas of production, endeavoured to retain the status quo of every industry and thus prevented creative destruction from taking its toll. Limiting the hours that machines could be used per week would not motivate anyone to innovate new methods of production. Unfortunately, Schumpeter wrote, depressions brought about 'reforms of institutions not intended to remedy the situation but suggested by the moral and economic evils of both booms and depressions' (Schumpeter 1934 [1968], p. 17). More to the point, businessmen sought those reforms as avidly as politicians as a way to get themselves out of their weakened position and to help them avoid taking the losses creative destruction inflicted on them. Although Schumpeter did not state this criticism of the NIRA, he surely implied it.

Schumpeter's implicit criticism of the NIRA was made explicit in the next essay in the book. Edward S. Mason (1899–1992) took direct aim at the NIRA in his essay titled 'Controlling industry.' On Mason's account, the NIRA aimed at increasing the purchasing power of labour, albeit at an increased cost of production for business. In return, business would receive increased demand for its products and protection from the anti-trust laws and unfair competition. As far as business was concerned, there was nothing new in these proposals, for they had been advocating in favour of them well before the New Deal existed. The New Deal simply used this business advocacy for political purposes by seeking the relaxation of anti-trust laws in the NIRA. Mason noted that this 'was a politically necessary segment of the National Industrial Recovery Act' (Mason 1934 [1968], p. 39).

The issue was whether business was making a Faustian bargain by subjecting itself to government control. None of the programmes for cooperation by business that had been set forth, such as the Swope Plan, contemplated government control; they would rely on businessmen acting morally. If businesses were left alone to organize their industries under the NIRA, their organizations might become permanent and thereby establish a vested interest that would be hard to displace. Mason observed, 'Our economic history is not lacking in examples of how the interests of particular producers may triumph over the commonweal. The Recovery Act gives promise of bringing this history up to date' (Mason 1934 [1968], p. 41).

The Roosevelt administration officials who spoke of the NIRA did so with a promise that it would deliver a new economic order where there would be a unified approach to economic affairs that was 'guided but not "regimented" by government.' Mason admitted the strong appeal of the catchphrases used to describe the NIRA such as calling it a 'cooperative effort' (Mason [1934] 1968, p. 42). The question was whether the NIRA could deliver on the ideas behind those catchphrases.

Mason then reviewed the evils that the NIRA was intended to address: unfair competition and the absence of planning of the overall economy. The problem with addressing unfair competition was that it was not easy to define. Certain types of competition were illegal under common law or under regulation of the Federal Trade Commission; still, they had not been eradicated. The NIRA codes listed unfair practices to be outlawed, many of which were specific to individual industries. Some of them were simply standard measures of competition. Indeed, Mason believed, 'By cut-throat competition business men oftentimes mean nothing more alarming than the selling of competing products at prices less than their own' (Mason 1934 [1968], p. 51). To the extent that the NIRA did eliminate unfair practices, Mason believed it would fulfil what to him was 'the sole justification of the Recovery Act' (Mason 1934 [1968], p. 47).

As for the planning elements of the NIRA, Mason noted that there was nothing in it that took legal steps towards planning. Many of the Roosevelt administration's spokesmen hinted that the NIRA would replace the market economy with planning. Moreover, all the codes included 'a planning committee whose function is the collection of the data necessary to the regulation of supply to demand' in each industry. At the same time, the NRA had a planning commission that could combine all the collected data from each industry to produce 'a balanced plan for the whole economy' (Mason 1934 [1968], p. 57). From the writings and speeches of high administration officials, Mason inferred that 'a strong group of Presidential advisors has the ideal of a planned economy close at heart' and they saw the NIRA as the best way to achieve planning (Mason 1934 [1968], p. 58). The problem was that the achievement of such planning would not work, because the data needed for planning to take place was not and could not be collected. Consumer demand was always changing, and some industries were declining; government could not stop these events from happening and efforts to try might well prevent new industries from emerging.

Planning would also have to allocate capital. Mason admitted that businesses had made many errors in how they used capital during the 1920s. These errors resulted from the problem that capital spending decisions were based on estimates of future economic conditions and it was only after the future did not live up to those expectations that it could be seen that errors had been made. The market economy was a ruthless corrector of those errors and Mason doubted that the government could do as well. He asked, 'Is it reasonable to suppose that a government bureau will be apt to make a sounder guess on the future currents of trade than the individual or institutional investor?' (Mason 1934 [1968], p. 61) If the government took on this responsibility, who would correct its errors?

In the final essay by a member of the Harvard economics department that we consider here, Douglass V. Brown took up the issue of 'helping labor.' He was especially concerned to combat the idea of 'work sharing' that he felt permeated the New Deal policies and the efforts of the NRA to set limits on working hours. He described the idea of work sharing as follows: 'For at least a hundred years the idea that unemployment arises from "not enough work to go around" has enjoyed intermittent popularity. What could be simpler than to cut the number of hours worked by each person to such a point that there will be enough to go around?' (Brown 1934 [1968], p. 70).

Brown found three faults with this idea. First, the process of work sharing would reduce the income of workers with jobs. No one, he continued, would accept a policy where one part of the working force had to relinquish a portion of its income to support another part that was not working. But work sharing came close to this, because it meant income sharing. Second, work sharing could potentially reduce national output and income. On Brown's reasoning, the workers with jobs were the best qualified parts of the labour force, given that businesses would lay off their least effective workers during a recession. Under work sharing, the hours of work gained by the unemployed would be less productive than the hours taken away from those asked to share their work. If total hours worked under work sharing were the same as before, total output would decline (Brown 1934 [1968], pp. 71–4). Third, the NIRA codes included provisions setting maximum hours to be worked in a week in order to increase employment. These provisions had an intention of increasing the purchasing power of workers, but Brown wondered how work sharing could increase total purchasing power if the total income of labour was merely shared rather than increased.

When looking at the other elements of the NIRA codes, Brown was equally sceptical about their efficacy. Efforts to raise wages would either increase business costs and cause additional unemployment or would result in higher prices and no addition to purchasing power. If workers were being exploited with low wages, an increase in wages might not cause unemployment. Brown argued that the sign of exploitation was high profits for business and since no business was earning high profits during the depression it was unlikely that they were exploiting their workers. More likely, efforts to implement a minimum wage, as the NIRA required, would be difficult to enforce. And if they were enforced, the higher wages for low-paid workers might come at the cost of higher-paid workers who could be 'discharged and rehired at a lower classification' (Brown 1934 [1968], p. 83).

Brown took a more positive outlook on other labour provisions of the NIRA. He applauded its provisions to eliminate child labour but indicated that they would be difficult to enforce. Regarding the NIRA's provisions for enhancing the formation of unions, Brown noted, 'Almost all students of labor problems are in agreement that wisely led organizations for collective bargaining can do much, not only for the economic and social betterment of labor, but also for the general improvement of the general welfare of the community' (Brown 1934 [1968], p. 85). Not many workers were organized into unions, but the labour provisions of Section 7A of the NIRA 'seem to assure a golden age for labor organizations' (Brown 1934 [1968], p. 86). Brown doubted that this golden age would take place. First, business could circumvent the rules of Section 7A by firing workers not for promoting a union but on the grounds of their inefficiency as workers. Second, workers would not join unions unless they were confident that they would gain from union membership and Brown believed that the 'leadership in American trade unions during the last decade has not inspired such confidence' (Brown 1934 [1968], p. 87). Union leaders had been corrupt and the old-line craft unions were not geared for signing up industrial workers to their ranks, assuming they even wanted to do so. As a result of all these difficulties in the methods being pursued by the New Deal through the NIRA in its efforts to help labour, Brown concluded that they would not work.

THE US CHAMBER OF COMMERCE HAS PROBLEMS WITH THE NRA

We saw in Chapter 9 that the US Chamber of Commerce supported many features of the NIRA, especially those elements that the writers in its journal *Nation's Business* construed as eliminating 'unfair competition' and helping businesses organize industry cooperation. Not every writer in *Nation's Business* supported the NRA codes of fair competition.

In December 1933 Forrest Q. Walker, economist for R.H. Macy, the retailing giant, referred to the NIRA as 'Price fixing via code.' The problem with the NIRA approach, according to Walker, was that it used terms that were not easily defined, such as cut-throat competition, to justify price-fixing. Walker made it clear that he thought price-fixing was a dangerous policy by writing, 'Price fixing by law was tried in many countries but the result was economic disaster.' To bolster his argument that prevention of 'cut-throat competition' was a guise for price-fixing, Walker asked just what it meant. Did it mean that a manufacturer who did not pay low wages but used advanced methods of production to reduce costs was a ruthless cut-throat? Were such strategies as 'loss leaders' an example of cut-throat competition or were they another form of advertising? The only point Walker would concede was that charges of unfair price cutting indicated 'objection to the practice by some one' (Walker 1933, pp. 39–40).

As time went on and business gained experience in working with the NIRA, the tone of approval for NIRA programmes in *Nation's Business* diminished. In September 1934, for example, Henry I. Harriman, president of the Chamber, presented an article on 'The future of the NRA.' The issue that really troubled Harriman and business about the NIRA was Section 7A. Section 7A guaranteed workers the right to collective bargaining by their chosen representatives and Harriman agreed with this guarantee. He also agreed that the right of workers to choose representatives with no interference by employers was important. He added, however, that workers 'be free from the coercive influence of labor unions or others.' Moreover, the right of the employer to hire whomever he wanted was a property right protected by the Fifth Amendment to the Constitution that prohibited the taking of property without due process. Therefore, he advised that any revisions of the NIRA include provisions that protected workers who wanted to organize unions from interference by employers and by unions and that did not place any limits on 'the right of an employer or of an employee to decide with whom he will enter into employment relations' (Harriman 1934, pp. 66–7).

This shift in the degree of approval the Chamber accorded to the NIRA may have reflected the possibility that the rank-and-file members of the Chamber were not as enthusiastic about the NIRA as the Chamber's leaders. In April 1935, in an article titled 'Two views of NIRA,' *Nation's Business* reported, 'A referendum vote by the member organizations of the US Chamber of Commerce showed a great majority favoring NRA's demise.' The article added, however, that this vote should not be taken to mean that everything the NRA had done was worthless. Rather, it meant that the NIRA needed to be revised to remove local business from the authority of the NRA, to let industry codes be approved or disapproved by the NRA but not let the NRA substitute its own codes and to modify Section 7A along lines proposed by Harriman as just noted. These revisions to the NIRA had been approved by the referendum of the Chamber's member organizations ('Two views of NIRA,' 1935, p. 66). The campaign for revisions to the NIRA was also contained in another article in *Nation's Business* in April 1935, (*Nation's Business* 1935, p. 69).

In June 1935 *Nation's Business* revisited the issues surrounding Section 7A of the NIRA in an article by Paul Hayward, *Nation's Business (1935)* According to Hayward, as soon as the NIRA and Section 7A were passed, the US went through a period of heightened industrial strife as workers used it to organize unions. Since the avowed purpose of the NIRA had been to enable management and labour to take combined action to increase employment, the period of strikes indicated that this purpose was being confounded. Much of the problem was that Section 7A was too vague to determine just what the union policy was, and several industry codes had interpreted it differently. The Labor Advisory Board had powers that were generally undefined. Senator Robert Wagner was introducing his Labor Relations Act (see Chapter 11) to remedy some of these problems, but Hayward argued that employers did not agree with the underlying assumption of the Wagner bill that labour and management were antagonistic and that management had superior bargaining power. He added that the Chamber had passed a resolution that said, 'Proposals such as those embodied in the labor relations bill would operate to disrupt rather than to promote proper relations between employer and employee and likewise retard the normal processes toward recovery' (Hayward 1935, p. 57).

In terms of our theme of the moral economy versus the market economy, the leaders of the US Chamber and the writers in *Nation's Business* took an ambivalent approach. We saw in Chapter 9 that they accepted some features of the New Deal and the NIRA that eliminated the supposedly immoral practices of unfair competition. Regarding relations between labour and management, however, the articles cited admitted little immoral behaviour on the part of business and where there was immoral behaviour, it was just as likely to come from unions as from business. The labour provisions of the NIRA, by putting government on the side of unions, were causing a moral hazard.

BROOKINGS REVIEWS THE NRA

Originally formed in 1916, the Brookings Institution is one of the oldest 'think tanks' in the US with a mission of investigating national policy issues. In 1935 the Brookings Institution took on the NRA in a lengthy (947 pages) study, *The National Recovery Administration: An Analysis and Appraisal* written by six policy analysts (Lyon et al. 1935).

Part I of the study took a look at the overall goal of the NRA as set forth in the NIRA. It quoted President Roosevelt as calling the NIRA 'the most important and far-reaching legislation ever enacted by the American Congress' and characterizing it as 'a supreme effort to stabilize for all time the many factors which make for the prosperity of the nation.' To do so, the law had a goal of 'the assurance of a reasonable profit to industry and living wages for labor' (Lyon et al. 1935, p. 3). This goal was consistent with the idea of a moral economy and the Brookings' scholars recognized that the citizens of the US were ready for heroic measures that included the federal government taking charge of economic revival. 'Most general in nature,' they added, 'was the much discussed concept of economic planning,' which would 'increase the amount of collective economic control' (Lyon et al. 1935, p. 4). Not everyone supported a complete system of national economic planning but it was felt that there was a need for greater planning in the economy. The Brookings' scholars indicated that this need for planning was to some degree due to a perception of a 'lack of balance' in the economy between production and consumption. The imbalance was caused in part by certain 'sick industries' and planning would help those industries and restore balance to the economy. The lack of balance was also viewed as being brought about in part by the predatory competition of individual businesses, with collective control over them being necessary for balance to be attained (Lyon et al. 1935, pp. 5–6).

The NIRA was set forth as a rapid response for the emergency and in a way where it became 'all things to all men.' The immediate goal of the NIRA was economic recovery with a secondary goal of economic reform, which the study referred to as a policy of 'recovery through reform.' The NIRA's labour components of shorter hours and higher pay had been sought by unions for decades during periods of prosperity as well as depressions. Business had long wanted relief from the anti-trust laws and now an emergency gave it to them (Lyon et al. 1935, pp. 751–2). Indeed, the Brookings' scholars gave prominence to the gains to business through the easing of anti-trust laws as a fundamental impetus for the NIRA (Lyon et al. 1935, pp. 20–21).

Part II of the study on the administration of the NIRA by the NRA detailed that within two years the NRA created a wide array of industry codes that were supposed to be written by collaboration of all elements of an industry and with everyone agreeing on the code there would be widespread compliance with it and little need for 'the coercive force of legal penalties' (Lyon et al. 1935, p. 58). Consequently, the NRA paid scant attention to enforcement, but the codes it approved did not always have the desired effect of securing support from members of an industry. Some businesses entered into codes to be exempt from the anti-trust laws, others became part of the code system through 'governmental coercion' and still others joined in with the hope of somehow gaining from the general promise of increased purchasing power. The Brookings' scholars nevertheless concluded that 'the expectation of "improving" prices by collective action among competitors was the central motivating force' behind business going along with the NRA codes (Lyon et al. 1935, p. 94).

Part III of the study dealt with labour provisions of the NIRA. The purpose of the labour provisions was to reduce unemployment and increase wages with a goal of providing everyone with 'living wages' and increasing the purchasing power of labour (Lyon et al. 1935, p. 303). The Brookings' scholars cited President Roosevelt for the philosophy of the labour codes as follows, 'The idea is simply for employers to hire more men to do the existing work by reducing the hours of each man's week at the same time paying a living wage for the shorter work week' (Lyon et al. 1935, p. 343). The problem the NRA faced in writing labour codes for wages, however, was that the wage structure was more complex than this simple idea seemed to indicate. Differences in wages existed due to geography and in terms of skill level, occupation and industry standards and once the NRA codes started changing some wages, the impact would be felt everywhere. What was needed was the regulation of all prices through planning. But the NRA was not a method for regulation of all prices in a coordinated way. As a result, the Brookings' scholars concluded, 'with few exceptions the handling of classes of wages above the minimum was and is inept' (Lyon et al. 1935, p. 364).

In Part IV on industrial relations the Brookings' scholars pointed out that the NIRA had three goals: minimum wage and maximum hour provisions consistent with fairness; collective bargaining as a legal right for workers; and mutual cooperation between management and labour. The last two goals were connected, with collective bargaining by labour acting as an impetus for better industrial relations and mutual cooperation. Working together, unions and business would bring about reduced work and higher wages under a premise 'that prosperity based on higher wages and shorter hours would be an enduring prosperity' (Lyon et al. 1935, p. 415). While the implication of the NIRA was that the federal government might regulate wages, the guiding intention was that by bringing about more equality of bargaining power between labour and management, collective bargaining would work in place of government. The Brookings' scholars found a fundamental conflict in this approach. The promotion of collective bargaining was a long-term structural reform in the market economy, while the economic recovery required short-term adjustments.

Part V of the study looked at the issue of the trade practice problem. The NIRA was indicative of Congress' stated aim 'to eliminate unfair competitive practices.' In signing the NIRA, President Roosevelt had said it would mean the 'elimination of piratical methods' and 'civilize industry.' In considering these worthy intentions of creating a moral economy, the Brookings' scholars observed:

> There is, in many quarters, an easy going assumption that it is easy to distinguish
> between the fair and the unfair; that a mere reference to 'unethical competition'
> or 'dishonorable' competition provides in itself the criteria of judging what is

'unethical' or what is 'dishonorable.' The history of six centuries of common law, the enactment of a large number of federal and state statutes, and the efforts of the Federal Trade Commission have all indicated the fallacy of this view. It has again been demonstrated by the experience of the NRA. (Lyon et al. 1935, p. 551)

The difficulty in resolving the issues surrounding the new morality for business was one of solving the 'larger problem of social justice' in the context of the traditional values of the US with their emphasis on individual liberty along with social responsibility. These values also had to deal with a market economy that was constantly changing (Lyon et al. 1935, pp. 552–3).

In the market economy businesses were always seeking a competitive advantage that would increase their profits. Any method that gave one business a competitive advantage might serve to harm another business, causing the sort of conflicts and cries of unethical behaviour that the NRA was being called on to resolve. Businesses often complained about 'losing the competitive advantages which they once held' and government agencies might decree that some business behaviour was 'detrimental to the public interest.' Consumers and labour might also complain and determining 'what is right, equitable, or fair' depended on whose standards were used (Lyon et al. 1935, p. 557).

Having presented evidence that the reform aspects of the NIRA had not worked, the Brookings' scholars in Part VI of their study considered whether it had succeeded as an economic recovery measure. They offered a summary of three ideas they attributed to advocates of the NIRA on how to end the depression: increase the purchasing power of labour through higher wages; eliminate the downward spiral of wages due to wage-cutting by business; and end ruinous price competition by business. They gave promi-nence to the idea of the need to increase the purchasing power of labour, however. To them, the purchasing power approach meant that businesses had to raise wages. Higher wages would translate into higher demand for goods and the expansion of production that required even more labour, creating an 'ascending spiral of recovery' (Lyon et al. 1935, pp. 757–8). The catch was that businesses needed to keep from raising their prices as fast as they raised wages. The Brookings' scholars cited President Roosevelt as arguing,

> I am fully aware that wage increases will eventually raise costs, but I ask that managements give first consideration to the improvement of operating figures by greatly increased sales to be expected from the rising purchasing power of the public.... If we now inflate prices as fast and as far as we increase wages, the whole project will be set at naught. (Lyon et al. 1935, p. 758)

The entire functioning of the NRA required that price increases lag behind wage increases; the expansion of sales would lower costs per unit and reduce the need for price increases.

The Brookings' scholars, however, argued that without higher prices businesses would not have the funds to increase wages. They considered how business could pay the higher wages through cutting down other expenses, and found none of their possibilities was feasible (Lyon et al. 1935, p. 769). The Brookings' scholars concluded, 'In so far as the NRA purchasing power theory called for a general increase in income of employees at the expense of the earnings of employers, it was, we believe, ill suited to the conditions prevailing when it was advanced' (Lyon et al. 1935, p. 771).

The Brookings' scholars then looked at what had happened to wages and prices under the NRA. To do so, they first put the NRA in a context of what had happened to wages and prices in the first four years of the depression. They found that from 1929 to 1933 prices had declined faster than wages from Hoover's exhorting business to hold the line on wages with the result that 'average real earnings per hour were higher in the first half of 1933 than in 1929' in most of the industries they surveyed (Lyon et al. 1935, p. 779). The problem of the depression was that many workers were not putting in full-time work at those higher real hourly wages. 'It did not seem to occur to the NRA,' the Brookings' scholars continued, 'that in some cases wage rates might be too high instead of too low.' Instead, the NRA seemed to assume 'that employers would buy more labor at a high price than at a low one' (Lyon et al. 1935, p. 782).

Increased wages meant that businesses had to raise their prices. The Brookings' scholars found that the control over prices that the NRA gave businesses allowed them to continue to raise prices to pay for higher wages in some cases and in advance of wage increases in other cases. This meant that 'the NRA raised hourly wage rates for some classes of employees by more than it raised living costs' but 'for other classes it raised the cost of living without any increase in compensation' (Lyon et al. 1935, p. 785). One group was benefited at the cost of another, but what was the overall impact? A review of the aggregate data on wages and prices showed that 'the codes apparently raised living costs on the whole concurrently with, or even in advance of, the hourly earnings of workers' (Lyon et al. 1935, p. 788). The Brookings' scholars summed up the dilemma of the NRA as follows: 'One group of workers may improve its relative position by higher wage rates and one industry may benefit itself by higher prices, but this is merely because wages and prices are not similarly raised elsewhere. When the game is played universally it is self-defeating' (Lyon et al. 1935, p. 808). The NRA efforts to put a floor under wages and prices very likely reduced production in the economy and prolonged the depression.

As a result of all of their analyses of the NRA, the Brookings' scholars' overall conclusion was that while the NIRA had granted President Roosevelt and his administration unprecedented power over the economy, 'the NRA on the whole retarded recovery' (Lyon et al. 1935, p. 873). In reaching this conclusion we may readily infer that they retained a belief in the benefits of the market economy over the moral economy. We may do more than infer, however, because at one point the Brookings' scholars did directly, albeit briefly, state their overriding concern with the entire programme of the New Deal and the NRA. They wrote:

> We have at present no knowledge that justifies us in using government regulation to check the amount of capital, labor, or natural resources that should flow into one industry rather into others. Sufficient study might reveal instances in which such regulation would be socially useful, but control should not be undertaken until such studies are made. If found socially desirable the serious administrative problems of such control should be faced before control is undertaken. (Lyon et al. 1935, p. 650)

The NRA had neither produced a study of the social usefulness of its regulations nor faced up to the difficulties of the design and administration of its codes being in the control of special interests groups predominantly from business but also from labour unions. None of these special interest groups had the fibre to realize the moral economy.

WALTER LIPPMANN AND THE NEW ROLE OF GOVERNMENT

Walter Lippmann had a career of over 50 years as a respected commentator on current events. His commentary, however, did not always present a consistent theme. We saw in Chapter 5 that in his earliest years he wrote ardently in support of government planning of the economy as a way to replace drift with mastery, while a decade later he believed that managerial capitalism in the form of well-run corporations was doing what was needed for keeping the economy stable. As the Great Depression and the government policies to combat it unfolded, he again switched gears and analysed what was being done by the government and how it could be justified.

One of his efforts at analysis was presented in a small book, *The New Imperative*, which he published in 1935. His first task was to explain what the new imperative of government was. He described it as the government holding 'itself consciously responsible for the maintenance of the standard

of life among the people' (Lippmann 1935, p. 1). Some might argue that this
new imperative was asking too much from government, but Lippmann
believed that government leaders had 'to attempt it whether or not they
succeed' (Lippmann 1935, p. 3). Others argued that in making this attempt,
the government was following the lead of Europe, as exemplified by either
communism or fascism. That was not the case, he insisted, because in the
US 'we are evolving a method of social control that is not that of laissez
faire and is not that of a planned and directed economy' (Lippmann 1935,
p. 7).

The new imperative was a break with the past in the US and Lippmann
went to great lengths to demonstrate that many of the changes it brought
about were initiated by Hoover and not Roosevelt. He found the two
presidents to be much closer to each other than either of them was to the
presidents before them. Moreover, he believed that Hoover's 'historic
position as an innovator has been greatly underestimated and that Mr.
Roosevelt's pioneering has been greatly exaggerated' (Lippmann 1935,
p. 13). He highlighted many of Hoover's policies and indicated that
Roosevelt had merely followed them.

One surprising case of this continuation of Hoover's policies by
Roosevelt was the NIRA, although a careful reader of our previous chapters
will not be totally surprised. Lippmann described the continuity as follows:

> As regards their relations to industry, if we strip the NRA of its ballyhoo, of the
> more or less unenforceable and unenforced labor provisions, we find the trade
> associations (which Mr. Hoover did so much to promote as Secretary of
> Commerce) freed of the menace of the anti-trust laws (which Mr. Hoover as
> President did so little to enforce). The NRA extended the principle of organ-
> ization to industries and trades that had not been organized previously. It
> tightened up the organization all along the lines. It made price-fixing and
> production control and marketing quotas more general, more effective, more
> respectable. (Lippmann 1935, p. 26)

To Lippmann, the NIRA made legal what had been a commonly accepted
practice by business long before Roosevelt took office and even its wage
policies followed a course set by Hoover.

The real radical was Hoover and the precedents he had set in 1929–30 in
making the government responsible for controlling business cycles, which
made it 'inconceivable that any of his successors should in another depression refuse to act' (Lippmann 1935, p. 35). Lippmann made it clear that he
did not necessarily agree with what Hoover and Roosevelt had done to
rescue the economy, but only that they had responded to the overarching

issue of whether the market economy could 'be preserved in working equilibrium by the compensatory action of the state' (Lippmann 1935, p. 37).

The market economy was ended, according to Lippmann, and his question was what would replace it. In looking at options, he indicated that he would 'rather have economic liberty than centralized direction and command' (Lippmann 1935, p. 48). As a result, he was not arguing that 'all social arrangements should be planned and directed by a highly centralized government' (Lippmann 1935, p. 49). He was in the camp that found government not to have the wisdom to be given that much power. He added, 'If we are not to be swallowed by an imperious state socialism in some of its many possible forms, then we have to govern successfully this capitalist democracy' (Lippmann 1935, p. 50). Lack of governing meant the drift that Lippmann warned of 20 years earlier. In place of the drift there must be a government that attained balance in the economy. Lippmann did not indicate that the New Deal was attaining that balance, but his finding that the NIRA represented a continuity between Hoover and Roosevelt can be taken as his indication that the New Deal was not as radical as many Americans thought.

STANDING UP FOR SMALL BUSINESS

In January 1935 *Congressional Digest* published two short articles on small business and the NIRA. The first, by Mark Sullivan, presented a case for differential treatment of small business by the NRA. Sullivan pointed out that what 'Mr. [Gerard] Swope might assent to in NRA might be bitterly rejected by the small business man.' Indeed, he continued, 'the policies of the New Deal tend to foster big business and harm little business.' The owners of small business were the last bastion of rugged individualism and the 'tendency to exterminate him by Government policies' was tragic. As evidence of that tragedy, Sullivan gave an example of an entrepreneur who sought to enter the ice business in a small town only to be turned down by an NRA appeals committee 'made up of three men already in the ice manufacturing industry.' In a second case the owner of a small chemical plant had to shut down because the NRA code for wages and hours doubled his costs. Sullivan called this type of programme one of oppression and cited one businessman writing to him that 'there is no more fear of Mussolini or of Hitler than we have of our own Government' (Sullivan 1935, pp. 22–3).

The same story was told in a second article on small business owners by Owen L. Scott. One such businessman who owned a large department store found that he had to increase the number of workers he employed to comply with the NRA hours codes, which increased his costs. The higher prices the codes offered him did not help because consumers began making purchases from catalogue outlets and smaller retail stores that were exempt from the NRA codes. He explained his problems to an NRA administrator who brushed him off with a comment, 'I never was interested in figures.' Meanwhile, he had to pay assessments 'for the support of the code authority' (Scott 1935, p. 23).

Both these articles tell the story of the difficulties owners of small business had in complying with the governmental regulations of the NIRA. Apparently there was no place in the moral economy for the individualism and freedom of action necessary for small business owners to survive. These cases are of particular interest, because it was the prosecution of the Schechters, owners of a small business, which led to the demise of the NRA, as we shall discuss in the next chapter.

CONCLUSION

The market perspective presented in the chapter recognized that some regulation of the market economy was necessary, but that the NIRA and the NRA had gone overboard in the regulations that the New Deal put in place. Their overall complaint, set forth by Slichter and the Brookings Study, was that the NRA codes greatly impeded the working of the market economy by reducing the flexibility of wages and prices to respond to market conditions. While never mentioned directly, they had in mind Say's Law where price changes upward in some industries and downward in others had been allowed to take place to get the economy back on track. The Brookings Study, for example, found that before the NIRA price declines had been allowed but wages had lagged behind, causing the real wages of workers to increase and profits to decline. By adjusting the policy through holding prices steady while increasing wages, the overall intent of the NIRA, curing underconsumption, remained contradictory. Profits would still decline and recovery would be thwarted.

The NIRA and the NRA codes also impeded another aspect of the market economy, the process of creative destruction. Schumpeter took the lead in making this charge, which included the idea that creative destruction also required the type of price adjustments that the NRA was forestalling. The goal of the NRA was reputedly to eliminate unfair competition, but Slichter, Mason and the Brookings Study argued that unfair competition was difficult to identify. Rather, the charge of unfair competition was often used by businesses to combat the way they were being harmed by the process of creative destruction. Government might respond to those charges because it was always listening to the pleading of special interest groups for targeted protection of their particular segment of the market economy. When the government intervened in the market economy at the behest of a special interest group, it crossed the line of what constituted legitimate regulation.

The advocates for the market economy also questioned whether overall regulation of the economy through planning could be effective. Slichter and Mason pointed out the difficulty planners would have in keeping up with ever changing demand conditions in the marketplace and the Brookings Study added that potential planners at the NRA overlooked how complex the wage structure of the market economy was. Its system of connecting its many parts by prices meant that if planners controlled one price, they would eventually have to control all prices, but market prices changed much too often from changes in demand and supply to be easily controlled. Even Lippmann, who had been an advocate of the planning of the moral economy, had become sceptical about the ability of the government to undertake the centralized planning of state socialism.

We saw in Chapter 9 that advocates for the moral economy attributed the Great Depression to a failure of the market economy. In this chapter the proponents of the market economy argued that in light of all the intervention in the economy by Hoover and then Roosevelt, it would be hard to place blame on the market economy and the real cause of the severity and duration of the depressions was the government programmes of the moral economy. As Lippmann recognized, government leaders felt a political imperative to do something to manage the market economy even though no one had devised a policy to do that effectively. Hoover had ended for all time the idea that the federal government would take a hands-off approach to the economy and Roosevelt had seconded him, despite the contrary evidence offered by market economists surveyed in this chapter.

11. The aftermath of the National Industrial Recovery Act

From 1933 to 1935 the NIRA had a brief but controversial career. We saw in the last two chapters how controversial it was, given the many ways in which it was interpreted – ranging from monopoly and fascism to a programme of cooperation by business, government, labour and consumers. Some of our economists, pundits, politicians and business leaders who advocated for the moral economy saw in it a hope for planning while others saw it as a betrayal of planning, depending on their vision of the moral economy. The friends of the market economy saw it as government blundering in the economy in ways that hindered the recovery from the Great Depression.

The controversy over the NIRA abated, to some degree, when the US Supreme Court voided it in 1935 in the Schechter Case. In this chapter we review the efforts that were made to evaluate where the NIRA had worked well and what had gone wrong with it. We start with the Court's decision to find the NIRA unconstitutional.

THE US SUPREME COURT REVIEWS THE NIRA

The US Supreme Court found the NIRA to be unconstitutional in the Schechter Case by a unanimous vote in a decision announced on 27 May 1935. In reviewing the facts of the case, we can see that the Court interpreted the NRA as overly intrusive, with the full weight and power of the federal government brought to bear on a small family business selling chickens. As part of its decision, the Court outlined the facts of the case. The Schechters operated a small wholesale poultry business in Brooklyn, NY, buying chickens in a produce market in New York City and selling them to retail butchers. They were convicted in a New York Federal District Court of 18 counts of violating the 'Live Poultry Code.' The Poultry Code had been established under the NIRA, which authorized the president to approve codes established by an industry association to promote 'fair competition' as long as no one in the industry was kept out of membership in the association and as long as the code did not form a monopoly or 'eliminate or oppress small enterprises.' Failure to comply with the code was a misdemeanour punishable by a fine of up to $500 for each offence and for each day the offence occurred (Schechter 1935, p. 2).

When business groups endeavour to form cartels in order to fix prices and eliminate competition, one of the problems they face is ensuring compliance by all firms in the group and even those not in the group. After all, once the cartel is formed and a price level and production quotas to sustain it are agreed upon, firms in the group have an incentive to cheat by selling at a price lower than the cartel price or selling more than their allotted quota to gain more business. As long as the cartel is voluntary, the firms that abide by the cartel have no means of retaliating against 'cheaters' except to reduce prices themselves, thereby ruining the cartel. The NIRA codes construed such behaviour as unfair competition, and the members of the code authority had legal power to curtail 'cheating' by non-compliant firms by having a US Attorney take them to court. The Schechters were charged with not reporting the range of prices they charged each day and with not adhering to the code's standards for a minimum wage of 50 cents an hour and a maximum work week of 40 hours (Schechter 1935, p. 3).

The Supreme Court recognized that the NIRA did not give a clear definition of 'fair competition' and that its intent was different from the common law definitions of 'fair competition.' It objected to Congress' delegating its legislative authority to define 'fair competition' to the writers of the codes who were often private citizens. Moreover, the Court did not accept the argument that the Schechters were engaged in interstate commerce. But what the Court really objected to was the unprecedented interference by the federal government and its delegates in the operations of business, pointing out that if the federal government could set standards for wages it could also set standards for other costs of business, with the result that 'all the processes of production and distribution that enter into cost could likewise be controlled' (Schechter 1935, p. 9).

The Court accepted that this control was inherent to the nature of the sort of national planning that it assumed to be the intent of the NIRA. It stated in its decision, written by Chief Justice Charles Evans Hughes, 'It is not the province of the Court to consider the economic advantages or disadvantages of such a centralized system. It is sufficient to say that the Federal Constitution does not provide for it' (Schechter 1935, p. 9). Thus, the experiment of national planning under the NIRA ended.

REXFORD TUGWELL EXPLAINS THE POLITICS OF SCHECHTER

Rexford Tugwell had been a confidante of the president for several years when the Schechter decision was reached. He was also likely the staunchest advocate for national economic planning in the New Deal, having called for planning nearly a decade before the New Deal began (see Chapter 6). In his memoir, *Roosevelt's Revolution*, Tugwell defended the NIRA as aspiring for an industrial policy through the cooperation of the components of an industry by 'the making of agreements to eliminate unfair practices among competitors'(Tugwell 1977, p. 80). A key factor in that aspiration, according to Tugwell, was that President Roosevelt had determined, after lengthy thought, that the time had come to develop a system of cooperation by business. The current business system maintained a divisive war with its workers and methods of cheating consumers had become widespread. Businesses did not try to determine what goods were in demand, which led to mistakes in capital allocation and the waste of industry that Tugwell had previously written about. There was a history of trying to bring businesses together through trade associations – Tugwell mentioned Hoover's work in the 1920s, the Swope Plan and Roosevelt's work with the Building Trades Council. From these experiences, the Roosevelt administration knew how to organize industry and Tugwell began working on draft legislation for the NIRA, as did Hugh Johnson. Soon they combined forces, drafted a legislative package and sent it to Congress. Congress modified the recommended legislation greatly, and Tugwell saw the most harmful change in 'the deletion of penalties for non-compliance with the codes of conduct' (Tugwell 1977, p. 81).

When the NIRA came into force, Tugwell anticipated that it would accomplish its mission of stimulating recovery. He found one flaw in its operation. The 'Blue Eagle' badge that was a symbol of compliance was too easily attained by business. As a result, many businesses accepted their 'Blue Eagle' badge of honour 'with the intention of allowing their competitors to comply while they held back' (Tugwell 1977, p. 82). From this flaw he saw the erosion of the effectiveness of the NIRA. Tugwell recognized, at least in his memoirs, that 'unless a firm and steady governmental pressure was exercised, the melee of code making would end by allowing monopolizers to fix prices without restriction. The effect would be just the reverse of what had been intended' (Tugwell 1977, p. 137).

When that reverse effect did take place, Tugwell attributed it to three factors. First, the business lobby remained powerful and Roosevelt could not stand up to it. Second, Johnson turned out to be a poor administrator who approved of codes that he should have sent back to the industry association for revision to eliminate their price-fixing provisions. Third, there were divisions within the Roosevelt administration and among Progressives over the efficacy of the NIRA. Tugwell characterized these divisions as being brought about by the followers of Justice Louis Brandeis. Brandeis had been part of the Wilson administration's pitch to help small business compete with larger firms and he was opposed to 'bigness' in itself. The NIRA was a blatant acceptance of 'bigness' and thus Brandeis was thought not to approve of the NIRA. Roosevelt had looked to Brandeis, when both were part of the Wilson administration, as an exemplary Progressive (Tugwell 1977, pp. 137, 145, 157, 281, 283, 285).

As for Roosevelt's attitude towards the NIRA, Tugwell found him to be torn by his respect for Brandeis and his belief that something like the NIRA was needed. Tugwell cited one speech of the president as indicating that while the NIRA was 'relaxing some of the safeguards of the anti-trust laws' it was protecting the public with 'new government controls' (Tugwell 1977, p. 137). At the same time, he found Roosevelt to be too compliant in giving his final approval to codes that contained monopoly practices and too reluctant to replace Johnson as head of the NRA when it became apparent that he was not up to the job (Tugwell 1977, pp. 147, 197, 279). As a result, Tugwell came to consider the NRA to be 'an uncontrolled riot' (Tugwell 1977, p. 280).

In seeing Brandeis and his followers in the Roosevelt administration as opposed to the NIRA, Tugwell indicated that 'Brandeis was certain that I represented the collectivism he saw in NRA' (Tugwell 1977, p. 284). He saw the Court's decision as Brandeis finally having his way by ending the experiment in collectivism that Tugwell had thought to be vital to the future of the US. As he put it, 'Roosevelt would find out about Brandeis when the court got its first chance at the NRA.' When it did, Brandeis clung to 'stubborn traditionalism' rather than seeing that the economy had changed and needed the collectivism that the NIRA was trying to attain (Tugwell 1977, p. 146).

BERNARD BARUCH QUESTIONS THE NIRA

By the 1930s, the prominent financier and speculator Bernard Baruch had become a stalwart in the Democratic Party, contributing to election campaigns and advising many of its leaders. He had also served the government in World War I by heading up the WIB; one of his connections from the WIB, General Hugh Johnson, became his business associate and good friend (Baruch 1960, p. 240). Once Roosevelt was nominated by the party, he fully supported his candidacy.

Baruch never held a government position during the New Deal, although he was often portrayed as a major influence in the Roosevelt administration. He did meet and offer his advice to the Brains Trust that came up with many of the ideas Roosevelt put into play. It was not clear how well his advice was taken. Baruch characterized himself as believing that government policies for ending the depression had to be based on solid economics, including a balanced federal government budget. He stated his overriding view as follows, 'Although I believe that government has a vital role to play in regulating the economy, and although I reject the outworn dogmas of laissez faire, I do not believe that government can decree prosperity or legislate us out of the consequences of our folly' (Baruch 1960, p. 244).

Where would he have placed the NIRA in this overriding view? Baruch noted that his experiences with the WIB made him interested in the notion of 'industrial cooperation under government controls for the public good' (Baruch 1960, p. 251). Consequently, he had advocated for something like the NIRA during the early years of the depression, before Roosevelt took office. Because several of his colleagues from the WIB, Johnson and Swope, had been instrumental in writing the legislation of the NIRA and administering it, Baruch often became viewed as aligned with it. To him, however, 'the NRA fell far short of its goal,' and he 'was often unhappy with the measures adopted by the NRA' (Baruch 1960, p. 252). The problem was that the NRA tried to do too much and in its efforts to end the depression forgot the lesson of the WIB that it was best to leave things alone that were working well. Baruch observed, 'moderation is not easy to follow in times of stress.' Government intervention would never suffice to bring about economic recovery. He added that government policies would not work 'until we pass a fiat changing the law of supply and demand' (Baruch 1960, p. 253).

What most concerned Baruch was that the New Deal might cause the US citizenry to lose its character and ability to take care of itself. This concern related to his observation that New Dealers had a maternalistic vision of government as a friendly place to which citizens could turn for help with any problem. He warned, 'When mature men rely on government to take care of them, they renounce their independence' (Baruch 1960, p. 254). Such a government would stifle initiative and diminish human incentive.

In holding this concern, Baruch took aim at the moral economy. In his utopia Bellamy had determined that human beings would take the initiative regardless of the incentives they were given to do so. But a dilemma of the moral economy, with its basis in household economics, is that one must ultimately leave the household with its beneficent parents and become an independent economic agent. That was why Baruch talked of 'mature men' who should not rely on government to solve all of their problems, and especially not the problems that the NIRA was designed to solve. In the end, Baruch remained where his business interests had led him, as an advocate of the market economy, and in his memoirs he candidly wrote, 'the fact remains that the New Deal did not end the depression' (Baruch 1960, pp. 256–7).

SENATOR ROBERT WAGNER, THE NIRA AND THE CONSTITUTION

Robert F. Wagner (1877–1953) was a career politician in New York City who served as senator from 1927 to 1949. He was a staunch New Dealer and participated in the drafting of the NIRA. In a radio broadcast on 13 June 1935 Wagner defended the NIRA in the aftermath of its being declared unconstitutional by the Supreme Court. He began his defence by describing the conditions of harsh competition that had existed before the NIRA and the damage it was doing to the economy. The main problem to bringing about a recovery was 'an outworn philosophy of government' that only allowed the federal government to regulate interstate commerce, narrowly construed. The NIRA expanded that philosophy and gave business 'an opportunity to bring order out of chaos, to manufacture and sell goods with a better knowledge of the market, and to restrain the demoralizing practices of the price slasher and the wage cutter.' The results had proved the value of the NIRA and Wagner found it 'unthinkable that in the face of these results, we should return to the destructive planlessness which existed' before the NIRA (Wagner 1935c, pp. 636–7).

The Supreme Court had made its decision in the Schechter Case and Wagner did not dispute its reasoning. Rather, he found the Court to have helped the NIRA by criticizing its wrongful delegation of power. But that error could be corrected. The Court's decision did not mean that the federal government had to accept the dire consequences a lack of action would bring. Wagner cited many letters he had been sent by owners of small business asking him to restore the good the NRA had achieved. Congress had responded by extending the NIRA to give it a chance to readjust to the Court's criticism and by starting the process to codify Section 7A of the NIRA through new legislation – what eventually became the National Labor Relations Act (see below). It was important to keep up the fight started with the NIRA to ensure 'the protection of the human element in industry,' to uphold 'a fair level of wages' and to stabilize business. These approaches to economic reform were 'the instrumentalities for social justice' and were not the concern of any one political party but 'the cause of humanitarianism in America' (Wagner 1935c, p. 639).

THE NEW REPUBLIC CHASTENS ROOSEVELT OVER THE NIRA

The New Republic had been a steady voice of Progressives for two decades prior to the New Deal and its editors had supported the cause of planning for most of that time. It took an ambivalent attitude towards the NIRA, finding it to be a positive approach to the economic recovery, albeit a confused and often counterproductive one.

When the US Supreme Court overthrew the NIRA in the Schechter decision, *The New Republic* took a closer look at the constitutional system in an article on 12 June 1935, titled 'The Supreme Court and the NRA,' written by Charles E. Clark. Clark believed that the US system, with its federalism, separation of powers and judicial review, made government action difficult except in emergency cases. He accepted that this constraint on the national government had been an original intention of the framers of the Constitution and was in accord with their distrust of government. He wondered, however, if that system was consistent with the modern world.

The Supreme Court had often taken an accommodating approach to the Constitution's provisions regarding government activities and supporters of planning should not passively sit by when the Court overruled New Deal legislation. Nevertheless, Clark faulted the Roosevelt administration for the way it had conducted the NIRA. New Deal legislation had always been susceptible to attacks on constitutional grounds, but the administration had done a poor job in defending itself. Clark observed, 'the Schechter case was a criminal conviction on a national crime of poultry distributors' who operated in a local area. It was hardly the right case 'upon which to risk the fate of the recovery legislation.' Instead, he went on, 'Had the government boldly pressed forward its strongest cases and won them – as it possibly may still win them – these defeats would not seem so overwhelming' (Clark 1935, p. 121). Had the Roosevelt administration used cases where the product was clearly within the bounds of interstate commerce, and Clark gave some examples, the NIRA might well have prevailed.

A week later, in its 19 June 1935 issue, *The New Republic* continued this theme of holding the Roosevelt administration accountable for the failure of the NIRA with three separate articles. The first, an editorial article, 'Ghosts of the NRA,' reviewed what the administration was trying to salvage from the NRA. One approach was to keep collecting the information the NRA had started to compile; the article believed that the NRA had done a poor job of gathering data and its approach would have to be improved for the data to be useful. Another approach was to replace the NIRA codes with agreements that were voluntary; that approach, however, would give even more control over industry plans to business than it had under the NRA, where there were at least some countering forces from the government and labour. More appropriate, the Congress aimed to reinstate the labour codes of the NRA through consideration of the proposed Wagner Act, and this approach the article approved (*The New Republic* 1935, pp. 153–4).

In the 'Washington notes' column of the same issue T.R.B. noted that the Schechter decision had not ruined the country after all. Roosevelt had tried to use the NRA to bring business to task, but had failed. Business groups, however, were telling the president that business had never cared for the NIRA codes, especially the compulsory labour codes (T.R.B. 1935, p. 164).

John T. Flynn also took a swipe at the NRA in his regular column, 'Other people's money,' for 19 June 1935. Progressives were attacking the Supreme Court for using the interstate commerce clause to limit 'the power of the central government over the economic life of the nation.' To Flynn, however, they were overlooking the reality of the NRA by thinking it was 'a great liberal revolution.' Instead, the NRA was a way for the president to delegate his power to business groups in order to give them control over industry planning. Flynn had warned of this delegation previously and now indicated that if the Court had let it continue, business domination of the economy would have grown more powerful over time, with the result that the US would have had 'the corporate state in all its essentials and the end of the democratic process in government would have arrived in this country' (Flynn 1935, p. 165).

BUSINESS VOTES WITH THE COURT

In much of the writing we have surveyed regarding the NIRA and the NRA it was argued that business gained from them and might thus want to see them continued. In June 1935, however, the business magazine, *Business Week*, offered evidence that business was happy to see the end of the NRA. The evidence came from a canvassing of 105 business leaders from all segments of industry and commerce in the US as presented in an article, 'Business votes with the Court.' The consensus of those business leaders was that the NRA had produced a 'tangled rule' that was part of the weakness of the New Deal. Those leaders told *Business Week* how they would respond to the end of the NRA.

In the immediate future business leaders indicated that they would retain some features of the NRA, such as not reducing wages or expanding hours without extra pay, no price cuts and maintaining other provisions of the NIRA codes that had proved useful. For the long term, business leaders wanted voluntary codes to keep their industry productive and prosperous. The need for voluntary codes reflected their desire that 'the government should abandon all attempts to badger, regiment or regulate all business' and it should not 'impede the free and unrestricted exercise of individual initiative in business.' The freedom of business to do what it thought was best in terms of earning a profit would do more to restore prosperity to the economy than government control of business. One business leader expressed relief that the Supreme Court had ended the New Deal experiment in 'state socialism.' He added, 'Private initiative will provide a higher standard of living for the masses, will reemploy more people faster, and will give greater security than state socialism' (*Business Week* 1935, 7–8 June, pp. 7–8).

STUART CHASE: PUBLIC BUSINESS AND THE NIRA

Of all the pundits we have considered in this book, Stuart Chase was probably the most creative. A prolific writer, he authored many books in support of his belief that the market economy required government planning to be efficient. Each book, however, stated the case from a different slant, and Chase's *Government in Business*, published in 1935 is no exception. In it Chase presented his advocacy for planning as part of a trend in the increase of 'public business.' Chase defined public business as the provision of government service as opposed to private business which aimed at profit. The important point for him was that the public businesses were growing as a percentage of the overall economy in part because of the inability of private business to provide many of the services that the population wanted. Chase saw a struggle between the private and the public business as the key issue of his day. He wrote,

> The New Deal is but a single engagement on a world-wide battle front. In Russia the forces of private income producing property are in disorderly retreat, but in all other industrial countries the struggle is grim and unremitting. Fascism in Italy and Germany is an unstable compromise between state control and private enterprise. (Chase 1935a, p. 2)

The US had been a laggard in this struggle until the WIB had shown that the government could plan the economy to get what it needed for fighting a war. The next step was to ask, 'If collective effort was an effective way to wage wars, why not to abolish poverty?' (Chase 1935a, p. 3).

The key ingredient of public business was its use of collective effort and Chase outlined many of the trends that were moving society towards collectivism. The most important trend was technology, which linked the various sectors of the economy so closely together that he found it difficult to see how industry could not be run collectively (Chase 1935a, pp. 23–4). To some degree, collectiveness was a part of the New Deal. Chase saw the beginnings of the collectivism of public business in Hoover's efforts to halt the depression. Previous presidents had not seen a 'part of their duty to take charge of the nation's economy' during a recession. Chase added, however, 'Mr. Hoover regarded it as his duty to interfere, and it was' (Chase 1935a, p. 33). What Hoover started, Roosevelt and the New Deal continued in greater force.

Of the forms of collective public business initiated by the New Deal, however, Chase especially looked askance at the NIRA (Chase 1935a, p. 34). To him, the NRA had 'started as an adventure in the collective control of industry, but became lost in the woods' (Chase 1935a, p. 43). Under it businessmen were supposed to work with their competitors and produce plans that would be good for the industry, and then work with the government to 'plan for the good of the entire nation.' Chase found this approach to have no practical value. He noted, 'Nine business men out of ten distrusted their competitors, and ninety-nine out of one hundred distrusted the government. Seeds of cooperation, no matter how thickly showered, could not grow on such stony ground' (Chase 1935a, p. 43).

The only positive components of the NIRA, with regard to the development of social control, were the labour elements of minimum wages, maximum hours and restrictions on child labour. Chase categorized the NIRA codes as a delegation of 'law-making authority to private business' and called it a 'doubtful blessing.' These aspects of the New Deal Chase found wanting from his 'new test for every economic activity, private or public. Is this business consistent with general economic security, or is it not?' (Chase 1935a, pp. 68–9). The NIRA failed to meet this test because it was a 'regulatory model' that foolishly attempted a partnership 'between state and private enterprise.' This approach might have worked in a few selected industries. Chase concluded, however, 'When practically the whole private sector was included, opposition became too massive to handle' (Chase 1935a, p. 225). The NIRA failed to attain the cooperative collectivization that it had promised and the Supreme Court was right to end it. The NIRA could only have worked if the government had acted 'as a senior partner whose decision was final' (Chase 1935a, p. 226).

THE COMMITTEE OF INDUSTRIAL ANALYSIS

When the US Supreme Court voided the NIRA, advocates for some form of government planning and control over industry likely wanted to see it re-enacted in a form that was consistent with the Constitution. Perhaps to provide Congress with a basis for new legislation to save the NIRA, on 1 April 1936 President Roosevelt issued an executive order creating a Committee of Industrial Analysis to undertake a summary of what results the NRA had produced. The Committee included the Secretaries of Commerce, Labour and Agriculture and four private citizens, John Maurice Clark, whom we have already met, William H. Davis, an attorney, George M. Harrison, president of the Brotherhood of Railway and Steamship Clerks, and George H. Mead, president of a manufacturing company and former chairman of the NRA Business Advisory Council.

Using reports and data collected by NRA staff, the Committee produced a 191-page report that looked at many features of the NIRA and its implementation by the NRA. The report included the words with which President Roosevelt outlined the overall intent of the NIRA: 'The idea is simply for employers to hire more men to do the existing work by reducing the work-hours of each man's week and at the same time paying a living wage for the shorter week' (Committee of Industrial Analysis 1937, p. 11). The NIRA also aimed at ending unfair competition as 'socially undesirable' (Committee of Industrial Analysis 1937, p. 5).

The Committee noted that the NRA had been set up to use 'voluntary agreements' to accomplish its objectives, but it found that 'little use of such agreements was made between labor organizations and industrial groups, and even less among industrial or business groups.' It had been anticipated that business would cooperate once immunity from the anti-trust laws had been granted, but most of the NIRA codes that had been put in place were made 'enforceable against a minority who disagreed, rather than voluntary agreements' (Committee of Industrial Analysis 1937, p. 9). Coercion would not seem to be consistent with a moral economy, but we must always remember that Edward Bellamy had promised, 'A man able to do duty, and persistently refusing, is sentenced to solitary imprisonment on bread and water till he consents' (Bellamy 1888 [1926], p. 128).

Bellamy's moral economy also included planning as a way to overcome the business cycle and to produce what people needed. The NIRA had elements of planning attached to it. Because of the heavy burden of approving the many codes that were submitted to it, the NRA, the Committee observed, was under a great deal of time pressure and added, 'It is difficult to picture the tremendous pressure of this urge for speed and the confusion that resulted from it. It is the predominant aspect of the inherent conflict between the recovery objective and the long-term planning object-ive of the NRA' (Committee of Industrial Analysis 1937, p. 21). Since economic recovery was the main goal of the New Deal, planning was pushed into the background under the NRA.

It had been hoped that the process of creating codes would become simpler as more codes were approved. Instead, the codes became more complicated and often had conflicting provisions in them (Committee of Industrial Analysis 1937, p. 24). There were also many requests for exemp-tion from the codes, over 5000 were submitted, and delays in processing them 'encouraged noncompliance' (Committee of Industrial Analysis 1937, p. 25). With all these difficulties, it was no wonder that long-term planning fell into the background.

In terms of the impact the NIRA had on bringing about economic recovery, the Committee was sceptical. For example, it reported that general labour codes for minimum wages and maximum hours had meant that 'labor income was strikingly expanded during a short period.' As a result, it added, 'New buying was in the hands of workers.' But it also noted, 'A rise in the cost of living occurred simultaneously, almost erasing the value of the increase in the individual worker's earnings' (Committee of Industrial Analysis 1937, p. 109). The Committee believed that wage increases con-tinued under the NRA and the net effect on the real wages was positive. Regarding the control of production, the Committee found that the NIRA codes had little control over production (Committee of Industrial Analysis 1937, p. 163). Efforts were made by the NRA to maintain a system of open pricing by requiring businesses to file their prices so competitors and consumers could make competitive choices, but the Committee found that 'the published indices suggest that the national level of prices was not affected by the trade practice programs'(Committee of Industrial Analysis 1937, p. 163).

From the above statements, we might easily conclude that the Committee deemed the NIRA and NRA to have been failures. We must temper that conclusion with recognition that the Committee did find positive accom-plishments from the NIRA and NRA. First, it noted, 'The child labor provisions of the codes immediately eased the lives of the children taken out of industry.' Second, it added, 'The NRA gave jobs to something like 2,000,000 workers by spreading work' (Committee of Industrial Analysis 1937, p. 179). Those workers earned higher pay but it was not clear to the Committee if their real wage had increased, because the impact of the NRA on prices was hard to calculate. Third, the NRA had produced 'a definite contribution toward the prevailing mood of the country' and business gained confidence, which was not less real 'because it may have been partly based on exaggerated expectations of what the codes would do' (Committee of Industrial Analysis 1937, p. 181). Businessmen also began 'to think more in terms of the common interests of their industry' (Committee of Industrial Analysis 1937, p. 182).

These contributions of the NRA had to be weighed against the difficulties it had encountered in meeting its goals. Here the Committee detailed several failures of the NRA. First, the NRA was not always able to get everything for labour that it wanted to achieve in the codes; the administration of the codes did not require labour's participation in writing the codes and business often got its way (Committee of Industrial Analysis 1937, p. 38). Second, the NRA could not resolve 'conflicts of interest among members of an industry as to their relative shares in production' (Committee of Industrial Analysis 1937, p. 141). Third, the NRA was understaffed and the Committee indicated that it had not been able to employ 'a large enough personnel with the exacting combination of qualities, background, and training required for NRA administration,' even though it had hired employees who were capable and devoted public servants (Committee of Industrial Analysis 1937, p. 183). Finally, the Committee concluded, any permanent programme for preventing the fundamental causes of depressions should not look for any policies derived from the NIRA experience. It wrote, 'The NRA experience appears to indicate that mere control of wages, prices, and trade practices is capable of playing a relatively minor part in such a fundamental program. Such a program needs to be comprehensive, and is more appropriate to a general governmental planning agency than to an organization limited to the field occupied by the NRA' (Committee of Industrial Analysis 1937, p. 191).

From this conclusion we may infer that for the Committee the NIRA and the NRA did not live up to the promise of the moral economy. Indeed, because the element of compliance was, in the Committee's estimate, very low, the NIRA may have contributed to inducing a nation of habitual lawbreakers. It was a case where moral imperative turned into moral hazard.

GEORGE H. MEAD OBJECTS TO THE LABOUR PROVISIONS OF THE NIRA

One of the members of the Committee on Industrial Analysis was a businessman, George H. Mead, president of a manufacturing company. At one point in the Committee's report, he issued a separate statement about the labour portion of the NIRA. We present his views, given in a separate statement in the Committee's report, in this section for they reflected a business concern about the NIRA and its labour provisions.

Mead began by indicating the importance of labour-management relations in the affairs of industry. The NIRA had produced a climate where employers were bound to take this question more seriously. Mead dissented from the attitude that the NIRA implied that only management treated workers badly. From his own review of the NRA's experiences, he indicated that 'coercion of employees can come from fellow employees and organizers as well as from employers.' By not recognizing this potential of abuse from other workers and union organizers, the NRA had put 'restraints upon the employer without placing restraints upon organizations of employees.' Because unions were often national organizations with centralized power, they had a greater potential for abuse than the NIRA contemplated. In addition, Mead insisted, management saw the potential for abuse because unions would put management-labour relations 'in the hands of professional labor leaders, not themselves workers.' Management did not want to deal with outsiders who did not know how a particular firm had to operate and thus interfered with the 'mutuality of interest' between managers and workers (Committee of Industrial Analysis 1937, p. 123). In short, Mead questioned whether union representatives were capable of the moral behaviour required of a moral economy.

JOHN MAURICE CLARK BACKS AWAY FROM PLANNING

John Maurice Clark, as described in previous chapters, had used two theories that he had developed, the theory of overhead costs and the theory of the accelerator, to point out areas where he believed that the market economy needed to be supplemented by planning. Clark was thus part of the Progressive Era's promotion of planning as a solution for depressions. As the 1930s wore on, however, Clark began to study planning and how it took place and began to revise his attitude towards it. He had seen how planning had worked in the Soviet Union under communism, in Italy and Germany under fascism and in the US under the NIRA. Clark did not regard these forms of planning as identical. He was neither a fan of communism nor of fascism and interpreted the NIRA as an attempt to balance the policies of the other two systems to avoid their glaring faults of a heavy-handed authoritarianism. It was a failed attempt, however. The severity of the Great Depression led Clark to consider that the market economy had some merit after all. To him, ending the depression required 'a freer flow of private capital' to increase demand, put labour back to work and restore economic growth (Clark 1939a, p. 521).

Planning was needed for society to meet human needs (Clark 1939a, p. 524). The problem with planning to Clark, however, was that the capabilities of workers had not developed to an extent where they could participate in it. Only business had developed the technical capability for planning, a point Walter Lippmann had made with regard to managerial capitalism. Following Lippmann, Progressives had believed that managers had gained the capability to plan in a way that took the interests of society to heart, rather than to plan in a way that helped their own firms. Clark now saw the flaw in this belief and argued that under the NIRA businessmen had captured the NRA and used it effectively to raise prices for business without a corresponding increase in wages for labour. Labour participation in the NRA had been weak, while its government administrators had proved ineffective. Without these countervailing forces to constrain them, business leaders had not been interested in planning as a cooperative venture (Stabile 1996, p. 154).

The issue for Clark was a big one. He asked, 'Can we control business or does it control us?' (Clark 1939a, p. 484). Under the NIRA, apparently, business was controlling the US, and unless the US went to the extreme of abolishing private property, which Clark certainly doubted, business would control any system of planning to serve its own purposes and not the interest of society as a whole (Clark 1939a, pp. 427–40). Planning and the moral economy were not compatible with private enterprise and the market economy.

Progressives had argued that through planning business, government and labour could collaborate effectively. As Clark saw it, labour was not ready to play its part in that system of planning. First, workers were becoming more reliant on union leaders to do their thinking for them, an outcome Clark found to be of doubtful value. Second, modern working conditions in large-scale factories had hindered the capability of workers to do anything more than rely on others to lead them. Clark stated the problem as follows, 'Modern life demands the highest qualities of character, personality and citizenship, but shows no clear tendency to develop such qualities' (Clark 1939a, p. 489). Clark pinpointed a cause for the low capability of workers that would have made Progressives flinch: scientific management. He wrote, 'F.W. Taylor's trained gorilla might be an efficient industrial worker, at some kinds of work, but he could not build a successful system of democratic social control' (Clark 1939a, p. 490).

As noted earlier, Progressive pundits had seen scientific management as imbuing business with a scientific spirit in thinking about how to plan production. They also saw scientific management as taking a more humane attitude towards workers. Clark now saw a flaw in this argument as well as in his own case for planning. National economic planning needed input from labour to be effective, but instead of developing the scientific outlook and moral character requisite to their participation in national economic planning, workers were being turned into automatons by scientific management as controlled by business. Consequently, they could not be relied on at all when it came to participation in planning and certainly not on a level equal to that of the expert, scientific managers of business. Nor had those scientific managers gained the socially minded character the Progressives had anticipated.

As a result of his critical analysis of the failure of planning under the NIRA, Clark greatly diminished his interest in planning and in his subsequent writings began to worry that unions were gaining too much power without the capability to use that power for the good of society (Clark 1957). The moral economy needed members with high moral character to function effectively. Progressives had believed that if humans were put under the influence of the moral economy, they would become moral or at least moral enough to make planning effective. Such was not the case on Clark's evaluation. The New Deal and the NRA had tried to plan the economy without having participants who had reached the level of moral thinking that Clark saw as incumbent on them to have, with the result that the NRA floundered in the middle zone where moral imperative becomes moral hazard.

WALTER LIPPMANN DISCOVERS THE MARKET

Walter Lippmann had been an advocate for planning for over 20 years before the New Deal began the NIRA. During those 20 years, however, he had drifted to an appreciation of the benefits of the market economy, as seen in his 1938 book, *An Inquiry into the Principles of the Good Society*. He attributed his new viewpoint to the influence of Ludwig von Mises and Frederich A. Hayek (Lippmann 1938, p. vii), two Austrian economists who did more than any other economist of the twentieth century to make the case for the market economy. In 1920 von Mises had written an article, 'Economic calculation in the socialist commonwealth,' in which he pointed out the difficulty a planning authority would have in finding out what consumers wanted to have produced (von Mises 1920).

Lippmann accepted this viewpoint, which indicated that he had recognized that humanity was being offered a false choice between 'security and liberty.' He continued, 'To escape from want they must enter a prison. To regularize their work they must be regimented' (Lippmann 1938, p. x). This was not a tolerable choice for humans to make and Lippmann chastised two of the thinkers surveyed in this book, George Soule and Stuart Chase, for thinking it could be made. Lippmann had joined them in a search to see if there were 'planners and managers who were wise and disinterested enough' to create a planned economy. His search led him to a recognition that planning might work in a static society, but since the industrial revolution science had been used to bring about a continual change in technology – the process of creative destruction – and planning could only work in an economy with 'a well-established routine which has to be altered only at rare intervals' (Lippmann 1938, p. 11). Pericles might have been able to plan the Athenian economy, but 'It would be rash, for example, to assume that Mr. Roosevelt can learn ... about the needs and desires of the people of the United States' (Lippmann 1938, p. 27).

Lippmann recognized that by allowing the specialization of tasks and the increased productivity that followed from it, the division of labour had brought about the industrial revolution and an increased standard of living for all members of society. For the division of labour to work effectively, however, market relations were paramount. Only through the market economy could the diverse body of workers find their niche in the division of labour. Proponents of the moral economy had 'beguiled themselves with the notion that they can plan this economy and administer it rationally.' Lippmann told them they were wrong. He wrote,

> The exact contrary is the truth. The modern economy is perhaps the least systematic of any that has ever existed. It is world-wide, formless, vast, complicated, and, owing to technological progress, in constant change. For that reason it is incapable of being conceived as a system, or of being replaced by another system, or being managed as an administrative unit. (Lippmann 1938, p. 362)

Lippmann had certainly learned from von Mises and Hayek that the market can gather information about human desires much more accurately than economic planners can. Planning would only work when the desires of the population were settled by an absolute state. That was why wartime planning by the WIB had been effective. It had taken place under a strong government that knew what needed to be produced to win the war.

Translating that effectiveness to a peacetime economy was not a simple task. Lippmann believed that Chase and Soule had not truly responded to this issue but they must have known it existed and been troubled by it. He wrote,

> They show that they are troubled because they denounce so vehemently the tastes of the people and the advertising that helps to form those tastes. They insist that the people have foolish and vulgar desires, which may be true ... . But I do not see how the purification of the public taste is to be worked out by a government commission. (Lippmann 1938, p. 97)

As long as society had an increasing standard of living, its members would spend an increasing part of their income on items that they did not need in an absolute sense like food, but on many items that intellectuals, Lippmann included himself, disapproved.

Planning was only feasible when everyone spent their money on generic forms of the basics – food, clothing, shelter and transportation. If, for example, each driver was happy with Ford's unchanging 'Model T' then plans for how many to produce each year were easy to construct. When the plan missed the target the difference could be adjusted by producing more or fewer in the following year. When drivers had a choice of a variety of car brands and models and colours within each brand that changed every year planning became much more difficult.

Like William Graham Sumner and Joseph Schumpeter, Lippmann had come to appreciate the process of creative destruction and the dilemma it posed for any government trying to regulate the economy. The market was a powerful, inanimate force that lacked humanity. Its discipline was merciless in terms of the way it used monetary incentives to tell people what to do and, just as important, what not to do. The process of creative destruction, for example, while it added to the vibrancy of economic life by creating new products, methods of production and industries, also destroyed the liveli-hood of persons in the industries it rendered obsolete. Those persons rather than accept their demise and force themselves to find a new way of earning a living turned to government for protection. And by helping them, the advocates for the moral economy generated a myth that 'the government can and should make them richer' (Lippmann 1938, p. 126). Lippmann understood very well, however, that the government could 'only redistribute what has been produced' (Lippmann 1938, p. 128).

Lippmann was not an advocate of the market economy, because he believed that there were problems in the functioning of the market that needed to be addressed (Lippmann 1938, pp. 174–5). First, he did not consider 'big business' to be consistent with the working of a free market (Lippmann 1938, p. 217). Second, when there was unequal bargaining power in the market economy, the government 'cannot be neutral' (Lipp-mann 1938, p. 222). This was especially the case with labour.

The solution of planning, however, relied on an authoritarian government telling consumers what to spend their money on. Lippmann was concerned with 'gradual collectivism' whereby democratic countries had for over half a century looked for 'relief from poverty and disorder by the use of collectivist measures.' He added that Progressives employed this gradual collectivism because 'they hope by the gradualness of their methods to avoid the violence of dictatorship' (Lippmann 1938, p. 106). Their approach was to use a series of democratic majorities who favoured one or more collective reforms to bring about a planned economy. In the process they served the needs of a series of special interest groups and operated under a theory they were treating all interest groups equally.

They were wrong in Lippmann's view and to support that view he considered the NIRA. He wrote,

> Under the National Industrial Recovery Act, industries were encouraged to organize themselves as agents of the state. To each of these groups there was then delegated the power to legislate not only for all who were engaged in that line of business but for all who might wish to engage in it. No clearer, no more naked illustration could be offered of what is meant by the statement that gradual collectivism means the conferring of privileges on special interests. (Lippmann 1938, p. 123)

The right to enact binding codes with the power of law behind it was a very special privilege granted to business under the NIRA and this interpretation of the meaning of gradual collectivism Lippmann further confirmed by the problem the New Deal had in granting it to other interest groups. Lippmann described it as follows:

> Ordinary considerations of justice, and the personal sympathies of many of the New Dealers required, for example, that if great industries like steel were to be given such extraordinary privileges, if great interests like that of the cotton planters were to be taken into partnership by the state, wage earners should also be given privileges. But the event showed that most wage earners were too weak to exercise the privilege which the government attempted to confer on them and that the government was not strong enough to make those privileges effective. (Lippmann 1938, p. 124)

Having given labour privileged status under the NIRA, the New Dealers found that this status had not worked out, even before the Supreme Court voided the NIRA.

STRATEGIES FOR LABOUR

With the end of the NIRA and its experiment with industry planning through the writing of codes that included fair wages, the leaders of the New Deal had to develop other strategies for labour. The obvious ones were to bolster the ability of workers to form unions and to pass laws stipulating that a minimum wage be paid. Both strategies had been part of the NIRA, and they became hallmarks of the New Deal that remain with us today. The National Labor Relations Act (NLRA) had an aim of establishing collective bargaining and the Fair Labor Standards Act (FLSA) legislated a minimum wage. In addition, the Social Security Act protected workers through the provision of unemployment insurance. In each case the laws were justified as necessary for a moral economy.

The National Labor Relations Act

As a staunch New Dealer, Senator Robert F. Wagner had introduced many of the key laws enacted during the 1930s. On 21 February 1935 he gave a speech indicating the need for the NLRA, which was also known as the Wagner Act. Wagner began the speech by pointing out that the New Deal recovery programme under the NIRA had been intended to give business and labour the freedom to work together in the struggle to end the Great Depression. To maintain the principle of 'equal treatment upon which a just democratic society must rest,' the NIRA had granted workers the ability to act cooperatively under union leadership under Section 7A (Wagner 1935a, p. 2371).

As a result, the US had faced a period of strikes that had not helped business, labour or the country. Moreover, when workers were not able to form unions when they wanted to, they could not 'participate in our national endeavor to coordinate production and purchasing power.' As a result, profits were outstripping wages and if that trend continued 'the whole country will suffer from a new economic decline' (Wagner 1935a, p. 2371). Because the NIRA was not helping workers, Wagner proposed a new national labour relations bill, which he indicated was simply enacting a principle of workers' rights to organize that was generally accepted by Congress.

In presenting the bill, Wagner went out of his way to allay any fears his fellow senators might have regarding the impact of the law he was proposing. His intent was not to create a 'labor dictatorship.' Rather, he sought 'to make the worker a free man in the economic as well as the political field' (Wagner 1935a, p. 2371). The bill, if enacted, would make the legal status of industrial relations much clearer, help to avoid industrial strife and 'improve business by laying the foundations for the amity and fair dealing upon which permanent progress must rest' (Wagner 1935a, p. 2372). New Dealers such as Wagner believed that business had bargaining power over workers and used it to pay low wages – a condition that was manifestly unfair from their perspective. It also helped that they could use the underconsumption argument to bolster their case for higher wages. Underconsumption had caused the Great Depression and higher wages brought by unions would end it.

Congress enacted the NLRA in May 1935. This law set up specific procedures for elections to recognize that workers wanted to form a union,

established penalties for businesses that did not follow the election procedures or that committed a set of unfair labour practices, and required that
businesses bargain in good faith with duly elected unions in a system of
collective bargaining. The NLRA also set up the National Labor Relations
Board (NLRB) to oversee that the procedures of the law were followed by
business and labour and to take legal action where the procedures were not
followed. In the four-and-one-half years following its founding the NLRB
oversaw 2500 union elections with a total vote of 1.2 million workers
(Stabile 1993, pp. 14–15). In a series of cases brought before the US
Supreme Court immediately after the NLRA went into effect a narrow
majority of the justices (usually 5–4) upheld it. In reaching these decisions
the Court held that unions 'were organized out of the necessities of the
situation; that a single employee was helpless in dealing with an employer;
… that union was essential to give labourers opportunity to deal on an
equality with their employers' (Supreme Court 1937b, p. 55). It was only
just to have unions that would negotiate fair wages for their members.

The Fair Labor Standards Act

In July 1933 Secretary of Labor Frances Perkins made a case for a
minimum wage law in a surprising place, the pages of *Nation's Business*.
She based the need for a minimum wage on the existence of sweatshops that
were coming into existence during the depression to produce items at the
lowest possible cost through the payment of low wages. Most retailers were
moral enough to want to buy from manufacturers who paid workers a living
wage, but if the store down the street was buying from a sweatshop and
selling at a lower price, a moral manufacturer would be at a competitive
disadvantage, would lose sales and be compelled to operate under sweatshop rules. The result would be 'lower wages in every other industry'
(Perkins 1933, p. 24). A minimum wage law would stop this race to the
bottom of reduced wages. It would protect both the exploited worker and
the 'responsible manufacturer' who was still 'trying to pay a living wage'
(Perkins 1933, pp. 24, 56).

For over three decades the Supreme Court had declared efforts by states
to enact minimum wage laws unconstitutional, usually on the grounds that
the laws interfered with the right of all persons to negotiate contracts freely
as in the case of the making of a wage contract between an employer and an
employee. When the issue of the minimum wage came to the Court again in
1937 through a challenge to the law of Washington state, the Court
approved it by a 5–4 vote, supporting it as a reasonable regulation 'adopted
in the interests of the community' (Supreme Court 1937a, pp. 22–3).

The Court's decisions on state minimum wage laws meant that the FLSA was constitutional when it was passed by Congress in 1938 to set minimum wages for workers and to place limits on the hours workers could work in a pay period. The minimum wage would set a standard for a tolerable if not decent standard of living for workers. In its original form the FLSA did not provide a uniform national minimum wage. Instead, industry and regional differences in the minimum wage, within a given range, would be established by an administrator in the US Department of Labor and advisory committees in each industry (Douglas and Hackman 1938, p. 514). In this respect the FLSA replicated the industry planning apparatus of the NIRA.

Unemployment Insurance

Unemployment insurance was raised at the federal level by President Roosevelt in a message to the Congress on 4 January 1935. He indicated that in the political world 'social justice' had become a key justification for a programme of economic security (Roosevelt 1935a, p. 226). Creative destruction was at the heart of the need for economic security. Roosevelt observed, 'Rapid changes – the machine, the advent of universal and rapid communication, and many other factors – have brought new problems' (Roosevelt 1935a, p. 226). For this reason he proposed unemployment insurance as 'security against the major hazards and vicissitudes of life' (Roosevelt 1935a, p. 227). Unemployment insurance would provide protection to workers who lost their jobs from business cycles or the destruction phase of creative destruction.

Wagner was responsible for proposing the legislation that became the Social Security Act, which included unemployment insurance. He believed that public opinion now accepted that 'men may become unemployed without having been shiftless and indolent.' Of the two main goals of the Act, unemployment insurance and old-age pensions, unemployment insurance was the most important because unemployment was the primary result of the depression and the unemployment insurance system would serve 'to minimize, if not to abolish, the likelihood of depressions.' The payment of unemployment benefits in the early stages of an economic downturn would 'release floods of purchasing power to check the decline and swing the cycle more quickly back to the prosperity level.' If unemployment insurance had been put into place a decade or so earlier, the payment of benefits might have reduced the severity of the Great Depression (Wagner 1935b, p. 294).

Unemployment insurance was part of a multi-faceted Social Security Act that went into effect on 14 August 1935 (Schieber and Shoven 1999, pp. 34, 37). To fund unemployment insurance, the federal government used a tax-offset plan where the federal government imposed a tax upon employers based on the total they paid in wages and salaries. If a state enacted an unemployment insurance law that met criteria established by the federal government, the payments made by employers for the insurance would serve as an offset against the federal tax that they would otherwise pay. In this way states that did not set up an unemployment insurance plan could not gain a competitive advantage over states that did set one up.

When the Social Security Act was put in place, much of the work to accomplish it had been undertaken by the Committee on Economic Security. In 1937 the Committee produced a report, *Social Security in America.* The Committee's report indicated in its first lines that 'the hazard of unemployment is one of the most serious and disastrous of the many risks which confront wage earners in an industrial society.' That risk had become especially acute during the Great Depression and private charity had not been adequate to alleviate the plight of the unemployed. Moreover, private charity was 'demoralizing to both the donor and recipient.' A system of unemployment insurance, however, was not demoralizing because it was 'received as a right' (Committee on Economic Security 1937, p. 3). By basing unemployment compensation on insurance principles, with workers contributing towards their coverage, the Social Security Act established its payments as a contractual obligation from the government to the unemployed worker and not as a benefit based on need. Efforts to reduce moral hazard included a waiting period before benefits could be paid, requiring a worker to be available for a potential job, making workers ineligible for 'quitting without good cause,' making workers ineligible 'in cases of discharges for misconduct' and a measure of a worker's 'willingness to accept new employment' (Committee on Economic Security 1937, pp. 125–6).

As with all the new programmes of the New Deal, the provisions of the Social Security Act were quickly challenged on constitutional grounds. In a case announced on 24 May 1937, *Charles C. Steward Machine Company v. Harwell G. Davis*, the US Supreme Court decided in a 5–4 vote that unemployment insurance was within the Constitution. The Court reasoned that the Great Depression had caused high unemployment with disastrous consequences on the lives of the unemployed, and 'the States were unable to give the requisite relief.' By the time the case came to the Court this situation had gone on for over seven years and the federal unemployment insurance programme was a way for the states to 'work together to a common end' (Supreme Court 1937c, pp. 65–71).

A STRATEGY FOR BUSINESS

Given the Supreme Court's overturning of the NIRA, Roosevelt could have sought an amendment to the Constitution that made programmes like the NIRA legal. He then could have enacted a new version of the NIRA, perhaps through modifications based on some of the evaluations presented in this chapter. Instead, Roosevelt did a turnaround and had the Justice Department pursue a vigorous prosecution of business for violations of the anti-trust laws. His chief prosecutor was Thurman Arnold.

After a short career in politics in Wyoming, Thurman Arnold (1891–1969) entered academia as a law professor, teaching at several schools before becoming a full professor at Yale Law School (1931–8). In 1938 he became assistant attorney general in the US Justice Department in the Antitrust Division, serving until 1943 when President Roosevelt appointed him as judge at the US Court of Appeals for the District of Columbia. After two years as a judge he resigned to form the law firm of Arnold & Porter, which remains a prestigious firm in Washington, DC.

During his career as a law professor Arnold wrote several books. We shall examine *The Folklore of Capitalism*, published in 1937. The folklore that concerned Arnold was that of the market economy and its underlying philosophy of laissez-faire. When folklore became well established it took on the status of a creed (Arnold 1937 [1968], p. 3). That was the problem the New Deal faced in its efforts to reorganize the economy and bring more government control to it. The Supreme Court, for example, had voided the NIRA because it held to the older creed that the government needed to stay out of the economy (Arnold 1937 [1968], p. 52).

Part of the problem was that the government had not developed a new creed that would allow it to take over the role that large businesses performed in the economy. In a statement of particular interest to the theme of this book Arnold did find one prophet of a new creed whom he apparently admired. He wrote,

> Edward Bellamy saw in the corporation itself a step toward Socialism. He thought of a future world of nationalized industry. He was the forerunner of the N.R.A. and the attacks on his preaching resembled very much the attacks on the recent National Recovery Administration. (Arnold 1937 [1968], p. 221)

Bellamy had championed the cause of the moral economy over the market economy, much as the NRA had. In both cases the hope had been that right thinking persons would get together and see the wisdom of change. The hope was misplaced, at least with the NRA, because, as Arnold observed, the right-thinking person 'chooses the reasoning of the Brookings Institution and throws out of the window the unsound theories of General Hugh Johnson' (Arnold 1937 [1968], p. 6).

In the ruthless days of the robber barons, large corporations suppressed competition by using any means to eliminate small firms. Once the battle was won and some of the large firms made up for their previous sins by being prosecuted for anti-trust violations, they became more respectable. The NRA had added to this respectability by putting curbs on competition that was not reasonable. But the NRA had not been able to go far enough because of the creed of the market economy. Centralized government could work in the US and anti-trust law that was truly aimed at controlling large corporations would be part of making centralized government work.

In his preface to the 1962 printing of *The Folklore of Capitalism* Arnold indicated that the philosophy that held in anti-trust was 'We no longer feel that government control of industry is something that will end in the destruction of individual liberty.' The courts had upheld the role of government agencies as having the capability to oversee business without having all of their decisions subject to review by federal courts. As a result, Arnold concluded, 'The amount of regulatory interference with business today which is represented by our vast government bureaus would have been unthinkable to a conservative in 1937' (Arnold 1968, pp. ix–x). Regulation of business was replacing the market economy with the moral economy.

CONCLUSION

The NIRA and the NRA had not worked out as their proponents had planned, even before the Supreme Court ended them. The Court objected to the centralization of economic control that the NRA apparently had, but it disapproved even more of the control it delegated to private businesses. The individuals surveyed in this chapter agreed that this delegation of control to business had given it too much power. Some, such as Tugwell and Chase, attributed the business dominance of the NIRA codes to weakness by the government. Others, such as Clark, found businesses' power over the NRA to be due to labour being incapable of participating equally with business in writing codes. None of them thought that the NRA had brought about national planning or economic recovery. Lippmann questioned whether planning was even possible.

The Roosevelt administration could have sought to amend the Constitution, which was a policy being suggested at the time (Lippmann 1937, p. 27). Instead, it ended a programme of voluntary self-regulation by all components of an industry with a policy of regulation of business by government agencies. The NLRA told business the terms under which it would interact with labour wanting to form unions and created the NLRB to be sure it did. The FLSA set a minimum wage that business must pay its workers along with the maximum hours it could make them work. The Social Security Act set up unemployment insurance and mandated that business pay taxes to support it. Critics of the NRA had argued that government participation in it had been too weak. The approach that followed the NRA strengthened government participation in business by making it the sole regulator.

Writing in *Nation's Business* Morris Edwards made it clear that business believed the NIRA offered it a deal of voluntary cooperation with its programme in return for the government refraining 'from any more drastic form of control.' If it would work to eliminate 'unfair competition' and to cooperate with labour business would give up some control over its management not to the government but to 'a group of proprietors among whom he has one voice' (Edwards 1933, p. 13). The deal had not worked. Recall from Chapter 7 that business's favourite approach, the Swope Plan, had proposed a number of items that had long been held dear by Progressives and forward-looking managers: a worker's compensation programme, life and disability insurance, pensions and unemployment insurance. The NIRA codes had been meagre in living up to this plan. When the Supreme Court called the NIRA unconstitutional, the Roosevelt administration turned to a system of regulation where business gave up control over its management to government agencies such as the NLRB and the Social Security Administration.

12. Keynes, fiscal policy and planning

The idea that government should use fiscal policy during an economic downturn, deliberately running a budget deficit to stimulate the economy, existed in the US before the Great Depression. We have seen in earlier chapters that Thorstein Veblen believed that military spending by the government had stimulated the economy during the Spanish-American War and Wesley Mitchell favoured the use of expenditures on public works to counteract the decline in spending that brought on a recession. During the 1920 presidential election campaign the Democratic Party candidate for vice-president, Franklin Roosevelt, had presented a programme of fiscal stimulus from government spending. This approach was also considered at the Presidential Conference on Unemployment called by Herbert Hoover as Secretary of Commerce. Bills to implement this counter-cyclical policy were introduced in Congress several times in the 1920s, but they were not enacted (Rothbard 2000, pp. 2881–911).

By the early 1930s the theory behind government spending programmes during a recession was 'pump-priming.' When a pump loses the pressure needed to draw water up from a well, it is necessary to pour water down the pump to get it started again. With foresight, a bucket of water will be left next to the pump to prime it. In a similar way, government would keep a reserve of money to get the economy started again. But when the initial priming does not work, the metaphor of pump-priming breaks down, for it involves a constant flow of water from multiple buckets to keep priming the pump and no one keeps that much water available.

A new and more robust theory of the economy and the government's role in it was needed. We have already seen that economic planning had been set out as one such theory, but in the US national economic planning had been limited to the efforts of the NRA. Those efforts had not proved effective even before they were voided by the US Supreme Court, and the federal government muddled along with a series of spending programmes that resulted in budget deficits. By the middle of the 1930s, however, that muddled approach would gain coherence through the writings of John Maynard Keynes.

JOHN MAYNARD KEYNES AND GOVERNMENT IN THE ECONOMY

John Maynard Keynes (1883–1946) must still be considered the outstanding economic influence of the twentieth century for the way in which he reoriented economics towards the aggregate approach of macroeconomics. Economic thinking would never be the same once Keynes's book, *The General Theory of Employment, Interest and Money*, was published in 1936. Keynes studied at Eton and Cambridge and then had a successful career as a civil servant in the Treasury Department of the UK. His Treasury duties brought him to the Paris Peace Conference at the end of World War I and when he objected to the economic penalties being imposed on Germany after the war by the political leaders of the victorious allies, his book, *The Economic Consequences of the Peace* (Keynes 1920), gained him worldwide recognition as an astute economic thinker. He was thus highly influential and any book he wrote on economics was bound to attract attention.

We cannot hope to do justice to a book as complicated and abstract as *The General Theory* in a brief review such as we are offering here. Fortunately, Keynes offered his own summary of his ideas, which we state briefly. His starting point was with the basic idea that when the economy grows and employment goes up, total real income in the economy will also go up. 'The psychology of the community,' however, would result in consumption not rising by as much as the rise in income. Total demand in the economy consisted of consumption and investment and when consumption did not rise as fast as income, investment had to make up the difference. When all of income was not spent on consumption it was because a portion of it was saved. The amount of savings did not determine investment, however. Instead, investment was determined by 'the inducement to invest,' which depended on 'the marginal efficiency of capital,' that is, the schedule of what business expected to gain from its use of investment in capital, compared to the interest rate. From the interaction of 'the propensity to consume' and 'the rate of new investment' there would be 'only one level of employment consistent with equilibrium' because any other amount of employment would mean that aggregate supply and aggregate demand would be out of balance. The level of employment determined by consumption and investment demand could be in equilibrium at a rate that did not give a job to every worker who wanted one (Keynes 1936 [1965], pp. 27–8).

Here we have the central feature of Keynes's general theory. The economy could be in equilibrium with balance between aggregate income and aggregate spending but not attain full employment. This feature went against the grain of thinking among economists that the market economy, if left alone, would tend to reach equilibrium at full employment. The difference between proponents of the market economy and Keynes was that they defended Say's Law and he attacked it. Although this difference would justify our putting Keynes in the moral economy camp simply from his attacks on the market economy, he often argued, as we shall see shortly, that he really wanted to save the best parts of the market economy.

A key element of Keynes's new economics was his popularization of the concept of the 'multiplier.' The point of the multiplier is to show how changes in investment by business can generate larger changes in income. If investment spending increases, for example, business is buying capital equipment, which creates jobs in companies that produce capital equipment. When the workers who get those jobs spend their earnings on consumption items, their spending generates jobs and income in consumer goods industries. Workers in those industries also spend their income and the process continues. It will not go on forever, however, because at each step in the process, due to Keynes's theory of consumption, workers will save a portion of their income and each step in the process will generate a smaller increase in income. Equally important, a decline in investment may cause a larger decline in income and bring about a recession.

The multiplier also applied to government spending and here was Keynes's rhetorical genius. Government spending of any type would stimulate the economy by giving people money to spend. When they spent that money on consumption goods, they would, through the multiplier effect, create jobs in the private sector. In addition, because of the multiplier, the income generated by government spending would be a greater amount than what the government spent. Taxes on that income would offset some of the government spending, with the result that the budget deficit might not be as large as originally planned.

It was through these ideas that Keynes hoped to challenge the basic assumptions of economists. Even though he challenged their assumptions, Keynes was not above making assumptions that they might challenge as well. For example, in the summary of his theory he qualified it with a brief statement of a key assumption on which it was based, 'a given situation of technique, resources and costs' (Keynes 1936 [1965], p. 28). Later in the book he elaborated on this assumption:

> We take as given the existing skill and quantity of available labour, the existing quality and quantity of available equipment, the existing technique, the degree of competition, the tastes and habits of the consumer, the disutility of different intensities of labour and of the activities of supervision and organisation, as well as the social structure including the forces, other than our variables set forth

below, which determine the distribution of income. This does not mean that we assume these factors to be constant; but merely that, in this place and context, we are not considering or taking into account the effects and consequences of changes in them. (Keynes 1936 [1965], p. 245)

In short, Keynes has abstracted away from the process of creative destruction that Sumner and Schumpeter thought to be the essence of the market economy. He has in consequence analysed a market economy that had more in common with John Stuart Mill's stationary state than with the dynamic economy of the early twentieth century. While it is a useful analytical tool to hold some variables constant in order to focus on the relationships among specific key variables, at some point a dynamic analysis must relax the assumption of *ceteris paribus* and let other things not remain equal.

Regarding the consumption function, for example, Keynes argued that as income rises consumption lags behind. To some degree, however, his argument depended on there being no new products to whet the psychology of consumers as he has assumed that no innovative products will emerge and consumer tastes would be constant even if they did. Yet changes in the available products or in consumer tastes must have some effect on the propensity to consume. More important, Keynes set forth an analysis of investment based on the schedule of the marginal efficiency of capital versus the rate of interest. In a static world the more capital a business has, the lower the return additional capital will bring, which makes the schedule of the marginal efficiency of capital have a downward slope; additional units of capital will earn a lower return than existing ones and it will take lower interest rates to spur investment. In the world of creative destruction, however, entrepreneurs will use additional units of capital in new ways that have the potential to earn a higher return than the existing units. Entrepreneurs would be willing to borrow at higher interest rates if they believed, as they usually do, that the marginal efficiency of the capital they were investing in their innovation would bring a return higher than the interest rate. Keynes allowed his schedule of the marginal efficiency of investment to shift upward only if there was a change in the 'animal spirits' of entrepreneurs. Yet, a spurt of innovation would have the same impact on investment, only Keynes kept it constant.

Keynes's partial justification for this assumption was that it accorded with the reality of the Great Depression. He observed that in the US in 1929 there had been five years of rapid capital expansion with the result that the income generated was so great that 'an enormous volume of new investment was required' and 'it became almost hopeless to find still more new investment on a sufficient scale to provide for such new saving as a wealthy community in full employment would be disposed to set aside' (Keynes

1936 [1965], p. 100). In a mature, affluent economy with high levels of income and corresponding high savings along with the accumulation of a large amount of capital, increases of investment would be difficult to find unless the process of creative destruction brought about new industries that needed capital equipment. If creative destruction had nothing new to offer at that moment, the result could well be a recession. We shall see below what Schumpeter thought of Keynes's ideas. For now we can say that they both seemingly agreed that when a period of investment brought about by creative destruction came to an end, the economy might decline. Schumpeter believed it was necessary to accept those periods of decline as the price we must pay for economic progress that came in clusters. Keynes wanted to do something about it and especially because he apparently doubted that the economy could count on new waves of innovation. The mature economy could be a stagnant one.

Given his background and his previous writings it is not surprising that Keynes wanted government to intervene in the economy to do something about economic recessions. What is surprising is that in *The General Theory* he offered precious little regarding just what he wanted government to do. We now identify Keynes with fiscal policy, using a government deficit to stimulate the economy. There are hints of this approach in *The General Theory* but we must look for them, because there is no chapter on what the government should do to end the Great Depression. We do find one such hint in his discussion of the propensity to consume. Keynes noted that the government's use of taxes to pay off its debt would reduce that propensity. Thus, a change of fiscal policy from borrowing to repaying debt through taxes would cause 'a severe contraction' in total demand while the reverse policy would cause a 'marked expansion' of that demand (Keynes 1936 [1965], p. 95). A few pages later he added the observation that when government 'willingly or unwillingly' was caused 'to run into a budgetary deficit' or to 'provide unemployment relief ... out of borrowed money,' the level of consumption would not fall at a rate comparable to the decline in income brought about by an economic downturn (Keynes 1936 [1965], p. 98).

As for government spending on public works, Keynes called it 'public investment.' He observed that the advantage it had over private investment was that there was a greater need for it. Thus, government provision of housing was often objected to as having a declining value. To Keynes, however, it was 'much easier to see an early satiation of the demand for new factories ... than of the demand for dwelling-houses' (Keynes 1936 [1965], p. 106). But government spending did not have to be on anything as useful as homes for low-income persons. Keynes insisted that 'pyramid-building, earthquakes, even wars may serve to increase wealth, if the education of our statesman on the principles of classical economics stands in the way of anything better.' These policies would end unemployment even though it would 'be more sensible to build houses' (Keynes 1936 [1965], p. 129). The point Keynes is making is that government expenditures, whether useful or wasteful, will generate income for the persons engaged in working on government projects and through the multiplier they would increase total demand and stimulate the economy. The investment multiplier applied to public investment by government as well as it did to private investment by business and increases in government spending would create private sector jobs.

One other approach to stimulating the economy was through monetary policy, reducing interest rates to encourage borrowing for investment. For many reasons related to his views on how interest rates were determined, Keynes doubted that monetary policy could influence interest rates and even if it could he doubted that lower interest rates could induce investment. Instead, he wanted the government, 'which is in a good position to calculate the marginal efficiency of capital-goods on long views and on the basis of general social advantage, taking an even greater responsibility for directly organizing investment' (Keynes 1936 [1965], p. 164). Government control over investment – we would call it planning – was needed because affluent countries like the US had accumulated so much capital 'that its marginal efficiency has fallen more rapidly than the rate of interest can fall,' causing economic decline. Decline was the fate of mature economies, Keynes added, when 'the propensity to consume and the rate of investment are not deliberately controlled in the social interest' (Keynes 1936 [1965], p. 219).

From this perspective, Keynes indicated that the government could influence consumption by its tax and spending policies and that investment could be controlled through a 'comprehensive socialisation of investment' in order to attain full employment. The socialization of investment, however, did not mean that the government had to engage in 'State Socialism which would embrace most of the economic life of the community.' Government ownership of the means of production was not needed as long as the government was able to control investment and establish a policy that produced full employment. The control over investment by government, however, would be tantamount to planning. To Keynes, the planning of investment by the government would control where capital was to be allocated. Once that planning was in place and effective, the market economy could handle the allocation of production in line with what consumers wanted and any errors in this allocation process due to misjudgements of consumer demand by business could be corrected by market forces and not 'by centralising decisions.' The controls over investment that Keynes called for would 'involve a large extension of the traditional functions of government' (Keynes 1936 [1965], pp. 378–9). Indeed, we must note, it would involve the government in investment planning and it is hard to see how businesses could respond to consumer demand unless the government gave it sufficient capital to do so. Keynes argued that the extension of government into control over investment would not have to alter the freedom and effectiveness of the market economy.

In terms of the theme of this book, the market economy versus the moral economy, Keynes claimed to be blending the two sides of the issue with a mixed economy of government planning of investment and private sector production of goods and services. He stated this blending clearly in an article, 'The dilemma of modern socialism,' in the 13 April 1932 issue of *The New Republic*. The dilemma to which he referred was that socialism had two aims, to follow sound economics and to undertake social pro-grammes that were not always sound economically but which were the right thing to do. Keynes reconciled the two aims by indicating that it was important to first do what was economically sound to ensure that society had enough resources to undertake those economically unsound social programmes. He added, 'I am convinced that those things which are urgently called for on practical grounds, such as the central control of investment, … will also tend to produce a better kind of society on ideal grounds' (Keynes 1932, pp. 227–8). By adhering to a policy of government control of investment, Keynes held a bias towards the moral economy of planning.

Keynes went to great length in *The General Theory* to argue that one strategy for ending the unemployment of the Great Depression, letting wages decline, was not acceptable. In the UK, at least, unions would not accept it. Instead, he believed that interest rates must fall. When interest rates became very low, however, they would no longer serve the function of allocating capital to its most productive use. That was why the socialization of investment was necessary, with government officials allocating capital in place of financial markets. Even though Keynes insisted that his socializa-tion of investment did not equate to state socialism or fascism he gave a revealing statement in the preface to the German edition of *The General Theory*: 'The theory of aggregate production that is the goal of the follow-ing book can be much more easily applied to the conditions of a totalitarian state than the theory of the production and distribution of a given output turned out under the conditions of free competition and a considerable degree of *laissez-faire*' (cited in Hazlitt 2011, pp. 4315–17).

Government control over investment would make sure that capital accu-mulation will be undertaken in the social interest much as the moral economy would do. Once those controls were effective, the market economy could be relied on to make decentralized decisions over how to use that capital. Here, however, Keynes encountered the dilemma of meshing social control with the freedom of markets: who will control the persons in charge of investment decisions? In pushing for his new economics Keynes pointed out the powerful influence of ideas, even obsolete ones. He wrote, 'Madmen in authority, who hear voices in the air, are distilling their frenzy from some academic scribbler of a few years back' (Keynes 1936 [1965], p. 383). But suppose they accepted Keynes's more modern academic scribbling, would that keep them from being any less 'madmen?' Keynes has done nothing less than argue for giving the control over investment and thus business to political leaders who might then use the power that control gave them to serve their own interests or the interest of the groups they represented. Control over investment would give them control over the process of creative destruction and we would have to wonder if politicians and government officials would give investment funds to entrepreneurs to innovate new products or methods of production that might destroy previous investments or harm special interest groups. They might instead engage in crony capitalism.

Keynes might have hoped that the social control of investment and consumption would be placed in the hands of virtuous civil servants, such as he had been in his days at the British Treasury. He hinted at this promotion of professional experts to greater authority when he once quipped, 'the *Class* war will find me on the side of the educated *bourgeoisie*' (Keynes 1925 [1932], p. 324, emphasis in original). His experiences at the Paris Peace Conference should have taught him to be more sceptical of the motivations of political leaders and their penchant for disregarding the advice of experts in the name of political expediency.

KEYNES AND THE NEW DEAL

Keynes's views on government spending and the social control of investment made him a kindred spirit of Roosevelt and his New Deal. Rexford Tugwell, who had mentored Roosevelt on economics, had argued for the socialization of investment in the 1920s. Moreover, we saw in Chapter 8 that Roosevelt had been taught in his economics classes at Groton and Harvard that public policy had to intervene where markets did not work, a point Keynes had often made well before he wrote *The General Theory*. What did Keynes think of the New Deal? We find a partial answer in two letters he wrote to Roosevelt about the New Deal policies.

The first was 'An open letter to President Roosevelt' published in the *New York Times* on 31 December 1933. In it Keynes complimented Roosevelt for giving hope to 'those in every country who seek to mend the evils of our condition by reasoned experiment within the framework of the existing social system.' If Roosevelt failed in his experiments, the hope for reasoned change would ebb and the old views of laissez-faire versus socialism would have to fight it out. Success would bring about a 'new economic era,' however (Keynes 1933).

Keynes worried that Roosevelt was risking failure due to his efforts to bring about both 'recovery from the slump and the passage of those business and social reforms which are long overdue.' It would be better if the New Deal were to focus on bringing about a recovery and using its success in the recovery programme to solidify its standing with the public and thereby bolster its chances for true reform. If reform 'upset the confidence of the business world' it would impede the recovery. The reform Keynes had in mind was the NIRA and he wrote of it, 'I cannot detect any material aid to recovery in NIRA, though its social gains have been large.' Indeed, Keynes believed the NIRA had been enacted 'in the false guise of being part of the technique of Recovery' (Keynes 1933).

In more recent times the slogan has been to not let an economic crisis go to waste but to use the opportunity it offers to push through social reforms. Here Keynes was advising against the policies behind this slogan even when he favoured them. Regarding the NIRA, he wrote to the President, 'I do not mean to impugn the social justice and social expediency of the redistribution of incomes aimed at by NIRA' But the NIRA aimed at artificially raising prices and Keynes believed that increased prices were not acceptable unless they came from increased demand and thereby brought about increased production and employment. That was a better approach than raising prices 'by restricting output' as the NIRA attempted to do (Keynes 1933).

The question was how to increase demand and Keynes offered a clear statement. Given the problems of trying to get consumers to spend more or to get business to invest more, the 'public authority must be called in aid to create additional current incomes through the expenditure of borrowed or printed money.' He elaborated on this policy, 'calling it the prime mover in the first stage of the technique of recovery,' and indicating that it called for increased government spending without raising taxes. He explained the policy in greater detail that anticipated his arguments in *The General Theory*:

> In a slump governmental Loan expenditure is the only sure means of securing quickly a rising output at rising prices. That is why a war has always caused intense industrial activity. In the past orthodox finance has regarded a war as the only legitimate excuse for creating employment by governmental expenditure. You, Mr President, having cast off such fetters, are free to engage in the interests

of peace and prosperity the technique which hitherto has only been allowed to serve the purposes of war and destruction. (Keynes 1933)

Apparently Roosevelt was not one of the 'madmen in authority' that Keynes complained about.

He might have changed his mind when he wrote a private letter to Roosevelt on 1 February 1938. By this time the Great Depression had experienced a very slow recovery that ended in a downturn in 1937. Keynes argued that the recovery, however slow, had been the result of the solving of the credit problems the world had faced in 1933, relief programmes for the unemployed, public works and other government investments, some investment by business and the momentum given to the economy by these factors. As the recovery proceeded, however, relief programmes were necessarily reduced. More important, public works and other government investments had 'been greatly curtailed in the past year.' These cutbacks in government had cost the economy its momentum and led to cutbacks in business spending and Keynes concluded that unless 'the above factors were supplemented by others in due course, the present [1937–8] slump could have been predicted with absolute certainty' (Keynes 1938).

The supplemental factors Keynes referred to were involved with the socialization of investment he had called for in *The General Theory* and the letter gives us a better idea of what he meant. He proposed, as one example, government programmes for building housing thereby having the government make investment decisions in this important area of the economy. He also expressed concerns about the New Deal efforts to regulate public utilities, and suggested, 'I think there is a great deal to be said for the ownership of all the utilities by publicly owned boards.' Public opinion might not be ready for this step in all parts of the country, he added, but that only meant caution in this sense: 'If I was in your place, I should buy out the utilities at a fair price in every district where the situation was ripe for doing so, and announce that the ultimate ideal was to make this policy nation-wide.' The same approach was needed with railroads, that is, 'Nationalise them if the time is ripe' (Keynes 1938). This programme of nationalization was part of the process where 'durable investment must come increasingly under state direction' (Keynes 1938). As he had done earlier, Keynes counselled that the planning programmes of the moral economy were needed to save the market economy.

SUMNER SLICHTER AND THE ADJUSTMENT TO INSTABILITY

Sumner Slichter was featured in Chapter 7 as a cautious advocate for experiments in economic planning. In 1936 he analysed fiscal policy in a paper, 'The adjustment to instability,' which he presented at the annual meetings of the American Economic Association. Slichter began his presentation with a question about the fundamental issue of the macroeconomic approach that was just emerging: 'What possibility is there that production and employment can be kept steadily growing in a world where virtually everything else is highly unstable?' (Slichter 1936, p. 196). The instabilities in the economy were caused by the unevenly timed innovations of the process of creative destruction, cycles of good and bad years in agriculture, unpredictable changes in consumer tastes, the advent of wars and continually changing political battles.

To analyse instability, Slichter turned to an approach similar to Keynes by dividing total spending in the economy into consumer spending, business spending and government spending. Setting aside government spending for the moment, he pointed out that if the profit outlook turned unfavourable, business would spend less. That would reduce the income of consumers. If they spent their savings on consumption items, it might offset the decline in business spending, which would restore profits and revive business spending. That was not what typically happened in a downturn, however. Instead, consumers cut back on their spending and made business conditions even worse (Slichter 1936, pp. 196–7).

To attain stability in a capitalist economy, the profit outlook had to be kept favourable or some change in spending that countered declines in business spending had to take place. One policy that might restore profits was the reduction of wages. When the prices of consumer goods were falling due to a lack of consumer demand, wages had to fall to keep costs in line with prices. Reductions in wages, however, would also cause a decline in spending on consumption items. Slichter summarized the situation as follows: 'The technical problem that confronts us is how to reduce the price of labor in a period of contraction without reducing labor income' (Slichter 1936, p. 207).

The system of unemployment insurance that had just been introduced in the US struck Slichter as a good method for keeping the income of workers stable when business spending fell (Slichter 1936, p. 208). The use of unemployment insurance would be especially effective because it came into effect the moment layoffs took place. He did not think that unemployment benefits could totally offset the decline in business spending because the level of compensation would necessarily be lower than the wages an unemployed worker previously earned. They also could not offset the decline in wages that employed workers experienced. As a result, Slichter proposed a 'labor income reserve,' a supplement to unemployment insurance that 'insured' workers from wage reductions (Slichter 1936, p. 208). Changing the unemployment benefit system in this manner would not be easy, and Slichter advised that if private negotiations between business and labour could not establish the principle, the government would eventually adopt it.

To Slichter, then, the best remedy for an economic downturn was wage reductions that were compensated for by a combination of unemployment and low-wage benefits. This remedy meant that the government had to 'assume the new function of economic manager' (Slichter 1936, p. 212). Slichter remained sceptical that the government would be an effective economic manager for quite a while, however, because economics had not developed a good understanding of the nature of economic management by government and because 'the process of management is likely to be so highly political that it will discourage rather than encourage enterprise.' He also worried that special interest groups would have too much influence over the government and set fiscal policies in the wrong direction. He thus concluded rather dourly, 'Unless the power of pressure groups can be restricted, economic management by the government will be devoted in large measure to promoting or protecting special interests, to protecting established enterprises and organizations against innovation and change, and to keeping prices rigid rather than to making them flexible' (Slichter 1936, p. 213). In short, Slichter doubted the government would be able to plan the economy in the manner Keynes had proposed.

ALVIN HANSEN INTERPRETS KEYNES

Alvin Hansen (1887–1975), professor of economics at the University of Minnesota, was one of the earliest and most important interpreters of Keynes's ideas in the US. His share of the Hicks-Hansen IS-LM model that synthesized Keynesian theory with the older approach remained a mainstay of macroeconomic teaching and analysis for a very long time. In the October 1936 issue of the *Journal of Political Economy* he gave an analysis of Keynes in an article, 'Mr. Keynes on underemployment equilibrium,' where his view of Keynes was not as favourable as it eventually became.

Hansen used the opening pages of the article to consider Keynes's claims in *The General Theory* that his ideas aimed at developing what he believed the classical economists had neglected, a general theory of employment.

They had assumed that the overall economy always tended towards equilibrium at full employment and it was this assumption that Keynes challenged. In an equilibrium position with full employment, consumption and investment had no impact on employment; increases in consumption meant decreases in investment or the reverse, but the total effect was no change in employment. When an economy was in equilibrium with unemployment, however, the level of investment and consumption did matter. Investment could change in the same direction as consumption and the two combined could increase or decrease the level of employment (Hansen 1936, pp. 669–70).

When investment and consumption declined in tandem and created unemployment, the problem for society was 'to bring under social control the determinants of equilibrium' (Hansen 1936, p. 670). The determinants, as Keynes had identified them, were the marginal propensity to consume, the marginal efficiency of capital and the rate of interest. These determinants all reflected the psychologies of consumers, businesses and financial markets and brought home the point that it was social conventions and institutions that were the key economic variables, not prices. How much individuals decided to save depended more on their attitude towards thrift than on the rate of interest, which caused the problem that Keynes identified of savings not automatically being equal to investment (Hansen 1936, p. 675). Without a change in the key elements of the marginal propensity to consume, the marginal efficiency of investment or the interest rate, the market economy would not reduce unemployment (Hansen 1936, p. 677).

Hansen questioned this result that the economy could stay in equilibrium with unemployment. First of all, he argued that equilibrium with unemployment required an assumption of rigid costs of resources including the wages of labour. There was evidence that the economy was heading in that direction but until it was apparent that costs were rigid, it was hard to say if Keynes's ideas were correct. Second, the process of creative destruction had 'the effect of raising the marginal efficiency of capital and thereby stimulating investment' (Hansen 1936, p. 680). If the future of the US saw stagnation of innovation, then Keynes's analysis was likely to prove correct.

If stagnation was the future, what should be done? Hansen made it clear that 'Keynes's proposals are designed to offer a substitute for a completely planned socialistic or communistic economy.' Keynes's solutions for a stagnant economy included 'socially controlled investment.' Hansen believed that the social control over investment went far 'in the direction of a planned economy and might, indeed, lead straight into thoroughgoing socialism.' Overall, Hansen worried that Keynes's policies would create an artificial and forced investment that would be different from the investment brought about by the process of creative destruction. As a result, he concluded, 'the continued workability of the system of private enterprise will be made possible, not by changes in prevailing economic institutions (such as those advocated by Keynes), but rather by the work of the inventor and the engineer' (Hansen 1936, p. 682).

Despite this conclusion, Hansen believed that regardless of the effectiveness of Keynes's proposals they were admired by many thinkers and policy makers and probably would be used to a greater degree in the future. To Hansen, the popularity of Keynesian fiscal policy was evidence that modern society was 'reverting to the behavior patterns of the precapitalistic period' where the emphasis was on leisure time with many holidays instead of a work ethic and the consumption of luxuries instead of thrift (Hansen 1936, p. 683). Hansen apparently preferred the values of the market economy and his later formulation of macroeconomics left out Keynes's proposal that government control investment.

JOSEPH SCHUMPETER REVIEWS KEYNES

By the 1930s, Joseph Schumpeter had become a fixture in the economic scene in the US. He had moved from Europe to become a professor at Harvard University and his international reputation rivalled that of Keynes. He brought all of this to bear on a review of *The General Theory* in the *Journal of the American Statistical Association* for December 1936.

Schumpeter began the review with praise for Keynes, detailing his new book's influence as generating 'the expectations of the best of our students' and kindling the interest of economists worldwide. From all of this interest, he felt he had to 'congratulate the author on a signal personal success' (Schumpeter 1936, p. 791). The book had generated some negative responses, and Schumpeter indicated that his review would be another negative one, but those negative reviews indicated the extent to which Keynes had challenged economic thinking.

Schumpeter's main complaint about Keynes was that while he claimed to be writing about theory, his primary concern was with policy and a specific policy of government intervention in the economy. That policy was written between every line in Keynes's book. Schumpeter believed that economics should be treated as a pure science that analysed economic conditions using data and faulted Keynes for not following this approach. As for the policy Keynes offered, he found it to be nothing new or interesting, writing 'everybody knows what it is Mr. Keynes advises.' The advice might be good for England in 1936, but Schumpeter considered it to be advice presented 'in the garb of general scientific truth' when it really had relevance 'to the unique historical situation of a given time and country' (Schumpeter 1936, p. 792).

To make his case, Keynes had employed some very specific assumptions to underline his points. As one example, Schumpeter gave Keynes's 'assumption that variations in output are uniquely related to variations in employment.' Statisticians who investigated the relationships between labour and total output would find this assumption hard to swallow. The only way Keynes could logically hold to it, moreover, required 'the further assumption that all production functions remain invariant.' We observed earlier the importance for Keynes of assuming that there were no changes in the economic variables associated with the process of creative destruction and not surprisingly Schumpeter strenuously objected to this assumption. He wrote, 'Now the outstanding feature of capitalism is that' production functions 'are being incessantly revolutionized. The capitalist process is essentially a process of change of the type which is being assumed away in this book' (Schumpeter 1936, p. 794). Keynes's use of this assumption was unrealistic.

Keynes also built his theory that unemployment could exist in equilibrium on the propensity to consume and on a falling inducement to invest. The propensity to consume went against statistical data on consumption, especially as fuelled by credit, and Schumpeter considered it to be beside the point for not considering why 'consumers' expenditure alternatively increases and contracts.' The declining inducement to invest was only possible because 'Keynes eliminates the most powerful propeller of investment, the financing of changes in production functions' (Schumpeter 1936, p. 794). In short, Schumpeter criticized Keynes for assuming what he needed to prove, that the market economy had become so stagnant that even the process of creative destruction was dying.

As for Keynes's policies of government intervention with spending programmes to stimulate consumption, Schumpeter offered a scathing rebuke. Keynes had discussed his policies in the spirit of Mercantilism, a pre-capitalist economic theory that called for government control over the economy. Schumpeter described the situation Keynes promoted as follows:

> Let him who accepts the message there expounded rewrite the history of the French ancien regime in some such terms as these: Louis XV was a most enlightened monarch. Feeling the necessity of stimulating expenditure he secured the services of such expert spenders as Madame de Pompadour and Madame du Barry. They went to work with unsurpassable efficiency. Full employment, a maximum of resulting output, and general well-being ought to have been the consequence. It is true that instead we find misery, shame and, at

the end of it all, a stream of blood. But that was a chance coincidence. (Schumpeter 1936, p. 795)

Why should we expect a better outcome from using the same approach in a market economy was the question Schumpeter asked of Keynes.

ARTHUR D. GAYER AND THE INVESTMENT MULTIPLIER

One of the elements of Keynes's economics was his popularization of the concept of the multiplier. The point of the multiplier is to show how changes in investment by business or spending by the government can generate larger changes in income. In a discussion of fiscal policy at the 1938 meetings of the American Economic Association, Arthur Gayer, professor of economics at Columbia University, presented a paper, 'Fiscal policies,' that addressed the theoretical and empirical issue surrounding the multiplier (Gayer 1938, p. 90). In the past arguments in favour of a policy of government compensatory spending had revolved around the use of spending on public works, but in recent years the idea had expanded to include nearly all government spending. In theory, the current justification for compensatory spending was the multiplier.

To Gayer, however, it was not possible to calculate in advance what the impact of an expansionary fiscal policy would be. Advocates of an expansionary fiscal policy argued as though the multiplier would always be positive. The crucial question in the use of an expansionary fiscal policy to fight a recession was 'whether its directly beneficial effects in stimulating consumption are outweighed or not by the injurious indirect effects that it may have on private investment through its repercussions on the budget, the bond market, building costs, the state of confidence, and future expectations' (Gayer 1938, p. 90). Expansionary spending may bring recovery in one area but produce decline in another. Gayer was raising the issue of 'crowding out,' where government spending may lead to higher interest rates and reduced business investment, causing a negative investment multiplier. Keynes's theoretical statement of the multiplier could not help policy makers know in advance how much income would be generated by a change in spending brought about through fiscal policy. The numerical value of the multiplier could only be calculated after the money was spent and the change in income it generated was calculated. Keynes had claimed more precision for the multiplier than was justified (Gayer 1938, p. 91). This lack of precision would hinder government efforts to use fiscal policy to plan the direction of the economy.

Gayer noted that since government spending during the depression had averaged only 6 per cent of national income, it was difficult to see how fiscal policy added stimulus to the economy. By taking into account the impact of the successive rounds of spending brought about by the multiplier, however, 'the resulting stimulus to business could very well have been of prime importance' (Gayer 1938, p. 101). Government spending had to continue because investment spending had not recovered sufficiently to get the economy moving again. Here, though he did not state this directly, Gayer argued in favour of Keynes's assumption that the economy, at least in the 1930s, was best viewed as a stationary state. Gayer put it this way, 'I refer to the possibility that an increasing secular difficulty may be confronting business today in finding promising channels for investment on an adequate scale. We are not justified in assuming without question that profitable new investment outlets will always automatically present themselves in abundance' (Gayer 1938, p. 106). At previous times, stagnation in the economy had alternated with periods of rapid investment and the 1930s may well be another period of stagnation. If this view was correct then government fiscal policy had an even greater task before it than compensating for a decline in spending due to the depression. Gayer concluded that the multiplier effect did work even though its total impact was difficult to gauge.

JOHN MAURICE CLARK APPRAISES FISCAL POLICY

John Maurice Clark has been a mainstay of our studies of the Progressive Era and the New Deal and we have closely followed his writings on the need for economic planning. We saw in Chapter 11 that he had turned away from planning. Instead, he became interested in compensatory fiscal policy and at the 1939 meetings of the American Economic Association he presented a paper, 'An appraisal of the workability of compensatory devices' that was published in the March 1939 issue of the *American Economic Review*.

The topic of his paper was the extent to which expansionary deficit spending could 'produce an industrial expansion, probably larger than itself' (Clark 1939b, p. 194). Fiscal policy was a plan of spending that served as a stimulus to increase output in the economy through the multiplier. Clark indicated that when he first encountered the theory of the multiplier he thought it contained an important explanation for how private spending brought about a recovery. In addition, the multiplier worked in both directions and was useful in explaining how a recession occurred. It also explained what 'might be expected from a sudden stoppage of the public outlays, unless some stimulus from another source had occurred in the meantime' (Clark 1939, p. 201). The recession of 1937–8 had been viewed by some economists as having been caused by a reduction in federal government spending. This interpretation of the negative multiplier effect suggested to Clark that an expansionary fiscal policy had to be ended gradually, depending on how much private investment increased.

This brought Clark to his key point, the impact deficit spending had on private investment. Following his own theory of the accelerator, Clark argued that 'public deficit spending, by increasing the demand for consumers goods, would naturally cause some increase in the demand for durable capital equipment; and this increase would come fairly promptly, without waiting for all the existing excess capacity to be called into use' (Clark 1939, p. 202). The total impact of government spending on investment, however, would depend on the attitude business took towards that spending; if they believed it would work that would enhance their expectations about the future and boost investment spending (Clark 1939, pp. 202–3). The usefulness of fiscal policy was extremely delicate in terms of its effects on business spending, especially if high taxes took away profits.

We can see Clark's disenchantment with planning in his approach to fiscal policy. Keynes had called for the socialization of investment, with the government finding ways to increase capital spending by business. Before the NIRA, Clark might have agreed with this approach. Instead, he argued that the multiplier effect, by increasing consumption, would be enough to spur investment through the accelerator process; the socialization of investment was not needed. Clark insisted that if the market economy was to be maintained, its participants had to be prepared to accept fiscal policy. His hope was that its flaws could be offset by thoughtful policies. There was danger in trying to manipulate the economy but there was also danger in not doing anything.

PAUL A. SAMUELSON RE-EXAMINES PUMP-PRIMING

Paul A. Samuelson (1915–2009) is especially known for his work in introducing Keynes's theories to countless college students in his popular textbook. In one of his earliest articles, 'The theory of pump-priming reexamined,' published in the September 1940 issue of the *American Economic Review*, he offered a preliminary statement of his approach to Keynes's theory. Like Clark, he focused on the interaction of the multiplier with the accelerator to increase investment.

He began the article by observing how the Great Depression had turned the attention of economists to the issues related to fiscal policy and the multiplier. The recession of 1937 further highlighted the multiplier as a way of assessing the impact of government spending on the economy (Samuelson 1940, p. 492). The key to the multiplier effect of government spending was the way it could influence private investment through the accelerator effect.

Part of what made investment so important in determining national income was that by paying out income to workers it added to consumption demand without adding immediately to the supply of consumption goods. Samuelson noted, 'The most favorable kind of investment from the standpoint of bolstering up the national income is that which does not increase the supply of consumers' goods for a long time to come' (Samuelson 1940, p. 497). Building construction was a good example of this type of investment. Government spending also took this form, because it increased income the same as investment did but without the production of additional consumption goods. As a result, expansionary fiscal policy could produce a large amount of stimulus from a small change in spending (Samuelson 1940, p. 498).

From this perspective, it might be readily concluded that the multiplier could be relied on to give a thorough analysis of the impact fiscal policy would have on national income. Samuelson resisted this conclusion, because it did not take into account the impact fiscal policy would have on investment by business through 'crowding out.' He wrote,

> It is conceivable that a dollar's worth of government investment might cause a simultaneous disinvestment of ten dollars on the part of private individuals, which with a marginal propensity to consume of two thirds would result in a total decrease in the national income of twenty seven dollars. The government Multiplier would therefore be negative even though the total investment Multiplier is positive. (Samuelson 1940, p. 500)

The issue was how government spending affected business investment.

If the economy and investment were in the stationary state as Keynes had assumed, government spending would increase consumption according to the multiplier. From Clark's accelerator process, Samuelson argued that the increased consumption would bring about new investment by business. The combination of private investment and public investment, through the multiplier effect, would bring about increased income, and Samuelson identified cases where investment and income would grow or taper off (Samuelson 1940, pp. 501–2). The case where investment and income would grow from a programme of government spending was what most economists meant by pump-priming. Samuelson indicated that most theories of pump-priming assumed that the economy was in a very stable state and a small programme of spending would push it into a different stable state at a higher level of employment. But pump-priming was just one of the cases Samuelson had set forth in looking at the relationship between investment and income and given his other cases where government spending did not lead to a permanent increase in income, 'No one should be seriously disappointed if a spending policy over a number of years does not create prosperity in perpetuity' (Samuelson 1940, p. 503). But it was also possible that the prosperity would continue. It all depended on the value of the multiplier and its relationship to the accelerator and since those were not knowable policy makers would have to be satisfied that there was a multiplier effect with regard to government spending and hope that it would bring about more investment through the accelerator.

The point Samuelson is making is that economics could not give policy makers definitive advice on how an expansionary fiscal policy would impact the economy and whether it could be relied on to bring about a recovery. The best that could be hoped for was that it would get the economy moving in the right direction. Like Clark, however, Samuelson did not consider Keynes's policy of government controlled investment.

DAVID MCCORD WRIGHT EXAMINES THE MULTIPLIER

One of the important issues related to fiscal policy is the effect of the multiplier from government spending to changes in income. In the November 1940 issue of the *Quarterly Journal of Economics* David McCord Wright (1909–68), economics professor at the University of Virginia, considered this problem in an article, 'The economic limit and economic burden of an internally held national debt.' Although Wright was mainly concerned with problems caused by a series of uninterrupted federal government budget deficits, here we are interested in his view of the multiplier.

The multiplier was related to the amount of debt the government ran up through continued deficits. Wright argued that the real issue in terms of the size of the national debt was the burden it placed on the economy due to the labour and other resources it drew from the private sector. When the economy had full employment, increases in government spending would bring about a smaller amount in output (in percentage terms) from the private sector. When there was unemployment of labour and other resources, government spending might not take any resources from the private sector, unless the spending programme was 'badly planned' such as happened when, 'by subsidizing a declining industry men may be kept in a line of endeavor which should be abandoned' (Wright 1940, p. 118). The fiscal policy might also be poorly timed and use resources that were needed in the private sector by the time the policy was implemented. There was no assurance that fiscal policy could plan the direction of the economy.

Keynes had argued that through the 'multiplier effect' that was key to his theory, 'the national money income will necessarily grow as a result of government spending' (Wright 1940, p. 121). The multiplier was controversial, however. Wright's view was that 'as a matter of theory Keynes's demonstration stands up.' There was some evidence that it held up in practice as well, but Keynes had indicated the possibility of declines in spending in other areas of the economy offsetting the multiplier effect. Wright noted that 'Economic prosperity is excessively dependent on a political and social atmosphere which is congenial to the average business man. If the fear of a … New Deal depresses enterprise this need not be the result either of a reasonable calculation or of a plot with political intent – it is a mere consequence of upsetting the delicate balance of spontaneous optimism' (Wright 1940, p. 122). This consequence could reduce the size of the multiplier and erode the prospects for government spending being self-financed through the multiplier whereby increased government spending would increase national income and thus increase government tax collections. Wright concluded,

> The New Dealers in this country may have done their cause a disservice by concentrating their arguments on pump priming and the multiplier. We should realize that there are weighty reasons for a spending program, not because you will somehow get three dollars for every dollar you spend through the government, but because you may lose from private enterprise three dollars for every dollar you do not spend. (Wright 1940, p. 123)

This conclusion meant that fiscal policy might be used to increase economic activity but there was no guarantee that the increase would take place. Wright ended his article with several examples to show what had to happen for increases in government spending to bring about increases in income and whether the increased national debt that resulted was a burden or not.

THE NEW REPUBLIC APPROVES FISCAL POLICY

As a leading magazine for Progressive politics, *The New Republic* generally approved of the New Deal and we have already described its views on the NIRA. As the Great Depression continued, it became increasingly interested in the role of government spending in bringing about a recovery. In this section we review articles from *The New Republic* that dealt with the issue of expansionary fiscal policy.

In the 18 December 1935 issue Stuart Chase took a look at fiscal policy in an article titled 'Recovery.' Chase found the basic cause of the depression to be that too much money was saved. Economic balance at full employment required that savings be channelled into investment (Chase 1935b, p. 162). When the level of savings was more than could be profitably invested, equilibrium in the economy only took place when income fell. Starting with President Hoover and continuing with President Roosevelt, government spending from borrowing had been used to restore employment. Both presidents had taken savings that were not being invested by businesses and put them in the hands of government agencies to spend (Chase 1935b, p. 164). This fiscal policy had not brought about a full recovery, however. Chase argued that as long as the private sector did not revive its spending, the federal government had to keep spending for 'as long as the government's credit holds out' (Chase 1935b, p. 165). Like other advocates of planning, Chase settled on fiscal policy as a viable alternative.

A second article, published on 3 February 1936, was titled 'All right, balance the budget!' and was written by Ferdinand Lundberg. With his tongue in his cheek Lundberg offered several plans for balancing the budget such as having businesses repay the loans they had received from the Reconstruction Finance Corporation and other agencies, the curtailment of the expansion of the navy, reduction of the public works programmes and the elimination of the civil conservation corps. These methods would eliminate jobs and 'industry, as everyone knows, could not give these persons employment' (Lundberg 1936, pp. 361–2). Those lost jobs were a potential danger from reduced government spending (Lundberg 1936, p. 363). An expansionary fiscal policy was needed to keep the economic system from collapse even if it did have to bail out businesses whose leaders opposed the New Deal.

A third article on fiscal policy, 'When and how to balance the budget,' appeared in *The New Republic* as an editorial on 5 May 1937. The article took the position that during a depression 'the budget not only is certain to be unbalanced but *ought* to be unbalanced' (*The New Republic* 5 May 1937, p. 372, emphasis in original). Deficits were needed during a depression because purchasing power was in decline from low levels of investment and the government needed to make up the shortfall by borrowing and spending. During prosperous times, however, the budget was more likely to be in a surplus. The total approach to fiscal policy was therefore to have the budget being 'balanced on the average over a period of years including all phases of the business cycle.' From this approach, the budget should be balanced only 'when recovery sets in and prosperity seems to be in prospect' (*The New Republic* 1937, p. 372).

Was recovery setting in at the time the article was being written in 1937? Apparently the editors of *The New Republic* thought so. They were concerned that continued borrowing by the federal government would make the national debt so large that the government might not be able to borrow additional money 'when depression next strikes us.' Thus, the article recommended that 'the budget ought now to be balanced and that debt retirement ought to begin at the earliest possible moment' (*The New Republic* 1937, p. 372). A balanced budget, however, did not have to mean the end of fiscal stimulus. Given the continued need for public relief as well as the need for many other programmes the federal government was undertaking, such as housing, a balanced budget at high levels of spending was needed.

A balanced budget at high levels of spending, however, did not necessarily mean higher taxes. Growth in incomes from the recovery would bring in extra tax collections, especially if they fell 'heavily on the higher brackets.' But no matter how increases in the higher tax brackets were 'justified on ethical grounds,' that policy would not raise enough revenue to get the budget in balance. Therefore, *The New Republic* argued, lowering the amount of income that was exempt from the income tax would 'include millions who now pay no income tax' and a small increase in their rates would give enough tax revenue to balance the budget at a high level of expenditure (*The New Republic* 1937, p. 372).

These tax increases need not harm the economy. As long as the government spent the taxes it collected it was no different from private spending in terms of its impact on the economy. In a line similar to Keynes's the editorial noted, 'Armament-making prosperity is recognized even by conservatives. There is no reason in the world why government spending for things that have uses other than for purposes of destruction should not have as stimulating an economic effect' (*The New Republic* 1937, p. 372).

A final article we have found in *The New Republic* on fiscal policy is another editorial, 'That debt controversy,' published on 19 January 1940. President Roosevelt had defended the fiscal policy of his administration by arguing that since national income had greatly improved over the previous seven years the debt was not a great burden on the economy. In addition, the president pointed out that if spending by the federal government was reduced too severely 'we are likely to encourage a recession, just as we did in the spring of 1937.' In support of the president, the editorial stated that the 'New Deal argument' was that when private borrowing declined, through 'public borrowing and spending' the government could 'stimulate employment and production when business will not or cannot' (*The New Republic* 19 January 1940, p. 231). The editors believed that although the growth of national income had improved under the New Deal, it could have been better, and concluded, 'Mr. Roosevelt should be apologizing that he has not spent more' (*The New Republic* 19 January 1940, p. 232).

CONCLUSION

Keynes presented an alluring prospect to Progressives and other advocates of planning that they could use government spending and the social control of investment to plan the direction of the economy and counteract the Great Depression. Thanks to the multiplier effect, increases in government spending would stimulate the economy when the recipients of government funds spent their money on consumption and created jobs in the private sector; a government investment fund would ensure that business would increase its capital spending in line with the expansion of consumption. The income from those new jobs, when taxed, would even offset the deficits that the government spending necessitated. The economists in this chapter, however, qualified the degree to which fiscal policy could stimulate the economy because the multiplier effect that Keynes had set forth was not precise enough in practice to make accurate predictions. They also backed away from the socialization of investment, arguing instead that the multiplier effect, to the extent that it worked, would function effectively through the accelerator to increase investment.

Regardless of their views on Keynes's ideas, it was clear to them that the deficit spending of the 1930s had not ended the Great Depressions. Advocates of Keynesian fiscal policy could readily agree with *The New Republic* that the fiscal stimulus from New Deal spending programmes was insufficient to bring about a full recovery. After all, the federal government deficits ranged from $2.3 to $3.5 billion from 1933 to 1940. Given that total federal government spending ranged from $5.1 to $10.1 billion during this period, as compared to national income of $56.4 to $101.4 billion, government spending would have been in the range of 10 per cent of gross domestic product (GDP). This was an increase compared to the 4–7 per cent of GDP under Hoover, but it would have taken a very large multiplier for the fiscal stimulus of the New Deal to have brought about full employment. Larger deficits were called for by the Keynesian theory.

In the October 1939 issue of the *Journal of Political Economy* Rutledge Vining of the University of Arkansas published an article, 'Suggestions of Keynes in the writings of Veblen,' to explore the connections between the ideas of Thorstein Veblen, which we have reviewed in Chapter 3, and Keynes. Vining characterized Veblen as agreeing with Keynes that the economy existed in a state of stagnation. He quoted Veblen as indicating that it was only the Spanish-American War in 1898 that restored prosperity and if that 'outside stimulus' was 'continued at an adequate pitch, the season of prosperity may be prolonged' (Vining 1939, p. 700). Veblen drew the conclusion that only government expenditures on war could be justified as a reason for running deficits large enough to end a depression. These social limits as to what was acceptable spending by the government apparently still held when Keynes wrote and Vining quoted his statements to the effect that spending on 'wars may serve to increase wealth, if the education of our statesmen on the principles of the classical economics stands in the way of anything better' (Vining 1939, p. 703). Thus, we have *The New Republic* along with Keynes and Veblen agreeing that military spending was a more politically acceptable form of fiscal policy then social spending on human needs.

This perspective coincides with the idea that it was not the New Deal but World War II that ended the Great Depression. Certainly government spending in the US rose dramatically during the war, with the federal budget during the war taking up about 40 per cent of total national income for the period of the war. As part of this spending, the government 'hired' over ten million men and women directly in the effort to win the war, with another 16 million individuals working in defence plants. Not surprisingly, the unemployment rate fell to a record low of 1.2 per cent in 1944. But the war also saw an economy completely controlled by the government, with overall production being planned by a War Production Board and then by the Office of War Mobilization. Prices were controlled by the Office of Price Administration, while the National War Labor Board regulated wages. Consumer goods were rationed through a coupon system that gave limited permission to consumers to purchase scarce goods and services. This was more than government spending combined with the socialization of investment. It was planning the economy. As was the case with the WIB of World War I, the planning was made relatively easy because the goal was simple: produce what was needed to win the war and ration everything else with coupons.

It would have been unprecedented and probably unthinkable for the New Deal to have put forth this level of stimulus in terms of spending and this degree of government planning and control during the Great Depression. No one, not even John Maynard Keynes, could have justified that amount of spending and control over investment in peacetime. Unlike World War I, however, when advocates of the moral economy used the WIB as a model for the planned economy, the lesson taken from World War II was that Keynesian fiscal policy, without the socialization of investment and planning, was the proper programme for ending the business cycle.

13. The New Deal and planning

For three decades before the New Deal, Progressives promoted the idea that government intervention in the economy was needed because the market economy could not solve the problems associated with the business cycle. Among those Progressives, the advocates of planning as a way to eliminate depressions thought they had their chance when the New Deal was put in place. The NIRA provided the potential for national economic planning, but it was never used to plan the economy. On that our economists, pundits, politicians and business leaders agreed.

In this chapter we look at how some of our proponents of planning and the moral economy interpreted the New Deal as a culmination of their ideas. How had it fallen short of their goals and where it was going were questions they asked. We also present the views of one advocate for the market economy. The persons whose ideas are reviewed in this chapter will be familiar to the reader by now and we start with the most familiar one of all, President Roosevelt.

ROOSEVELT EXPLAINS HIS OVERALL POLICY

By all accounts Franklin D. Roosevelt was a polished public speaker. Throughout his years as president he put his speaking abilities to use in a series of radio broadcasts to the people of the US called the 'Fireside Chats.' In those Fireside Chats the president explained the basis for many of his policies from the NIRA to the strategy for fighting World War II. Among those explanations he included occasional comments on his overall policy, answering the questions about what he believed had caused the Great Depression and outlining his views on what role the government should play in rescuing the US from it.

In a Fireside Chat on 28 June 1934, for example, he placed the source of the Great Depression on a lack of a moral economy. He spoke, 'Much of our trouble today and in the past few years has been due to a lack of understanding of the elementary principles of justice and fairness by those in whom leadership in business and finance was placed' (Roosevelt 1934a, pp. 424–6). That theme of justice and fairness continued in the broadcast of 28 April 1935, when Roosevelt stated that the programmes of the New Deal 'contemplate the enrichment of our national life by a sound and rational ordering of its various elements and wise provisions for the protection of the weak against the strong' (Roosevelt 1935b, pp. 737–9). As a specific reason for the depression, Roosevelt stated the cause as underconsumption. The US had created a very productive economy. Indeed, it was too productive because farms and factories could produce more than could be sold at reasonable prices and fair profits. A system that produced poverty in the midst of abundance was certainly immoral.

A solution to the problem of underconsumption was the NIRA, which aimed at getting production in line with consumption through guidance by government. On 30 September 1934 Roosevelt explained his approach to business in relation to government: 'Men may differ as to the particular form of governmental activity with respect to industry and business, but nearly all are agreed that private enterprise in times such as these cannot be left without assistance and without reasonable safeguards lest it destroy not only itself but also our process of civilization' (Roosevelt 1934b, pp. 502–5). The chief intervention by the New Deal with business was the NIRA and it had worked in getting people back to work through 'the establishment of fair, competitive standards and because of relief from unfair competition in wage cutting' (Roosevelt 1934b, pp. 537–9). Roosevelt declared, 'We are definitely rebuilding our political and economic system on the lines laid down by the New Deal – lines which as I have so often made clear, are in complete accord with the underlying principles of orderly popular government' (Roosevelt 1934b, pp. 542–6).

Some individuals might 'complain that all we have done is unnecessary and subject to great risks.' But Roosevelt replied to them: 'In our efforts for recovery we have avoided on the one hand the theory that business should and must be taken over into an all-embracing government' and avoided 'the equally untenable theory that it is an interference with liberty to offer reasonable help when private enterprise is in need of help' (Roosevelt 1934b, pp. 598–617). The New Deal would avoid the all-encompassing planned moral economy of Edward Bellamy and the market economy of William Graham Sumner to produce a mixed economy that was a partnership among all the stakeholders in industry and agriculture. Roosevelt observed on 6 September 1936, 'Private enterprise is necessary to any nation which seeks to maintain the democratic form of government' (Roosevelt 1936, pp. 827–8). By giving workers a decent standard of living and economic security Roosevelt sought 'to avoid the growth of a class-conscious society' in the US (Roosevelt 1936, p. 859). The overriding goal of his policies, as explained by Roosevelt on 12 October 1937, was 'such governmental rules of the game that … industry will all produce a balanced abundance without waste' (Roosevelt 1937, pp. 1077–8).

Because the Great Depression was an emergency as great as any faced in the US during wartime, Roosevelt referred to the New Deal as 'our program for the national defense of our economic system' (Roosevelt 1938, p. 1350). In his defence of the US economic system, however, Roosevelt had to change it. On his telling, the changes included an infusion of elements of the moral economy into a market economy. As a result, Roosevelt could claim that he was moving the US towards the mixed economy of government intervention, drawing that fine line between the moral economy and the market economy.

REXFORD TUGWELL AND THE FUTURE OF PLANNING

Rexford Tugwell has been another of the mainstays of this study, having espoused the cause of national economic planning well before his days as an active member of the New Deal. Even though the type of economic planning he fought for had not been implemented during the New Deal, he never gave up hope that it would eventually be used. He made this point in two articles in *The New Republic*. In doing so, he also gave his thoughts on what the New Deal had accomplished,

The first article, on 9 December 1936, titled 'The future of national planning,' posed the question of how the US should develop a system of planning. Tugwell began by rejecting the idea that the US would 'set up some kind of economic council which would tell us what to do' as a 'doctrinaire and essentially naive' approach to the problem. The inhabitants of the US did not like being told what to do unless they took part in deciding it. This attitude reflected the country's democratic spirit. Advocates for planning typically reacted to this democratic spirit with 'the premise that dictatorships are more effective in economic affairs.' This premise led them to the conclusion that 'communism, or it may be fascism, is a superior competitive instrument and must eventually displace democracy' (Tugwell 1936, p. 162).

Tugwell did not agree with this conclusion because to him it was much too rigid. A doctrinaire approach to planning must always fail because eventually the facts of economic life will change to the point where doctrine becomes useless. During the Great Depression the accepted doctrine was that 'The purchasing power of consumers has to be enlarged until it suffices to take off the market the goods that an expanding industry can supply.' The problem in putting this doctrine to good use by expanding consumer purchasing power was that business leaders in the US were dictators 'within their own sphere.' While their dictatorial powers allowed for effective 'intra-industry planning' it did not permit 'inter-industry planning.' The self-interest of businessmen in taking care of their own firms did not allow for national planning and Tugwell believed that businessmen preferred to keep it that way. For democracy to continue, it had to curtail the small-scale dictatorships of businessmen (Tugwell 1936, pp. 162–3).

The voters of the US had re-elected Roosevelt because they wanted him to use his powers to ensure that democracy won out over the dictatorships of business. The cooperation of business was essential to the future of planning but that meant businessmen had to accept democracy's influence over their individual decisions. Even though business and labor were not yet cooperating in bringing planning to industry, the New Deal through its approval by the voters was preparing the way for business to accept the need for its 'economic statesmanship' (Tugwell 1936, pp. 163–4).

On 26 July1939 Tugwell returned to the issue of what the New Deal had wanted to accomplish in the way of planning with an article, 'We have bought ourselves time to think.' The article was part of a series in *The New Republic*, 'After the New Deal.' Tugwell began the article by indicating there was a feeling of frustration among New Dealers over how little they had accomplished. Tugwell reminded them of all the good they had accomplished in terms of giving relief to the poor and the unemployed, even if they had not achieved all the changes in the economy that Progressives had wanted.

Those changes in the economy harkened back to World War I and the planning of the economy by the WIB. The war and the WIB had 'resulted in national organization on a unitary scheme' and that brought about 'immense advances toward industrial unity.' The increase of production took precedence over profits. When the war ended, however, 'profit was reestablished in the shrine' (Tugwell 1939, p. 324). Progressives had hoped that the crisis initiated by the Great Depression would bring about the same type of unity and that the New Deal was the vehicle to accomplish it. They sought to use collective methods, and Tugwell noted that those methods were merely 'a social arrangement in which the new industrialism can operate' (Tugwell 1939, p. 325). Modern industry was an interconnected whole that had to be operated collectively to operate at all.

The problem was that there was resistance to change among many important groups in the economy. Certainly business objected to what the New Deal aimed to accomplish. As a result of this resistance, the work of the New Deal 'was done haltingly and not with claims of discovery and shouts of virtue.' Significantly, the New Deal had begun 'the important task of changing habits and bringing policy within the influence of modern thought.' Tugwell made it clear that this modern thought included the idea that 'collective institutions will emerge from collective facts' with the result that 'profits must be subordinated to production.' Again, business leaders and their followers might resist those collective facts, but they were up against 'a vast-scale modernism which no resistance can stop' (Tugwell 1939, p. 325). The function of the New Deal was thus to prepare the way for this modern, collective economy that technology required.

WALTER LIPPMANN CONFRONTS COLLECTIVISM

As the New Deal continued to move along, with policies that did not end the Great Depression, in 1938 Walter Lippmann became disenchanted with planning and more interested in the market economy. As noted in Chapter 11, he attributed his new viewpoint to the influence of Ludwig von Mises and Frederich A. Hayek (Lippmann 1938, p. vii). Lippmann's discontentment was with the 'dominant dogma of the age,' collectivism.

Under collectivism Progressives were 'unanimous in holding that the government with its instruments of coercion must, by commanding the people how they shall live, direct the course of civilization' (Lippmann 1938, p. 4). Such government might work in a static society, but since the industrial revolution science had been used to bring about a continual change in technology – the process of creative destruction – and planning could only work in an economy with 'a well-established routine which has to be altered only at rare intervals' (Lippmann 1938, p. 11). Apparently Lippmann had also learned from von Mises and Hayek that government intervention in the economy necessarily led to socialism. Consequently, he was concerned with 'gradual collectivism' whereby democratic countries had started a trend to control the market economy through 'the use of collectivist measures' (Lippmann 1938, p. 106). This gradualist approach consisted of a series of collective reforms to bring about a planned economy by serving the needs of a series of special interest groups.

From this view Lippmann recognized the dilemma of trying to build the moral economy of planning. Going full scale into a moral economy as Edward Bellamy had proposed required a dictatorship with the authority to ensure that everyone behaved morally, as defined by the authority of the dictator. But a gradual building up of the moral economy, through a piecemeal taking away of the functions of the market and giving them to the government, could become a policy of appeasing special interest groups, turning a moral imperative into a moral hazard. Through his recognition of these issues, Lippmann came back to the attitude of William Graham Sumner that the economic liberalism started by Adam Smith 'was the necessary philosophy of the industrial revolution' (Lippmann 1938, p. 373).

GEORGE SOULE ASSESSES THE NEW DEAL

George Soule has been a common voice in this book, given his long and consistent commitment to planning and the moral economy. Like many of the persons we have featured, there has always been a question of how strongly his voice was heard in the US during the 1930s. A partial answer to this question may be offered through the recognition he was given in January 1939, when he was invited to give the Storrs Lectures on Jurisprudence at the Yale School of Law. The overall title of the lectures was 'An economic constitution for democracy.'

In the first lecture, 'The peril to democracy,' Soule began with the idea that the New Deal was over and that it had changed the structure of the US economy in ways that were irreversible. By saying the New Deal was over, Soule did not mean that its impact was at an end with what he supposed would be Roosevelt's last years of office. Rather, the New Deal would vanish from the minds of the people of the US because its changes had been so complete. He wrote,

> It is not probable that many of the New Deal measures will be repealed or even substantially amended. Nor can it be said that they will pass into forgetfulness without continuing to exert an important influence on our society. What will appear, however, is that they have been assimilated into the background; they are beginning to be taken for granted even by many of their traditional opponents. (Soule 1939, p. 2)

Once a programme was taken for granted, it became part of the political and economic environment like the air we breathe. This was the programme of gradual collectivism that Lippmann described.

Soule assessed the New Deal to highlight its failure to end the depression in his second lecture, 'The legacy of the New Deal.' From his perspective, the business cycle of the 1930s, especially the recession of 1937–8, was 'almost exactly paralleled by the increases and decreases of governmental spending of borrowed funds' (Soule 1939, p. 41). Soule concluded, 'Pump priming works as long as we keep priming the pump, but fails as soon as we stop pouring water in' (Soule 1939, p. 42). Soule argued that a lack of consumption spending had brought about the depression and this lack had to do with the unequal distribution of income. He summed up the idea as follows:

> Depression in consumers' goods industries therefore argues either that a great many potential consumers do not receive large enough wages, salaries, or income from raising crops (if they are farmers), or that the prices of goods offered for sales and production are too high. The problem of increasing sales

and production is clearly one of raising incomes of consumers on the one hand or reducing prices on the other, or both. (Soule 1939, p. 47)

In a similar way, for business to invest, prices of goods and services had to be sufficiently high and the costs of resources sufficiently low for it to earn a profit on its investment.

Any policy to bring about an economic recovery had to get all these prices and the incomes those prices produced in a proper balance. Starting with the NIRA, the programmes of the New Deal to establish prices for consumer goods produced by industry had 'been confused and relatively ineffectual' (Soule 1939, p. 53). The result was that the New Deal had not been able to use the control of prices to increase production nor to produce a greater equality of income (Soule 1939, pp. 54–5). As he put it, 'The problem is rather one of making internal readjustment among price relationships, of knowing which prices ought to rise, which ought to fall, and which ought to remain unchanged' (Soule 1939, p. 59). The New Deal had not developed a consistent policy to solve this problem. Because of its failure to solve this problem, which amounts to having the planners of the moral economy being able to do the job the market economy was supposed to do, the New Deal had not done enough to eliminate unemployment.

In his last lecture, 'The new economic constitution,' Soule took on the failure of the New Deal to end the depression. The problem to him was that 'we fall back into depression the moment the government ceases to spend more than it receives in taxes, that is, the moment its economic budget is balanced' (Soule 1939, p. 65). There was a new view being espoused by younger economists that government deficit spending must be made constant and there was no need to worry about the increases in the government debt that continual deficit spending would create (Soule 1939, pp. 72–5). Soule had discovered Keynesian fiscal policy and believed it was part of 'a world-wide tendency for government to take over economic functions when private enterprise resigns them' (Soule 1939, p. 76). If private businesses did not invest and expand, government would have to replace it.

This conclusion led Soule to an additional conclusion that if the government was going to intervene to stimulate the economy with public investments, it had to enter the sphere of private enterprise (Soule 1939, p. 83). If the building of factories was more important for job creation than the typical government infrastructure project, then the government should build factories. It was already directly investing in areas previously the domain of private enterprise, such as housing and electricity generation. Soule believed it would soon have to take over the railroads and it would do even more. In this way, government ownership of industry, or at least a part of it, would enable the government policies for stimulating the economy to be more effective (Soule 1939, pp. 89–90).

Soule has brought us back to the moral economy of Edward Bellamy with government ownership and operation of industry serving to bring a better world for all citizens. Like Bellamy, Soule had no doubt that the personnel to manage this moral economy already existed and there was no need to be concerned that government ownership would reduce efficiency (Soule 1939, p. 91). Government under the New Deal had shown it could build more affordable housing than the private sector and the Tennessee Valley Authority showed that it could produce energy. The problem with the New Deal was that it had not gone far enough in bringing about this moral economy, because it had stopped short of planning and government owner-ship of the means of production. The New Deal had not brought the US to that point, but it had begun the process that would eventually lead to it.

JOSEPH SCHUMPETER LOOKS FORWARD

Joseph Schumpeter's theory of the role of the entrepreneur in the process of creative destruction informed everything he wrote. In 1942 he took a long-term look at the past and future of the market economy in his most popular book, *Capitalism, Socialism and Democracy*. The book made several important points regarding our interest in the moral economy and the New Deal.

First, regarding the effectiveness of planning an economic system, his answer to the question 'Can socialism work?' was a resounding, 'Of course it can' (Schumpeter 1942 [1962], p. 167). In offering this answer Schum-peter had in mind a form of socialism quite similar to Bellamy's moral economy, with a centralized authority in control of the economy and industrial councils planning production. The central authority would be able to determine what needed to be produced through surveys of the population as well as past indications of how members of that population spent their equal shares of income on consumer items. Of course there would be shortages and not everyone would get what they wanted in the way of consumer goods, but a majority would most of the time (Schumpeter 1942 [1962], pp. 167–82).

As for the way in which socialism might come about, Schumpeter also came close to Bellamy by indicating that it could be accomplished peace-fully through a political vote. One of the dilemmas of the market economy was that except for businessmen, it had few strong supporters. Business had a great influence over the government of the countries where the market economy was the strongest, such as the US, but that influence was waning.

The rise of large corporations had reduced the size of the business community and diminished its effectiveness as a voting bloc (Schumpeter 1942 [1962], p. 142). The remnants of the leaders of the market economy were also amenable to compromise with efforts to regulate them.

Moreover, capitalism created sufficient wealth for the development of a large group of intellectuals 'whose interest it is to work up and organize resentment, to nurse it, to voice it and to lead it' (Schumpeter 1942 [1962], p. 145). These intellectuals never attained the employment conditions and income comparable to corporate managers, which intensified their personal resentment. Many of them joined the labour movement to serve as its intellectual leaders. We can readily infer that Schumpeter, at least by implication, was criticizing the New Deal. After all, intellectuals heavily favoured it.

Schumpeter, however, remained in the camp of the market economy and defended it. The key to that defence was the process of creative destruction and the amount of economic growth it produced. In the US from 1870 to 1930 the economy had grown by an estimated 3.7 per cent per year. Suppose, Schumpeter asked, it grew at 2 per cent a year for the 50 years following 1929. The 1930s had been a decade of 'subnormal prosperity.' But part of the problem was that the economy and business were adjusting 'to a new fiscal policy, new labor legislation, and a general change in the attitude of government to private enterprise' (Schumpeter 1942 [1962], p. 64). Schumpeter asked his readers not to construe his comments as a criticism of the New Deal, but they merely indicated that any transition to a new political order was bound to disrupt economic performance.

Once the market economy adjusted to the New Deal it could be expected to return to a trend of annual economic growth of 2 per cent. As a result, per capita income in the US would double in 50 years. Critics might argue that much of that income gain would go to the wealthy, but Schumpeter insisted that the relative shares of total income of labour and capital were stable over time. Moreover, the mass production of the large corporations made many consumption items available to the less affluent more than ever before in history and he believed that trend would also continue. The result he forecast was that over the next 50 years if capitalism were permitted to grow at its long-term trend, it would 'do away with anything that according to present standards could be called poverty' (Schumpeter 1942 [1962], p. 66). To Schumpeter, this meant that the market economy would do a better job of ending poverty than the programmes of the New Deal or the moral economy of planning. The market economy and the process of creative destruction represented the best chance humanity had for ending poverty.

CONCLUSION

In his analysis of the New Deal Raymond Moley (1886–1975), an original member of Roosevelt's Brains Trust, indicated that it had not achieved 'the subordination of private interests to collective interests' that had inspired Edward Bellamy to write (Moley 1939, p. 14). This meant that the New Deal did not bring about a moral economy of government ownership of the means of production combined with planning, nor even planning without government ownership. Instead, it created a mixed economy that included more moral behaviour through guidance by government. That was President Roosevelt's assessment of what he had accomplished. By bringing about this change, the New Deal had established a more moral economy.

His followers who advocated planning did not share this belief. Tugwell remained committed to planning as long as it could be brought about without the need for a government dictatorship; the general approach of the WIB would be the best approach even though it had not been tried under the NIRA. Still, Tugwell believed that the New Deal had begun changing the habits of thought of the citizens of the US, making them more amenable to the idea of planning. George Soule agreed that the New Deal philosophy of government intervention in the economy had gained social acceptance, but its efforts at planning had been confused and ineffective in ending the depression. Instead, the government was using Keynesian fiscal policy as its counter-cyclical approach. Soule approved of this new economics and, unlike the economists surveyed in Chapter 12, he agreed with Keynes's desire for the socialization of investment and the nationalization of key industries.

Advocates for the market economy questioned the effectiveness of the New Deal. Lippmann came to an appreciation of the value of the market economy, especially in handling the process of creative destruction. He worried, however, that by appealing to special interest groups, politicians would continue another process, gradual collectivization, that would counteract the process of creative destruction. Schumpeter also worried that the new economics would diminish the process of creative destruction. Still, even in its diminished state the process of creative destruction had the potential to bring everyone in the US above the 1930s poverty line within 50 years.

The next 50 years have proved Schumpeter and Lippmann to be more right than Tugwell and Soule. The process of creative destruction has continued at a pace that even Schumpeter would have to admire and economic growth surpassed the 2 per cent he hoped for. At the same time, gradual collectivization in the form of the programmes of fiscal policy and the welfare state has continued to grow, much as Lippmann worried about, but it has not ushered in the planning that Tugwell and Soule foresaw. Instead, we have the mixed economy that Roosevelt said he sought and it has become increasingly difficult for both sides in the debate over morals and markets to determine whether creative destruction or gradual collectivization are responsible for either the downturns that the economy still suffers or the recoveries that still follow them. Since business cycles are now the joint responsibility of government and business, they are difficult to construe as a fault of the market economy. Rather, they would now seem to be inherent to the mixed economy and we must still wonder if the moral economy of planning could end them.

14. Epilogue: the moral economy in the twenty-first century

The New Deal was ended by the time the US entered World War II, but its legacy remains with us. As George Soule so aptly put it, the programmes of the New Deal 'have been assimilated into the background; they are beginning to be taken for granted even by many of their traditional opponents' (Soule 1939, p. 2). History has proved the aptness of Soule's statement. Aside from the NIRA, the social programmes we have discussed in this book, the NLRA, the FLSA, unemployment insurance as part of the Social Security Act, regulation of business and Keynesian fiscal policy remain in place as unassailable policies along with a host of other programmes we have not discussed such as the Federal Housing Administration, the social security pension system and federal welfare assistance. Advocates for the market economy may well lament that they can never get rid of Roosevelt's system.

There is one aspect of the New Deal that they may not lament: the US does not have a system of national planning as was proposed by many whom we have called proponents of the moral economy. Soule may represent those proponents in his prediction that the government would soon have to take over the railroads and use fiscal policy to build factories. In this way, government ownership of industry, or at least a part of it, would enable the government policies for stimulating the economy to be more effective (Soule 1939, pp. 89–90). Edward Bellamy had thought that the people of the US would see the folly of their being dominated by large businesses and the economic crises they provoked and would willingly have the government nationalize them and use planning to maintain a stable economy. Instead, the New Deal proved that there was no broad-based support for the federal government to undertake national economic planning; its ownership of industry was out of the question.

As a result, the US has evolved along the lines suggested by Walter Lippmann with his concept of 'gradual collectivism' whereby democratic countries used a series of small collective reforms to bring about a planned economy (Lippmann 1938, p. 106). In the process they served the needs of a series of special interest groups and operated through a piecemeal taking away of the functions of the market and giving them to the government. We

249

see this in the expansion of social security pensions and unemployment insurance to more occupations than the original Act provided, the extension of unemployment benefits, the introduction of federal healthcare programmes such as Medicare and Medicaid, the development of food stamps and a host of other entitlements, and the use of a quasi-socialization of investment by the government regarding General Motors and alternative energy producers, to give two recent examples. The US has reached a point where the federal government spends 25 per cent of GDP. Because there is no overall federal government planning of the expansion of this collectivism, we might criticize it for being 'plan-less.' But within each federal agency planning takes place. The problem is in coordinating the plans of all agencies. Thus, we may have an energy plan, a job stimulus plan, a deficit reduction plan, a healthcare plan, a tax plan, environmental regulation plans, a housing plan and a large number of job retraining plans but no overall plan that ties the individual plans together. Coordination of the overall economy remains dependent on the market activities of individual businesses seeking to make profits, including the way in which they accommodate to the myriad plans of the government. Because the plans of the government are often changing and always uncoordinated, they wind up interjecting a large element of uncertainty into every business. But that is the trend of federal government intervention in the economy.

In this Epilogue we focus on the way this uncoordinated government intervention in the US economy has played out in the first decade of the twenty-first century through consideration of the writings of three advocates of the moral economy: Barack Obama, Paul Krugman and Robert Reich. We shall add to their ideas our own thoughts on what an advocate for the market economy would say about the moral economy they describe.

BARACK OBAMA'S MORAL ECONOMY

Barack Obama (1961–) has had a remarkable rise to becoming president, helped as was Franklin Roosevelt by an economic downturn that was an outlier among all the business cycles that have hit the US. We shall not, however, analyse how Obama has handled the economy, especially since at the time of writing the verdict is not yet in on whether his policies have worked. Instead, we focus on his underlying philosophy and its relationship to the moral economy as presented in his book, *The Audacity of Hope: Thoughts on Reclaiming the American Dream* (Obama 2006).

We see elements of that philosophy in the prologue to the book, when Obama writes of 'a set of ideals that continue to stir our collective conscience' (Obama 2006, p. 8). The idea of a collective conscience is a key ingredient of the moral economy, and using it Obama can express his anger 'about policies that consistently favor the wealthy and powerful over average Americans' (Obama 2006, p. 10).

The wealthy, then, are not included in this shared set of values. Rather, they are a special interest group that has used government to feather their own nests. Their individualism in pursuit of their own advantage puts them at odds with the majority of the US who believe in the moral economy. Looking backward, Obama finds that the New Deal had limits in terms of building that moral economy. The New Deal coalition was held together by 'a vision of fair wages and benefits, patronage and public works, and an ever-rising standard of living' (Obama 2006, p. 26). Unfortunately, advocates of the moral economy were not effective in promoting this agenda and making it clear that they were engaged in helping all members of society.

This neglect came to a head during the economically slow period of the 1970s, when liberals in government failed 'to give middle class voters any sense that it was fighting for them.' As a result, they allowed for an opening by the advocates of the market economy, as personified by Ronald Reagan, to supplant the New Deal vision by attacking government programmes. Moreover, Obama notes, Reagan was on to something. He writes, 'For the fact was that government at every level had become too cavalier about spending taxpayer money. Too often bureaucracies were oblivious to the costs of their mandates. A lot of liberal rhetoric did seem to value rights and entitlements over duties and responsibilities' (Obama 2006, p. 31). In short, liberalism had become side-tracked from the moral economy's emphasis on mutual responsibility, a key value in the US. The advocates of the market economy gained an edge as a result.

Because of this edge the administration of President George W. Bush pushed the market economy too far. Obama describes their ideology as follows, 'There is the absolutism of the free market, an ideology of no taxes, no regulation, no safety net – indeed, no government beyond what's required to protect private property and provide for the national defense' (Obama 2006, p. 37). Advocates of the moral economy responded by refusing to use market principles at all. This split between the market economy and the moral economy, Obama continues, reflects a split in the culture of the US. We prize individualism but 'Our individualism has always been bound by a set of communal values' (Obama 2006, p. 55). The trick is to balance the conflicts between these values by finding where to draw the line between individual action versus communal responsibility, between the moral economy and the market economy. The key to that balance is in attaining a sense that we are all equal and can understand each other through empathy. Obama writes, 'It's hard to imagine the CEO of a company giving himself a multimillion-dollar bonus while cutting health-care coverage for his workers if he thought they were in some sense his equals' (Obama 2006, p. 67).

Human understanding, shared values and mutual responsibility can balance individualism and bring us to the moral economy. Obama expresses admiration for the workings of the market economy. The US has been 'consistently hospitable to the logic of the marketplace' and has produced a business culture that brought about 'a prosperity that's unmatched in human history' (Obama 2006, pp. 149–50). But business and the market economy cannot handle all of the problems society faces. As a prime example of such a problem, pertinent to the issues of this book, Obama points to the process of innovation and creative destruction.

To him, the process of creative destruction was causing 'a fundamental economic transformation' in the US. Because of advanced communications, capital can move around the world in search of low-cost areas to produce. This mobility of capital has led to global competition and lower-cost products for consumers in the US. It has also caused economic instability and uncertainty for millions of workers in the US – the destructive phase – and great wealth for the entrepreneurs in charge of innovation and those with the skills the innovation requires. Advocates of the market economy want to further the process by privatizing as much of government as possible and leaving it to the market to take care of the destructive part of creative destruction. Leaving it to the market is not an option, however. Obama writes, 'But over the long term, doing nothing probably means an America very different from the one most of us grew up in. It will mean a nation even more stratified economically and socially than it currently is' (Obama 2006, p. 148). What can the government do to revitalize the moral economy?

Obama's chief answer is that it can undertake 'those investments that can make America more competitive in the global economy' (Obama 2006, p. 159). Those investments include spending on infrastructure related to education, science and technology, and energy independence. Most of these investments are typical of what the government has spent on for much of the past 50 years. Energy independence is a new one, however, and Obama explains in detail the need to get away from using fossil fuels. Instead, the US needs to have the government invest in alternative energy such as ethanol and fuel efficient cars (Obama 2006, p. 177). In pursuing this policy, Obama has brought us back to the moral economy of John Maynard Keynes and his call for the social control of investment; at least the idea that the government should invest in businesses that produce alternative energy is a step in that direction. It is not clear, however, the extent to which Obama would follow Keynes all the way to social control over all investment and the planning that would come as a consequence.

Obama believes that the US is facing an economic transformation equal to what Roosevelt faced. Roosevelt handled that economic change by bringing the country 'to a new social compact – a bargain between government, business and workers that resulted in widespread prosperity and economic security for more than fifty years' (Obama 2006, p. 177). Roosevelt appreciated that he was creating a middle-class society whose consumption of goods and services would make the US prosperous. He also recognized that with the economic security of a social safety net individuals could afford to take risks by changing jobs when their previous one was threatened. The New Deal needs to be updated with the extension of the safety net to include healthcare, to help displaced workers get retrained for new careers, to strengthen unions through changes in the NLRA and to expand unemployment insurance to wage insurance, 'which provides 50 per cent of the difference between a worker's old wage and his new wage for anywhere from one to two years' (Obama 2006, p. 181).

Obama then asks the big question, 'How do we pay for it?' (Obama 2006, p. 187). His answer, however, is vague. We could easily pay for all the new and enhanced programmes he was proposing, Obama noted, if we had maintained the budget surpluses that President Bill Clinton had managed to secure. Instead, President Bush had spent them all on tax cuts for the wealthy, running up huge deficits of over $300 billion and increasing the public debt of the US to a massive $9 trillion. The real answer, then, is to restore taxes to their previous level, if not higher. After all, he went on, 'The rich in America have little to complain about' (Obama 2006, p. 192). They have done well due to creative destruction and globalization making the distribution of income as unequal as it has ever been in the last 100 years. Obama recognized that the wealthy had worked hard, created jobs and given value to consumers. But he also believed 'that those of us who have benefited most from this new economy can best afford to shoulder the burden of ensuring that every American child has a chance for the same success' (Obama 2006, p. 193).

In speaking this way, Obama has indicated his philosophy that the moral economy must take precedence over the market economy. For the market economy counterpoint, we return to William Graham Sumner. In Chapter 2 we noted that to Sumner it was acceptable for a person such as himself to exercise 'my own sympathies under my own reason and conscience' to help others but it was not acceptable 'what another man forces me to do of a sympathetic character, because his reason and conscience approve of it' (Sumner 1883b [1982], p. 136). Humans owed each other help and sympathy out of personal feelings, but not out of governmental edict. How the affluent used the moral opportunities their wealth gave them was up to them. To Obama, however, they had a moral obligation to help others even if they had to be forced to do so.

What is missing from this approach is the planning that goes along with the moral economy. Do all of the programmes Obama is suggesting fit together? In particular, will the persons whose activities are being influenced act in the way the programs require? Healthcare reform, to give one example, requires that the individuals to be covered take the steps to prevent their health from deteriorating as the result of activities that they can control. As we have mentioned several times in this book, Edward Bellamy was not above using coercion in his moral economy indicating that an individual who did not go along with the plan would be sentenced to 'solitary imprisonment on bread and water till he consents' (Bellamy 1888 [1926], p. 128). If the wealthy are to be coerced to share their wealth in the name of fairness, should the plan also coerce the beneficiaries of healthcare to eat properly, to name one possibility?

In addition, there is no way to determine if the wealthy will behave as the plan requires them to. If their taxes are increased, the wealthy must cut back on something, consumption, saving or investment. As noted in Chapter 8, Rexford Tugwell once explained to Roosevelt that 'the price system actually was a system' (Tugwell 1968, p. 81). Efforts to regulate one sector of this system will cause all other sectors to respond to the regulated sector in ways that are not predictable. Once the government intervened in one set of markets where the incomes of the wealthy are determined it would have to control all other markets through planning. Advocates of the market economy might agree with Tugwell, but they would do so from the perspective, raised by Ludwig von Mises, that planning could not solve the task Tugwell set for it.

PAUL KRUGMAN'S LIBERAL CONSCIENCE

Paul Krugman (1953–) has had a career that makes the rest of us in economics envious. He has been awarded the Nobel Prize in Economics for his work in technical economics, while also serving as a well-known pundit by writing for the *New York Times*, authoring best-selling books and appearing regularly on television talk shows. Here we shall examine one of his best-selling books, *The Conscience of a Liberal* (Krugman 2009).

Krugman begins the book by indicating that its theme is the need in the US for a new New Deal. Because of the economic crisis taking place as he was writing, the US faced conditions similar to what existed when Roosevelt became president. Part of the problem was the return to the market economy and greed brought about by the Bush administration. That return led to the crisis and Krugman quotes Roosevelt as saying, 'We always knew that heedless self interest was bad morals; we now know it is bad economics.' He adds, 'And that line has never rung truer' (Krugman 2009, p. xiv).

Krugman is clearly in the camp of the moral economy, at least in the form created by the New Deal. He describes that form as follows:

> In the early years after World War II, with the memory of the great depression still fresh, most economists believed that keeping the economy on track required an extensive role for the government. Mainstream economics rejected calls for a planned economy, but did accept the need for government intervention to fight recessions. (Krugman 2009, p. 116)

This view meant that they supported the mixed economy of morals and markets where Keynesian fiscal policy would take care of recessions without the social control over investment that Keynes recommended. Not surprisingly, Krugman's solution to the economic crisis at the time he was writing is 'large-scale fiscal stimulus' with an estimate that $600 billion in spending would be needed (Krugman 2009, p. xviii). The mainstream economists of the 1930s, as described in Chapter 12, would remind him that if the multiplier and accelerator did not respond in the way he predicted, his estimate might be off.

As was the case with the New Deal, the economic crisis of 2007–9 also provided the opportunity for completion of many items the New Deal left unfinished. In Krugman's case that meant 'major health care reform' (Krugman 2009, p. xix). Before looking at healthcare, however, he takes his reader on a long tour of the economics of inequality, describing how the policies of the New Deal and after brought about greater equality of income and prosperity for over a generation. The moral economy of fiscal Keynesianism worked well. But then the US tilted back to the market economy and greater inequality became the trend over the last two decades.

One explanation for the divergence of pay among workers, experts and corporate leaders is the process of creative destruction. Innovations in technology, market advocates might argue, have rewarded entrepreneurs, corporate leaders and workers with technological skills while they have destroyed old-line manufacturing skills of the traditional blue-collar worker and reduced their wages. Krugman disagrees, writing, 'There's remarkably little direct evidence for the proposition that technological change has caused rising inequality' (Krugman 2009, p. 133). Instead, he attributes the increase in inequality to social and political factors. He describes the process as follows, 'High incomes shot up not because of an increased demand for talent but because a variety of factors caused the death of outrage' (Krugman 2009, p. 145). Corporate executives were able to use their position to give themselves and their technical experts higher incomes while slowing the growth of wages for lower-level workers and they got away with it because no one complained, certainly not weakened labour unions. Moreover, the federal tax code, which had previously taxed the affluent at higher rates than lower-level workers and thus increased equality, had been changed by a series of tax cuts into a more level system (Krugman 2009, p. 157). Although Krugman does not say this bluntly, he implies that the gains of the affluent have been immoral and it is acceptable for the moral economy to reclaim them to help the less well-off.

We see this implication in his discussion of healthcare reform. He starts the discussion with the moral argument of the market economy that it is not the job of the government to take money from one group to help another group with healthcare insurance. He does not refute this argument but points out that it is rejected by most voters who believe that everyone in the US should have healthcare. He concludes, 'The moral case for universal health care isn't in dispute' (Krugman 2009, p. 215).

Krugman also takes on the market economy through his view of private health insurance companies. Because of their quest for profits, health insurance companies do as much as possible to avoid paying claims. To do so, they use 'risk selection' to deny coverage or charge higher premiums for person who are likely to have high claims, which to him means persons who really need the coverage. They also deny claims if they can make the case that the person has a pre-existing condition. Krugman does not blame morality for this approach, but the market economy. Under market incentives 'a nice insurance company' that did not screen out high risk individuals would wind up with most of those persons denied coverage by other not-as-nice companies and would become bankrupt (Krugman 2009, p. 221). Universal coverage through a government programme would solve this problem and avoid many of the costs involved with risk selection and claim investigations. Universal coverage would also be the new New Deal that Krugman desired. By paying for universal healthcare through the tax system, this new New Deal would also reduce the inequality in after-tax incomes.

In short, Krugman's new New Deal would have a healthcare plan that used taxes on the wealthy to provide open-ended medical services to everyone, regardless of costs, with a promise that the plan would eliminate the unnecessary costs created in the healthcare system by the market economy. Elimination of the 'unnecessary costs' of the market economy have always been part of the rhetoric of the moral economy. Proponents of the market economy would counter that because of the issue of moral hazard, the open-ended nature of the plan would lead to costs that were endless.

ROBERT REICH AND MORAL RESPONSIBILITY

Robert Reich (1946–) has had a long career in government and academia. His most notable public service was as Secretary of Labor in the Clinton administration. He is the author of numerous books and a participant on numerous television talk shows. In his writings and commentary he has always espoused the cause of the moral economy through a wide-ranging discussion of the negative features of the market economy. He has been especially adamant in denouncing the immorality of corporate scandals (Reich 2004, pp. 1068–262).

In place of that immorality, Reich argues for a public morality that includes responsible behaviour in economic activities. Of interest to us in this Epilogue, he is especially concerned with responsible behaviour regarding the use of social insurance. To him, social insurance contributes to fairness in society, with a basic premise that 'we are all in the same boat together' (Reich 2004, p. 1465). Life is full of risk and misfortune, which may happen to anyone. Social insurance redistributes money from those lucky enough to avoid risk to the unlucky ones who do not. Because we all recognize that misfortune may befall any of us, we all tacitly agree to help each other.

In the economy the biggest risk most individuals face is from the transformation of the economy from creative destruction. Because of creative destruction, Reich argues, the global economy is being transformed from manufacturing to services. In the US this has meant the decline of blue-collar jobs. In their place the US economy is being divided into two general occupations: knowledge workers who earn high incomes and personal service workers who earn low incomes. The relative incomes of these two groups is the result of market forces, Reich acknowledges, and it has helped produce the disparities of income that worry advocates of the moral economy (Reich 2004, pp. 1800–50).

To reduce this disparity, we need economic growth brought about by high productivity workers. For workers to become more productive, however, they will need enhanced education and better healthcare. Government programs to provide that education and healthcare will be expensive, however (Reich 2004, pp. 1950–90). Higher-income individuals ought to be willing to pay for those programmes, if for no other reason that they may some day need them. Even knowledge workers can be knocked from their high perches by the process of creative destruction and could thus benefit from social insurance.

Advocates for the market economy argue that when social insurance bails people out of their difficulties, it also creates the problem of moral hazard. If individuals know they will be bailed out they will not take precautions to keep from needing the bailout. Reich describes the issue as follows, 'Unemployment insurance can invite more unemployment; welfare more welfare; generous health insurance, more health care' (Reich 2004, pp. 1528–30). The dilemma that results is that social insurance must 'square the natural human tendency to be less careful when protected against the full consequences of one's actions with the need for some protection' (Reich 2004, pp. 1535–7). The market economy perspective stresses the need for responsibility while the moral economy approach focuses on protection.

Reich's approach is to find a balance between responsibility and protection by helping individuals with their losses but by not helping so much if they fail 'to take reasonable precaution' (Reich 2004, p. 1144). One approach would be to have the government attach more strings to the recipients of entitlements. In this way the moral economy's premise of mutual responsibility would be supplemented by the incentives of the market economy. Reich thereby shows how far gradual collectivism has taken us in the mixed economy: it is now the moral economy that should be supplemented by the market economy instead of the reverse. (Reich 2004, pp. 1068–262).

CONCLUSION

We began this study of markets, planning and the moral economy with a discussion of the market economy versus the moral economy. Our theme has been that proponents of the moral economy believed that planning could solve the problems caused by business cycles. We presented Edward Bellamy as the quintessential advocate of the moral economy of planning in the US. Not all of the persons we have included in this study were influenced by Bellamy but we have seen that several prominent advocates for the moral economy of planning – Thorstein Veblen, Rexford Tugwell, Thurman Arnold and Raymond Moley – directly indicated an appreciation for Bellamy's philosophy. Other advocates for planning followed him implicitly if not in name.

The other source of inspiration for planning native to the US was the WIB of World War I. Tugwell, Stuart Chase, Gerard Swope and George Soule looked backward to the WIB as a model of how to achieve planning of the economy. Their efforts concluded with the NIRA as a system of planning through a partnership among business, government and labour. The partnership proved unwieldy, however, and was failing even before the US Supreme Court declared it unconstitutional. Some advocates for planning such as John Maurice Clark attributed the failure of the NIRA to the problem that none of the partners in planning, business, government and labour, had developed the moral and technical capability to engage in planning that rose above special interest politics to truly consider the general welfare of the country. Clark's interest in planning subsided, as did that of Walter Lippmann. By the time Keynes came along with his fiscal policy of government spending plus the socialization of investment, economists, pundits and political leaders were willing to adopt programmes of government spending, but not the planning of investment.

Instead, the US government has combated business cycles with the fiscal policy of running budget deficits to stimulate the economy along with Lippmann's gradual collectivism through expansion of the welfare state. Both policies take place in the absence of planning. Indeed, planning might be a detriment to them, because planning includes a formulation of priorities and limits on what the government can achieve at any given moment. It is doubtful, for example, that a system of planning worthy of the name would have tried to end a severe recession such as began in 2008 while also implementing a programme of national healthcare. The result, a large increase in the government's budget and deficit along with a sizable increase in the public debt of the US, would be hard for effective planners to tolerate.

But we do not have effective planners in the US and advocates for the market economy would argue that effective planners are a contradiction in terms. Not Franklin Roosevelt, Barack Obama nor Paul Krugman, as intelligent as they were and are, can possibly understand or calculate the wants and needs of a diverse population such as the US has. The best they can do is continue the process of gradual collectivism by catering to the wants and needs of special interest groups by taking from William Graham Sumner's forgotten man and giving to members of the groups they have privileged. Sumner would warn them, however, that their policy of income redistribution will set up a conflict between gradual collectivism and the process of creative destruction. The moral economy aims at security through economic stability while creative destruction leads to instability and no security for anyone, even the wealthy. Whether proponents of the moral economy can gain the wisdom to walk the fine line between morals and markets such that the process of creative destruction, which has been the key to economic progress, is not impeded by gradual collectivism is still an open question. One thing is certain: the gradual collectivism of the moral economy has not ended the business cycle.

Bibliography

AEA (1931), 'The business depression of nineteen hundred and thirty – discussion', *American Economic Review*, **21**, March, 183–201.

Allen, Robert Loring (1993), *Irving Fisher: A Biography*, Cambridge: Blackwell.

Anderson, Paul Y. (1934), 'New Year's gift for the NRA', *The Nation*, **138**, 3 January, 17–18.

Arnold, Thurman (1937), *The Folklore of Capitalism*, reprinted 1968, New Haven, CT: Yale University Press.

Baruch, Bernard M. (1921), *American Industry in the War: A Report of the War Industries Board*, reprinted in Richard H. Hipplehauser (ed.) (1941), New York: Prentice Hall.

Baruch, Bernard M. (1960), *Baruch: The Public Years*, New York: Holt, Rinehart and Winston.

Bellamy, Edward (1888), *Looking Backward*, reprinted 1926, Boston, MA: Houghton Mifflin Co.

Bellamy, Edward (1898), *Equality*, reprinted 2005, Amazon Kindle.

Broun, Heywood (1926), 'Introduction', in Edward Bellamy, *Looking Backward*, Boston, MA: Houghton Mifflin Co., pp. i–iv.

Brown, Douglas V. (1934), 'Helping labor', in *The Economics of the Recovery Program*, reprinted 1968, Freeport, NY: Books for Libraries Press, pp. 64–89.

Business Week (1935), 'Business votes with the Court', June, 7–8.

Chase, Stuart (1925), *The Tragedy of Waste*, New York: The Macmillan Co.

Chase, Stuart (1929), *Prosperity: Fact or Myth*, New York: Charles Boni.

Chase, Stuart (1932), *A New Deal*, New York: The Macmillan Co.

Chase, Stuart (1935a), *Government in Business*, New York: The Macmillan Co.

Chase, Stuart (1935b), 'Recovery', *The New Republic*, 18 December, 162–6.

Clark, Charles E. (1935), 'The Supreme Court and the N.R.A.', *The New Republic*, 12 June, 120–3.

Clark, John Maurice (1923a), *Studies in the Economics of Overhead Costs*, Chicago, IL: University of Chicago Press.

Clark, John Maurice (1923b), 'Some social aspects: an application of overhead cost to social accounting, with special reference to the business cycle', *American Economic Review* **13**, March, 50–59.

Clark, John Maurice (1926), *The Social Control of Business*, Chicago, IL: University of Chicago Press.

Clark John Maurice (1934a), *Strategic Factors in Business Cycles*, New York: The National Bureau of Economic Research.

Clark, John Maurice (1934b), 'Economics and the National Recovery Administration', *American Economic Review*, **24**, March, 11–25.

Clark, John Maurice (1939a), *The Social Control of Business*, 2nd edn, Chicago, IL: University of Chicago Press.

Clark, John Maurice (1939b), 'An appraisal of the workability of compensatory devices', *American Economic Review*, **29**, Supplement, Papers and Proceedings of the Fifty-first Annual Meeting of the American Economic Association, March, 194–208.

Clark, John Maurice (1957), *Economic Institutions and Human Welfare*, New York: Alfred A. Knopf.

Committee of Industrial Analysis (1937), *The National Recovery Administration*, Washington, DC: US Government Printing Office.

Committee on Economic Security (1937), *Social Security in America*, Washington, DC: US Government Printing Office.

Committee on Elimination of Waste in Industry of FAES (1922), *Waste in Industry*, Washington, DC: Federated Association of Engineering Societies.

Compton, Wilson (1934), 'Putting a code to work', *Nation's Business*, **22**, June, 41–2 and 53–4.

Coughlin, Charles E. (1934), 'The National Union for Social Justice', radio address, Sunday, 11 November, Social Security Online History Pages, accessed 14 June 2012 at www.socialsecurity.gov.

Coughlin, Charles E. (1935), 'A reply to General Hugh Johnson', radio address, Monday, 11 March, Social Security Online History Pages, accessed 14 June 2012 at www.socialsecurity.gov.

Coughlin, Charles E. (1936), 'Roosevelt and ruin', radio address, 19 June, accessed 14 June 2012 at www.austincc.edu/lpatrick/his2341/rooseveltandruin.htm.

Croly, Herbert (1914), *The Promise of American Life*, New York: Macmillan Co.

Dickinson, John (1934), 'The recovery program', in Clair Wilcox, Herbert F. Fraser and Patrick Murphy Maling (eds), *America's Recovery Program*, reprinted 1970, Freeport, NY: Books for Libraries Press, pp. 23–44.

Dorfman, Joseph (1972), *Thorstein Veblen and His America*, Clifton, NJ: Augustus M. Kelley.

Douglas, Paul H. and Joseph Hackman (1938), 'The Fair Labor Standards Act of 1938 I', *Political Science Quarterly*, **53**, December, 491–515.

'Editorial' (1920), 'A great event in engineering history', *Industrial Management*, **60**, July, 74.

'Editorial notes' (1916), *The New Republic*, 17 May, 75–6.

Edwards, Morris (1933), 'The truce on the Sherman Law', *Nation's Business*, **21**, July, 13–16.

Fisher, Irving (1906), *The Nature of Capital and Income*, reprinted in 1930, New York: The Macmillan Co.

Fisher, Irving (1911), *The Purchasing Power of Money*, (assisted by Harry G. Brown), New York: The Macmillan Co.

Flynn, John T. (1935), 'Other people's money', *The New Republic*, 19 June, 165.

Flynn, John T. (1938), 'Other people's money', *The New Republic*, 2 February, 363.

Folsom, Burton W. and Alan Sklar (2009), *New Deal or Raw Deal?: How FDR's Economic Legacy has Damaged America*, Amazon Kindle.

Ford, Henry (1922), *My Life and Work*, Project Gutenberg eBook.

Foster, William Trufant and Waddill Catchings (1924), *Money*, 2nd edn, Boston, MA and New York: Houghton Mifflin Co.

Foster, William Trufant and Waddill Catchings (1925), *Profits*, Boston, MA and New York: Houghton Mifflin Co.

Foster, William Trufant and Waddill Catchings (1928), *Business Without a Buyer*, Boston, MA and New York: Houghton Mifflin Co.

Foster, William Truffant and Waddill Catchings (1930a), 'Mr. Hoover's road to prosperity', *Review of Reviews*, **81**, January, 50–52.

Foster, William Truffant and Waddill Catchings (1930b), 'Riotous saving', *Atlantic Monthly*, **146**, November, 667–72.

Foster, William Truffant and Waddill Catchings (1931a), 'Must we reduce our standard of living?', *The Forum*, **85**, February, 74–9.

Foster, William Truffant and Waddill Catchings (1931b), 'In the day of adversity', *Atlantic Monthly*, **148**, July, 101–6.

Frey, Donald (2009), *America's Economic Moralists: A History of Rival Ethics and Economics*, Albany, NY: State University of New York Press.

Fried, Albert (1999), *FDR and his Enemies*, New York: St Martin's Press.

Fusfeld, Daniel R. (1956), *The Economic Ideas of Franklin D. Roosevelt and the Origins of the New Deal*, New York: Columbia University Press.

Gantt, Henry Laurence (1916), 'What is industrial preparedness?', *The Engineering Magazine*, September, 804–8.

Gayer, Arthur D. (1938), 'Fiscal policies', *American Economic Review*, **28**, supplement, Papers and Proceedings of the Fiftieth Annual Meeting of the American Economic Association, March, 90–112.

Goldberg, Jonah (2007), *Liberal Fascism: The Secret History of the American Left, From Mussolini to the Politics of Meaning*, New York: Doubleday.

Hansen, Alvin H. (1936), 'Mr. Keynes on underemployment equilibrium', *Journal of Political Economy*, **44**, October, 667–86.

Harriman, Henry I. (1934), 'The future of the NIRA', *Nation's Business*, **22**, September, 27–8 and 65–7.

Hayward, Paul (1935), 'The troubled path of 7 (a)', *Nation's Business*, **23**, June, 31–2 and 57–60.

Hazlitt, Henry (2011), *The Failure of the 'New Economics': An Analysis of Keynesian Fallacies*, Amazon Kindle.

Hoover, Herbert (1921), 'What America faces', *Industrial Management*, **61**, April, 225– 8.

Hoover, Herbert (1922), *American Individualism*, Garden City, NY: Doubleday, Page & Co.

Hoover, Herbert (1929), 'State of the union address', 3 December, Amazon Kindle.

Hoover, Herbert (1930), 'State of the union address', 2 December, Amazon Kindle.

Hoover, Herbert (1931), 'State of the union address', 8 December, Amazon Kindle.

Hoover, Herbert (1932), 'State of the union address', 6 December, Amazon Kindle.

Hoover, Herbert (1934), *The Challenge to Liberty*, New York: Charles Scribner's Sons.

Hoover, Herbert (1938), *Addresses upon the American Road: 1933–1938*, New York: Charles Scribner's Sons.

Hoover, Herbert (1951), *The Memoirs of Herbert Hoover: Vol. 2, The Cabinet and the Presidency, 1920–1933*, New York: The Macmillan Co.

Johnson, Hugh S. (1934), 'Administration of NRA', *Saturday Evening Post*, **206**, 14 July, 10–11 and 89–92.

Johnson, Hugh S. (1935a), 'The Blue Eagle from egg to earth', *Saturday Evening Post*, **207**, 19 January, 5–7 and 68–76.

Johnson, Hugh S. (1935b), 'In commerce we are one country', *Vital Speeches of the Day*, **1**, 8 April, 445–8.

Keynes, John Maynard (1920), *The Economic Consequences of the Peace*, London: Macmillan.

Keynes, John Maynard (1925), 'Am I a liberal?', in *Essays in Persuasion*, reprinted 1932, New York: Harcourt, Brace and Company, pp. 323–38.

Keynes, John Maynard (1932), 'The dilemma of modern socialism', *The New Republic*, 13 April, 227–9.

Keynes, John Maynard (1933), 'An open letter to President Roosevelt', *New York Times*, 31 December, accessed 14 June 2012 at http://newdeal.feri.org/misc/keynes2.htm.

Keynes, John Maynard (1936), *The General Theory of Employment, Interest and Money*, reprinted in 1965, New York: Harcourt, Brace & World.

Keynes, John Maynard (1938), 'Letter of February 1 to Franklin Delano Roosevelt', accessed 14 June 2012 at http://delong.typepad.com/egregious_moderation/2008/12/john-maynard-ke.html.

Krugman, Paul (2009), *The Conscience of a Liberal*, New York: W.W. Norton & Co.

Laidler, Harry (1917), 'War collectivism and wealth conscription', *The Intercollegiate Socialist*, April–May), 4–7.

Lippmann, Walter (1914), *Drift and Mastery*, reprinted 1961, Englewood Cliffs, NJ: Prentice-Hall.

Lippmann, Walter (1916), 'Integrated America', *The New Republic*, 19 February, 62–6.

Lippman, Walter (1929), *A Preface to Morals*, reprinted 1964, New York: New York Times.

Lippmann, Walter (1932), *Interpretations, 1931–1932*, Allan Nevins (ed.), New York: The Macmillan Co.

Lippmann, Walter (1935), *The New Imperative*, New York: The Macmillan Co.

Lippmann, Walter (1937), *The Supreme Court: Independent or Controlled?*, New York: Harper & Brothers Publishers.

Lippmann, Walter (1938), *An Inquiry into the Principles of the Good Society*, Boston, MA: Little, Brown and Co.

Long, Huey P. (1985), *Kingfish to America: Share Our Wealth, Selected Senatorial Papers of Huey P. Long*, Henry M. Christman (ed.), New York: Schocken Books.

Lorwin, Lewis L. (1932), 'Planning in Western Europe', in Felix Morley (ed.), *Aspects of the Depression*, Chicago, IL: University of Chicago Press, pp. 147–55.

Lundberg, Ferdinand (1936), 'All right, balance the budget!', *The New Republic*, 3 February, 361–3.

Lyon, Leverett S., Paul T. Honan, Lewis L. Lorin, George Terborgh, Charles L. Dearing and Leon C. Marshall (1935), *The National Recovery Administration: An Analysis and Appraisal*, Washington, DC: The Brookings Institution.

Mallery, Otto T. (1932), 'Forward planning of public works to stabilize employment', in Felix Morley (ed.), *Aspects of the Depression*, Chicago, IL: University of Chicago Press, pp. 87–95.

Mason, Edward S. (1934), 'Controlling industry', in *The Economics of the Recovery Program*, reprinted 1968, Freeport, NY: Books for Libraries Press, pp. 38–63.

May, Stacy (1932), 'Federal planning', in Felix Morley (ed.), *Aspects of the Depression*, Chicago, IL: University of Chicago Press, pp. 175–84.

McCrea, R.C. (1913), 'Schumpeter's economic system: review of Das Wesen und der Hauptinhalt der Theoretischen Nationalokonomie by Joseph A. Schumpeter and Theorie der wirtschaftlichen Enlwicklung by Joseph A. Schumpeter', *Quarterly Journal of Economics* **27**, May, 520–9.

Mill, John Stuart (1848), *Principles of Political Economy*, reprinted 1969, New York: Augustus M. Kelley Publishers.

Mitchell, Wesley Clair (1913), *Business Cycles*, reprinted 1970, New York: Burt Franklin.

Mitchell, Wesley Clair (1922), 'The crisis of 1920 and the problem of controlling business cycles', *American Economic Review*, **12**, March, 20–32.

Mitchell, Wesley Clair (1935), 'The social sciences and national planning', *Science*, New Series, **81**, 18 January, 55–62.

Mitchell, Wesley Clair (1936), 'Intelligence and the guidance of economic evolution', *Scientific Monthly*, **43**, November, 450–65.

Moley, Raymond (1939), *After Seven Years*, New York: Harper & Brothers Publishers.

Morley, Felix (ed.) (1932), *Aspects of the Depression*, Chicago, IL: University of Chicago Press.

Namm, Benjamin H. (1934), 'The war on cut-throat prices', *Nation's Business*, **22**, April, 60–1.

The Nation (1934), 'Bombs bursting in air', **138**, 30 May, 606.

The Nation (1934), 'Saving the good in the NRA', **139**, 5 September, 256.

Nation's Business (1932), 'A panorama of economic planning', **20**, February, 29–32.

Nation's Business (1933), 'Business agrees to regulate itself', **21**, June, 13–14 and 17–18.

Nation's Business (1935), 'Business wants a new NRA', **22**, February, 69.

Nation's Business (1935), 'Two views of NIRA', **23**, April, 66–7.

The New Republic (1918), 'After the war – reaction or reconstruction', 19 January, 331.

The New Republic (1935), 'What to do with the N.R.A.', 20 March, 144–6.

The New Republic (1935), 'Experts judge the N.R.A.', 1 May, 325–7.

The New Republic (1935), 'Ghosts of the N.R.A.', 19 June, 153–4.

The New Republic (1937), 'When and how to balance the budget', 5 May, 372–3.

The New Republic (1940), 'That debt controversy', 19 January, 231–2.

New York Times (1929), 'Fisher sees stocks permanently high', 16 October, 2.

Obama, Barack (2006), *The Audacity of Hope: Thoughts on Reclaiming the American Dream*, New York: Three Rivers Press.

Olsen, Mancur (1965), *The Logic of Collective Action: Public Goods and the Theory of Groups*, Cambridge, MA: Harvard University Press.

Parker, Randall E. (2007), *The Economics of the Great Depression: A Twenty-first Century Look Back at the Economics of the Interwar Era*, Cheltenham, UK and Northampton, MA, USA: Edward Elgar.

Perkins, Frances (1933), 'Why we need a minimum wage law', *Nation's Business*, **21**, July, 23–5 and 56.

Reich, Robert (2004). *Reason: Why Liberals Will Win the Battle for America*, Amazon Kindle.

Richards, Calvin P. (1935), 'N.R.A. chiselers and sculptors', *The New Republic*, 5 June, 92–5.

Richberg, Donald M. (1917), 'Democratization of industry', *The New Republic*, 12 May, 49–51.

Roosevelt, Franklin D. (1932a), address at Oglethorpe University, 22 May, accessed 14 June 2012 at newdeal.feri.org/ speeches/1932d.htm.

Roosevelt, Franklin D. (1932b), campaign speech in Atlanta, GA, 24 October, *Atlanta Constitution*, 25 October, accessed 14 June 2012 at georgiainfo.gallileo.usg.edu/FDRspeeches/FDRspeech32-2.htm.

Roosevelt, Franklin D. (1933a), 'First Inaugural Address', 4 March, 1–9, accessed 14 June 2012 at www.archives.gov/education/lessons/fdr-inaugural/.

Roosevelt, Franklin D. (1933b), 'Fireside Chat of May 7', reprinted in *The Fireside Chats of Franklin Delano Roosevelt* (2004), Amazon Kindle, pp. 67–180.

Roosevelt, Franklin D. (1933c), 'Fireside Chat of July 24', reprinted in *The Fireside Chats of Franklin Delano Roosevelt* (2004), Amazon Kindle, pp. 180–294.

Roosevelt, Franklin D. (1934a), 'Fireside Chat of June 28', reprinted in *The Fireside Chats of Franklin Delano Roosevelt* (2004), Amazon Kindle, pp. 397–492.

Roosevelt, Franklin D. (1934b), 'Fireside Chat of September 30', reprinted in *The Fireside Chats of Franklin Delano Roosevelt* (2004), Amazon Kindle, pp. 492–620.

Roosevelt, Franklin D. (1935a), 'Messages to the new Congress', *Vital Speeches of the Day*, **1**, 14 January, 226–9.

Roosevelt, Franklin D. (1935b), 'Fireside Chat of April 28', reprinted in *The Fireside Chats of Franklin Delano Roosevelt* (2004), Amazon Kindle, pp. 620–742.

Roosevelt, Franklin D. (1936), 'Fireside Chat of September 6', reprinted in *The Fireside Chats of Franklin Delano Roosevelt* (2004), Amazon Kindle, pp. 742–870.

Roosevelt, Franklin D. (1937), 'Fireside Chat of October 12', reprinted in *The Fireside Chats of Franklin Delano Roosevelt* (2004), Amazon Kindle, pp. 1025–146.

Roosevelt, Franklin D. (1938), 'Fireside Chat of June 24', reprinted in *The Fireside Chats of Franklin Delano Roosevelt* (2004), Amazon Kindle, pp. 1318–452.

Roosevelt, Theodore (1916), *Theodore Roosevelt: An Autobiography*, New York: Macmillan.

Rothbard, Murray N. (2000), *America's Great Depression*, 5th edn, Auburn, AL: The Ludwig von Mises Institute, Amazon Kindle.

Sachs, Alexander (1934), 'National Recovery Administration policies and the problem of economic planning', in Clair Wilcox, Herbert F. Fraser and Patrick Murphy Maling (eds), *America's Recovery Program*, reprinted 1970, Freeport, NY: Books for Libraries Press, pp. 107–92.

Samuelson, Paul A. (1940), 'The theory of pump-priming reexamined', *American Economic Review*, **30**, September, 492–506.

Schechter (1935), *A.L.A. Schechter Poultry Corporation v. United States, 295 U.S. 495*, 27 May, accessed 14 June 2012 at http://caselaw.lp.findlaw.com/cgi-bin/getcase.pl?court=us&vol=295&invol=495.

Schieber, Sylvester J. and John B. Shoven (1999), *The Real Deal: The History and Future of Social Security*, New Haven, CT: Yale University Press.

Schumpeter, Joseph (1927), 'The explanation of the business cycle', *Economica*, **2**, December, 286–311.

Schumpeter, Joseph (1928), 'The instability of capitalism', *Economic Journal*, **38**, September, 361–86.

Schumpeter, Joseph A. (1934), 'Depressions', in *The Economics of the Recovery Program*, reprinted 1968, Freeport, NY: Books for Libraries Press, pp. 3–21.

Schumpeter, Joseph (1936), '*The General Theory of Employment, Interest and Money* by John Maynard Keynes', *Journal of the American Statistical Association*, **31**, December, 791–5.

Schumpeter, Joseph A. (1942), *Capitalism, Socialism and Democracy*, 3rd edn, reprinted 1962, New York: Harper Torchbooks.

Schumpeter, Joseph A. (1964), *Business Cycles: A Theoretical, Historical and Statistical Analysis of the Capitalist Process*, abridged edn, New York: McGraw-Hill.

Scott, Owen L. (1935), 'Further plea for little business', *Congressional Digest*, **14**, January, 23–4.

Shlaes, Amity (2007), *The Forgotten Man*, Amazon Kindle.

Slichter, Sumner H. (1932), 'Limitations on planning', in Felix Morley (ed.), *Aspects of the Depression*, Chicago, IL: University of Chicago Press, pp. 185–96.

Slichter, Sumner H. (1934), *Towards Stability: The Problem of Economic Balance*, New York: Henry Holt and Co.

Slichter, Sumner H. (1936), 'The adjustment to instability', *American Economic Review*, **26**, supplement, Papers and Proceedings of the Forty-eighth Annual Meeting of the American Economic Association, March, 196–213.

Smiley, Gene (2003), *Rethinking the Great Depression*, Chicago, IL: I.R. Dee, American Ways Series.

Smith, Adam (1759), *The Theory of Moral Sentiments*, reprinted in David D. Raphael and Alec L. Macfie (eds) (1976), Oxford: Clarendon Press.

Soule, George Henry, Jr (1932a), 'The idea of planning', in Felix Morley (ed.), *Aspects of the Depression*, Chicago, IL: University of Chicago Press, pp. 137–46.

Soule, George (1932b), *A Planned Society*, New York: The Macmillan Co.

Soule, George (1934), *The Coming American Revolution*, New York: The Macmillan Co.

Soule, George (1939), *An Economic Constitution for Democracy*, New Haven, CT: Yale University Press.

Stabile, Donald R. (1984), *Prophets of Order*, Boston, MA: South End Press.

Stabile, Donald R. (1986), 'Herbert Hoover, the FAES, and the AF of L', *Technology and Culture*, **21**, October, 819–27.

Stabile, Donald R. (1987), 'The DuPont experiments with scientific management: efficiency and safety', *Business History Review*, **61**, Autumn, 365–86.

Stabile, Donald R. (1988), 'Veblen's analysis of social movements: Bella-myites, workers, and engineers', *Journal of Economic Issues*, **22**, March, 211–26.

Stabile, Donald R. (1993), *Activist Unionism: The Institutional Economics of Solomon Barkin*, Armonk, NY: M.E. Sharpe.

Stabile, Donald R. (1996), *Work and Welfare: The Social Costs of Labor in the History of Economic Thought*, Westport, CT: Greenwood Press.

Stabile, Donald R. (2000), 'Business and professional organizations', in David O. Whitten and Bessie E. Whitten (eds), *Handbook of American Business History*, Vol. III, Westport, CT: Greenwood Press, pp. 419–65.

Stabile, Donald R. (2008), *The Living Wage: Lessons from the History of Economic Thought*, Cheltenham, UK and Northampton, MA, USA: Edward Elgar.

Stewart, William Kilborne (1928), 'The mentors of Mussolini', *American Political Science Review*, **22**, November, 843–69.

Sullivan, Mark (1935), 'Presenting the case for "little business"', *Congressional Digest*, **14**, January, 22–3.

Sumner, William Graham (1879), 'The influence of commercial crises on opinions about economic doctrines', reprinted in *The Forgotten Man and Other Essays* (1969), Freeport, NY: Books for Libraries Press, pp. 213–38.

Sumner, William Graham (1883a), *Problems in Political Economy*, New York: Henry Holt and Co.

Sumner, William Graham (1883b), *What Social Classes Owe to Each Other*, reprinted 1982, Caldwell, ID: The Claxton Printers.

Sumner, William Graham (1883c), 'The forgotten man', reprinted in *The Forgotten Man and Other Essays* (1969), Freeport, NY: Books for Libraries Press, pp. 465–98.

Sumner, William Graham (1885), 'Protectionism, the -ism that teaches that waste makes wealth', reprinted in *The Forgotten Man and Other Essays* (1969), Freeport, NY: Books for Libraries Press, pp. 9–114.

Sumner, William Graham (1887a), 'Strikes and the industrial organization', reprinted in *The Forgotten Man and Other Essays* (1969), Freeport, NY: Books for Libraries Press, pp. 249–56.

Sumner, William Graham (1887b), 'What makes the rich richer and the poor poorer', *Popular Science Monthly*, **30**, reprinted in Albert Galloway Keller (ed.) (1914), *The Challenge of Facts and Other Essays*, New Haven, CT: Yale University Press, pp. 63–77.

Sumner, William Graham (1896a), 'Cause and cure of hard times', reprinted in *The Forgotten Man and Other Essays* (1969), Freeport, NY: Books for Libraries Press, pp. 149–56.

Sumner, William Graham (1896b), 'Industrial war', *The Forum*, **2**, September, reprinted in Albert Galloway Keller (ed.) (1914), *The Challenge of Facts and Other Essays*, New Haven, CT: Yale University Press, pp. 93–102.

Sumner, William Graham (1902), 'The concentration of wealth: its economic justification', *Independent*, April–June, reprinted in Albert Galloway Keller (ed.) (1914), *The Challenge of Facts and Other Essays*, New Haven, CT: Yale University Press, pp. 79–90.

Sumner, William Graham (1904), 'Reply to a socialist', *Collier's Weekly*, 22 October, reprinted in Albert Galloway Keller (ed.) (1914), *The Challenge of Facts and Other Essays*, New Haven, CT: Yale University Press, pp. 53–62.

Sumner, William Graham (1914a), 'The challenge of facts', in Albert Galloway Keller (ed.), *The Challenge of Facts and Other Essays*, New Haven, CT: Yale University Press, pp. 17–52.

Sumner, William Graham (1914b), 'The state as an "ethical person"', in Albert Galloway Keller (ed.), *The Challenge of Facts and Other Essays*, New Haven, CT: Yale University Press, pp. 199–204.

Sumner, William Graham (1969), 'The cooperative commonwealth', in *The Forgotten Man and Other Essays,* Freeport, NY: Books for Libraries Press, pp. 441–64.

Supreme Court (1937a), *West Coast Hotel Company v. Parrish*, 29 March, in Arthur Steiner (ed.), *Significant Supreme Court Decisions: 1934–1937*, 2nd edn, New York: John Wiley & Sons, pp. 21–6.

Supreme Court (1937b), *National Labor Relations Board v. Jones & Laughlin Steel Corporation*, 12 April, in H. Arthur Steiner (ed.), *Significant Supreme Court Decisions: 1934–1937*, 2nd edn, New York: John Wiley & Sons, pp. 49–57.

Supreme Court (1937c), *Charles C. Steward Machine Company v. Harwell G. Davis*, 24 May, in H. Arthur Steiner (ed.), *Significant Supreme Court Decisions: 1934–1937*, 2nd edn, New York: John Wiley & Sons, pp. 65–71.

Swope, Gerard (1931), 'The Swope Plan', Appendix A in Antony C. Sutton, *Wall Street and FDR*, accessed 14 June 2012 at www.reformation.org/wall-st-fdr-app-a.html.

Taylor, Frederick W. (1911), *The Principles of Scientific Management*, reprinted in 1919, New York: Harper & Row.

Thomas, Norman (1934), *The Choice Before Us: Mankind at the Crossroads*, reprinted 1970, New York: AMS Press.

Tily, Herbert J. (1934), 'Business under the NRA', in Clair Wilcox, Herbert F. Fraser and Patrick Murphy Maling (eds), *America's Recovery Program*, reprinted 1970, Freeport, NY: Books for Libraries Press, pp. 193–206.

T.R.B. (1935), 'Washington notes', *The New Republic*, 19 June, 164.

Tugwell, Rexford Guy (1927), *Industry's Coming of Age*, New York: Columbia University Press.

Tugwell, Rexford Guy (1930), 'Review of *Our Business Civilization* by James Truslow Adams, *This Ugly Civilization* by Ralph Borsodi, and *Men and Machines* by Stuart Chase', *Annals of the American Academy of Political and Social Science*, **152**, November, 417–19.

Tugwell, Rexford G. (1932), 'Responsibility and economic distress', in Felix Morley (ed.), *Aspects of the Depression*, Chicago, IL: University of Chicago Press, pp. 129–36.

Tugwell, Rexford G. (1934), 'New strength from the soil', in Clair Wilcox, Herbert F. Fraser and Patrick Murphy Maling (eds), *America's Recovery Program*, reprinted 1970, Freeport, NY: Books for Libraries Press, pp. 45–68.

Tugwell, Rexford G. (1936), 'The future of national planning', *The New Republic*, 9 December, 162–5.

Tugwell, Rexford G. (1939), 'We have bought ourselves time to think', *The New Republic*, 26 July, 323–5.

Tugwell, Rexford G. (1968), *The Brains Trust*, New York: The Viking Press.

Tugwell, Rexford G. (1977), *Roosevelt's Revolution: The First Year – A Personal Perspective*, New York: Macmillan Publishing Co.

Tull, Charles J. (1965), *Father Coughlin and the New Deal*, Syracuse, NY: Syracuse University Press.

Veblen, Thorstein (1899), *The Theory of the Leisure Class*, reprinted 1973, Boston, MA: Houghton Mifflin Co.

Veblen, Thorstein (1901), 'Industrial and pecuniary employments', *Publications of the American Economic Association*, 3rd Series, **2** (1), February, reprinted in *The Place of Science in Modern Civilization and Other Essays* (1932), New York: Viking Press, pp. 279–323.

Veblen, Thorstein (1904), *The Theory of Business Enterprise*, reprinted 1935, New York: Charles Scribner's Sons.

Veblen, Thorstein (1908), 'On the nature of capital', *Quarterly Journal of Economics*, **23**, November, reprinted in *The Place of Science in Modern Civilization and Other Essays* (1932), New York: Viking Press, pp. 352–86.

Villard, Oswald Garrison (1934), 'The gifts of the New Deal', *The Nation*, **138**, 3 January, 8.

Vining, Rutledge (1939), 'Suggestions of Keynes in the writings of Veblen', *Journal of Political Economy*, **47**, October, 692–704.

von Mises, Ludwig (1920), *Economic Calculation in the Socialist Commonwealth*, trans. G. Sandler (1990),, Auburn AL: The Ludwig von Mises Institute, pp. 1–47.

Wagner, Robert F. (1935a), 'Speech on the National Labor Relations Act', 21 February, *Congressional Record*, 74th Congress, 1st session, vol. 79, 2371–2.

Wagner, Robert F. (1935b), 'Toward security', *Forum and Century*, **93**, May, 294–6.

Wagner, Robert F. (1935c), 'N.R.A. legislation and the Supreme Court', *Vital Speeches of the Day*, **1**, 1 July 1, 636–9.

Walker, Forrest Q. (1933), 'Price fixing via code', *Nation's Business*, **21**, December, 39–41.

Walling, William English (1914), *Progressivism – And After*, New York: The Macmillan Co.

Ward, Paul W. (1935), 'NRA – haven for cake-eaters', *The Nation*, **140**, 10 April 10, 411–14.

Ware, Colston E. (1932), 'Planning in Russia', in Felix Morley (ed.), *Aspects of the Depression*, Chicago, IL: University of Chicago Press, pp. 156–65.

The New Republic (1935), 'What to do with the N.R.A.', 20 March, 144–6.

The New Republic (1937), 'When and how to balance the budget', 5 May, 372–3.

Wicker, George Ray (1911), 'Review of Das Wesen und der Hauptinhalt der Theoretischen Nationalokonomie by Joseph Schumpeter', *American Economic Review*, **1**, June, 318–20.

Wilcox, Clair, Herbert F. Fraser and Patrick Murphy Maling (1934), 'Introduction', in Clair Wilcox, Herbert F. Fraser and Patrick Murphy Maling (eds), *America's Recovery Program*, reprinted 1970, Freeport, NY: Books for Libraries Press, pp. 7–19.

Wolman, Leo (1934), 'Labor under the NRA', in Clair Wilcox, Herbert F. Fraser and Patrick Murphy Maling (eds), *America's Recovery Program*, reprinted 1970, Freeport, NY: Books for Libraries Press, pp. 89–106.

Wolman, Leo, J.M. Clark, Mollie Ray Carroll, Frank G. Dickinson and Arthur D. Gayer (1930), 'Public works and unemployment', *American Economic Review*, **20**, Papers and Proceedings of the Forty-second Annual Meeting of the American Economic Association, March, 15–29.

Wright, David McC. (1940), 'The economic limit and economic burden of an internally held national debt', *Quarterly Journal of Economics*, **55**, November, 116–29.

Index